Double
Takes

Contemporary French Culture and Society

edited by

Richard J. Golsan,

Mary Jean Green,

and

Lynn A. Higgins

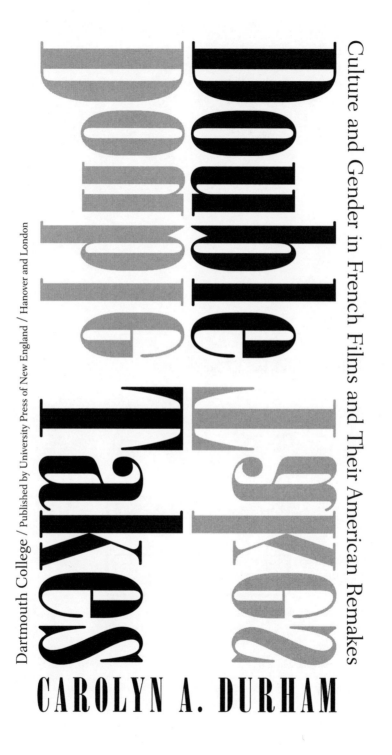

Double Takes

Culture and Gender in French Films and Their American Remakes

Dartmouth College / Published by University Press of New England / Hanover and London

CAROLYN A. DURHAM

Dartmouth College

University Press of New England, Hanover, NH 03755

© 1998 by the Trustees of Dartmouth College

Printed in the United States of America

5 4 3 2 1

CIP data appear at the end of the book

Publication of this work was

supported in part by a grant

from The Henry Luce III Fund for

Distinguished Scholarship at the

College of Wooster.

To Jennifer, Kathryn, and John

Contents

Illustrations

Acknowledgments

I am grateful to the College of Wooster for supporting research leaves in 1990–91 and 1995–96, which allowed me to complete much of the research and the initial writing that led to this book, and for providing additional funding from the Henry Luce III Fund for Distinguished Scholarship to enable me to do necessary research in Parish and to help me purchase some of the book's illustrations. I want to thank my colleagues and students for the many ways in which they have challenged and encouraged my thinking and my scholarship. In particular, I thank my student assistants, Chris Becker and Ken Walczak, who patiently helped me track down references and resources, and my students in three successive classes of "Comparative Sexual Poetics," whose careful reading, interesting writing, and thoughtful discussions stimulated my own thinking about literature and film.

I wish to recognize the editors of *French Review, Jump Cut,* and *The Modern Language Journal* for their willingness to publish earlier versions of portions of the analyses that appear in chapters 4, 5, and 8. Conferences sponsored by the University of Louisville and the Wichita State University also provided a forum for presenting work in progress. I thank the members of the editorial staff of the University Press of New England for the encouragement and the remarkably efficient assistance they provided at all stages of the editing process. Terry Geeksen of the Film Stills Archive of the Museum of Modern Art was very helpful in my search to locate illustrations for the manuscript.

Like all books, this one could not have been written without the support of some very special people. I am grateful to Dudley Andrew and Steven Ungar and to all of the participants in the 1995 NEH summer seminar for their support during the months in which I began to work seriously on this project. Conversations with Ginette Adamson, Yolanda Patterson, Elizabeth Joiner, Michèle Bernatchez, Michael Pretina, Christine Girard, Catherine Pelché, Michèle Valencia, and Judy Miller, despite the distance that usually separated us, always provided an affectionate and stimulating context for sharing ideas. Closer to home, Carolee Taipale, Nancy Grace, and Debra Shostak offered me the many pleasures of close friendship on a daily basis. I am particularly grateful to John Gabriele, who shares with me not only his life and his children but also his love of language, literature, and scholarship, and who, not least of all, can always make me laugh.

Double
Takes

Introduction

Disneyland Comes Home to Paris

Since Disney opened its newest amusement park at Marne-la-Vallée on April 12, 1992, Euro Disney has continued to show up in all the wrong places. The first, of course, was Marne-la-Vallée itself. Disney's preference for a region where the winters are relatively cold and rainy, over the year-round sunshine of southern Spain, seemed particularly odd in light of the equally chilly intellectual climate of nearby Paris. Most memorably denounced by Ariane Mnouchkine as a "cultural Chernobyl," Euro Disney, sight unseen, quickly became the main attraction for opponents of "American cultural imperialism" (Corliss, "Voilà" 82). Film critic Serge Toubiana, for example, interrupted his introductory essay to the May 1992 issue of *Cahiers du cinéma* to open an uncharacteristically vitriolic "parenthesis on Euro Disney." Toubiana portrays the amusement park as definitive proof of America's successful colonization of Europe: "We get the message: it is America that delimits and demarcates the European space in which we live—Disney-Marne will drain off millions of visitors from everywhere in Europe! This act on the part of America is one of unprecedented violence" (39).[1] Other Paris intellectuals issued similar warnings, in the wake of Euro Disney, of the impending "Disneylandization" of France's own aesthetic and cultural patrimony (Kuisel 228).

Viewed from the United States, what seemed most out of place was not Euro Disney itself but the reaction it provoked in France. As Richard F. Kuisel notes, the same space that the Disney Corporation defended as "mere entertainment" was "scrutinized" by the French as "an important cultural phenomenon" (229). It is hard to imagine a better illustration of this difference in perspective than the most recent and, by far, the most incongruous place in which Euro Disney has yet been found: between the covers of its very own *Guide vert Michelin*. Surely the very antithesis of a "cultural Chernobyl," the narrow, green Michelin guidebooks, instantly recognizable worldwide, have rather the reassuring stature of cultural artifacts. In a gesture that might well descend directly from Caesar's famous partitioning of Gaul into three parts,

Double Takes

Michelin has long divided modern France into the twenty-four "great touristic regions," each covered by one or more of its guidebooks. With the arrival of *Euro Disney Resort* amidst France's former provinces and traditional historical regions, the geography of the entire country is significantly altered. In this newly revised context, the capital of France appears as an appendix on "Local Tourism"; and Versailles, Reims, Fontainebleau, and the wine cellars of Champagne figure among the "principal tourist attractions near Euro Disney." If one were looking for an example of a demarcation of European space that represented "an act of unprecedented violence," to recall Toubiana, surely one would single out Michelin well before Disney—or Caesar.

Paradoxically, it is less as anomaly than as carbon copy that the Euro Disney text disturbs; the greatest discord emanates from its superficial resemblance to the other *Guides Michelin*. The Disney guide speaks the same language as all the previous books in the collection and follows an identical format. After the description of the topographical particularities and a discussion of the historical importance of the region, its principal sights are described and, more importantly, ranked. This means that such three-star attractions ("Worth the trip") as Big Thunder Mountain, Phantom Manor, and Pirates of the Caribbean presumably hold an interest equal to that of the Louvre and the Arc de Triomphe and superior to that of the Centre Georges-Pompidou. The latter merits only two stars ("Deserves a detour"), bringing it down to the level of The Main Street Electrical Parade and "Le Chateau de la Belle au Bois Dormant" (Sleeping Beauty's Castle). Similarly, those who have the leisure to explore single-star events ("Interesting") can choose either Peter Pan's Flight or a walk in the Jardin des Tuileries.

At about the same time that Disney-Michelin re-placed Disney-Marne within France's cultural patrimony, French theater director Ariane Mnouchkine revised her widely quoted condemnation of the amusement park: "I remain opposed to the Euro Disney development, although frankly I don't give a damn about the place. Television seems to me to be a much more menacing cultural Chernobyl" (qtd. in Cohen, "When You Wish"). Although Mnouchkine does not single out any particular nation as responsible for this new source of cultural decay and disaster, guilt by association makes it probable that she still has the United States very much in mind. Certainly American sitcoms, soap operas, and films not only appear frequently on French television, where the Disney Channel itself has been available since 1995, but also provide the primary models for imitation at the local level. In any event, Mnouchkine's statement usefully identifies a politics of displacement, which she is far from the only one to practice, in which Euro Disney serves discursively to refer to *another* place, one, like the Michelin guide, both similar and different.

Most often, as is implicit in the case of Mnouchkine and explicit in that of

Serge Toubiana, for whom Euro Disney was only a "parenthesis," this "symbol of American *entertainment*" brings us back to Hollywood and the American movie industry (39).[2] Although Toubiana certainly points out that the presence of American films in eight out of ten movie theaters is the one thing that cities as different as Madrid, Prague, Rome, and London all have in common, he actually objects less to the fact of American domination in Europe than to the particular form it takes:

> [The American model] conceives of difference only through integration, cultural enlistment, the absorption of one language into another—supposedly universal—in which everything is based on performance. This cultural language, which engenders the melting pot, nonetheless has absolutely no fear of braving that which still retains a few traces of civilization by offering the only possible solution: popularization. (41)

This is clearly a complex statement, and one that I suspect its author would be pleased to learn is remarkably difficult to translate into English.[3] At the same time, however, and largely because of the language in which Toubiana chooses to express his critique of a linguistic model that he also presumes to be distinctively American, his words raise a number of interesting questions and reveal some potential sources of cross-cultural ambiguity and contradiction.

In the last ten to fifteen years, and increasingly in the last five, a number of studies have appeared in both scholarly works and the popular press that suggest that France is undergoing a major identity crisis.[4] Despite the diversity that such texts represent in terms of origin and intended audience, they reveal widespread agreement that the current French malaise stems primarily from two relatively new preoccupations, one internal—the growing number of immigrants and citizens of Arab descent within France—and one external —France's role in the future construction of Europe. In both cases, concern clearly centers on questions of integration: on the one hand, the fear that an Arab population *will not* be assimilated into France; on the other hand, the fear that France *will* be assimilated into Europe. Those who interpret France in this way, almost all of whom are either British, American, or of bicultural background, also concur, however, that their French counterparts often prefer to project France's everyday social and political concerns into the realm of the cultural and to substitute an invasion from abroad for the domestic and continental space in which these problems actually unfold. To cite a single example of this recurrent analysis, in the conclusion to *Seducing the French: The Dilemma of Americanization*, Kuisel notes the decline of French anti-Americanism during the 1980s when "Frenchness faced external immersion in Europe as well as internal subversion from immigration. Americanization no longer had exclusive rights to the charge of endangering national identity"

(228). Subsequently, however, and Kuisel once again singles out the 1992 opening of Euro Disney as the catalyst of change, America began to reemerge as a menace of a particular kind: "In the 1990s the dilemma about Americanization focuses, now more than ever, on the issue of culture" (230).

In this context, Toubiana's statement serves, in part, as exemplary illustration, for it seems to point in several different directions at once. Certainly the immediate concern of *Cahiers'* noted film critic lies with the cultural threat that the production and distribution practices of Hollywood represent for France's native film industry. Simultaneously, however, Toubiana's identification of the "American model" with the process of "integration," particularly in conjunction with his explicit reference to the all-American image of the "melting pot," also recalls the political and social worries that plague contemporary France. *Visible* difference is quite literally what distinguishes France's new immigrants from all those so readily welcomed in the past. (Cultural metaphors may displace their referents and still reproduce anxieties associated with the real world.) Ironically, it is precisely in the area of culture that it seems most surprising that the American ideal of integration should be perceived by Toubiana—and indeed the French in general—as both foreign and to be feared. The Michelin guide to Euro Disney, for example, might lead us to think that the model Toubiana describes could be qualified as French just as appropriately as American. What effect does *Euro Disney Resort* produce if not that of "the absorption of one language into another—supposedly universal"? The Michelin guide, as we have seen, takes a specific place, whose dominant reference is American visual culture, and rewrites it into France's still strong verbal and literary tradition. In the process, a foreign icon is enlisted as an official, if symbolic, representative of a concept of civilization in which the conflation of "French" and "universal" has long been understood: "French difference, superiority, and universal mission [are] all bound up in the term *civilisation*" (Kuisel 236). Indeed, Jean-Marie Rouart, the literary critic of *Le Figaro*, objected to Euro Disney precisely on the grounds that France "must stand for universal cultural values" (Cohen, "When You Wish").

One could argue, of course, and no doubt many French cultural analysts would want to, that what I have just described is not at all a model of integration *à l'américaine*—in which Disneyland (and those of Arab descent) could move to France and still retain significant aspects of their native cultural origins—but rather a model of assimilation *à la française*—in which the amusement park (and the immigrant population) necessarily abandon all signs of foreignness in order to become fully French.[5] Toubiana speaks of these processes in terms of language acquisition; similarly, contemporary anthropologists frequently describe cross-cultural analysis as a form of translation or "version" (see Carroll, *Cultural* 9–10). The word *version* exists in both French and English to designate an essentially identical translation procedure, but there is an interesting variation in how the two languages define the term. What French perceives as translation *into* the mother tongue, English describes as translation *from* another language. This kind of reversal of perspective, which occurs often between the two languages, appears to reproduce the difference between the processes of assimilation and integration. In this context, to repeat a distinction of my own, one could say that America offered France its "version" of Euro *Disney*: a Disneyland translated, that is, *transferred*, intact, from California to Marne-la-Vallée. France, in contrast, wanted its own "version" of *Euro* Disney: a Disneyland translated, that is, *transformed*, into "Frenchness" itself. These two versions of the same event reflect a cross-cultural gap that is presently bridged only by the bilingual and bicultural oddity of the Michelin guide to Euro Disney. This may change sometime in the next few years when a movie theme park, on the model of the Disney-MGM attraction in Florida, is scheduled to open at Marne-la-Vallée. This addition to Euro Disney promises to produce an ensemble somewhat more consistent with the original French "version" of such a place.

That the already close ties between France and Disney/Hollywood are shortly destined to become even closer seems only appropriate. *Version* also refers to an adaptation of a given text, as in *"Three Men and a Baby* is the Hollywood version of *Trois Hommes et un couffin."* Here too Euro Disney intervenes to designate a cultural practice that is no doubt a more direct and immediate target of Toubiana's critique of the "American model": Hollywood's current passion for remaking original French films. Although such cultural borrowing is far from new, its prevalence has made it increasingly remarkable of late. In the *New York Times* alone, Vincent Canby was already complaining in early 1989 about Hollywood's penchant for "swallowing up other countries' movies with a desperation unknown in the past" ("Movies Lost"), and by 1994 three different reviewers had emphasized within a matter of months the banality of this form of inspiration. Roger Cohen refers to "what has become an almost standard practice" ("Aux Armes"), Janet Maslin to "that all American art form known as 'le remake'" ("A Bahamian Vacation"), and Molly Haskell to the "remake craze" (qtd. in Young 17). If French critics tend to make Euro Disney representative of "America" as a whole, the comments I have just quoted do something similar in reverse. "Hollywood," in the case of the penchant for remaking French films, more exactly designates Touchstone Pictures, the studio owned by the Disney Corporation, which has shown particular zeal in purchasing the rights to remake French comedies. In some sense, then, the fear that "Disneylandization" would not only pollute French soil at Marne-la-Vallée but actually endanger France's own cultural and aesthetic patrimony as well seems to have been realized.

If Euro Disney was a "cultural Chernobyl," the 1993 General Agreement on Tariffs and Trades (GATT) promised to be the cinematic equivalent of

The Invasion of France by American movies. Paris, March 1996, author's photo.

Euro Disney. Indeed, Richard Pells describes the crisis, which coincided with the arrival in France of Steven Speilberg's *Jurassic Park,* as the proverbial last straw in the context of the triple threat posed by the amusement park, France's Arab population, and American movies: "In the wake of Euro Disney, along with the flood of immigrants from North Africa, the dinosaurs represented one more assault upon French uniqueness" (269). In practical terms, the battle was informed less by cultural issues than by economic questions of distribution and production. In 1993 American movies accounted for nearly 60 percent of box-office receipts in France and an even higher percentage of video rentals. Although the figures are still higher for Europe as a whole, where U.S. products represent 80 percent of the movies shown and 75 percent of television programming, France also represents the largest film industry in Europe, thanks, at least in part, to a system of subsidies and quotas. France produces approximately 150 films a year with the help of a 13 percent tax on all movie tickets sold within France, whether to foreign or to domestic films. The resulting monies, which created a government fund of approximately $350 million in 1994, are used to subsidize French filmmakers, film festivals, and film schools. France also enforces a 60 percent quota of European content on French television, two-thirds of which must be specifically French (see Goodell; Cohen, "Aux Armes"; and Corliss, "Fellini").

At the same time, foreign-language films represented less than 1 percent of the total U.S. box office in 1996 (Corliss, "Fellini" 68), down from a 1969 peak of 4 percent and down a full percent from only two years earlier when France alone could still lay claim to 1 percent of the U.S. market (Cohen, "Aux Armes). Less than 1 percent of prime-time shows on American television are foreign-made, and France in any form is virtually nonexistent on U.S. television screens. (It is true that a fair amount of foreign coverage is devoted every May to the Cannes film festival, but such reporting does not necessarily focus either on France or on the French in any significant way.) In the United States, cultural "commodities" have become the most lucrative export after aerospace technology. Estimates of foreign revenues are routinely figured into the production budgets of American films, and in 1993 Hollywood earned $4 billion in Europe alone (Goodell 132). Pells believes that French anger over this imbalance of trade has been heightened by Hollywood's recent remake practice, which virtually eliminates the possibility that original French films will ever be shown in the United States, either in theaters or on video (Pells 269).

During the final stage of negotiations over the international free trade agreement, in which France ultimately won the right to retain the system of quotas and government subsidies that protect its film industry, the same arguments that had informed the Euro Disney debate over culture resurfaced with the same intensity. Paris intellectuals and politicians once again insisted that the preservation of a distinctively French national and cultural identity was at stake, what no less an authority than then president François Mitterrand claimed as "the right of every country to create its own images" (Goodell 135). Hollywood, in turn, repeated the American conviction that the "entertainment" it sells worldwide constitutes no threat to others, since it "has nothing to do with culture" (Valenti). Yet on-site inspection in both countries might rather suggest at least a blurring of traditional boundaries, if not their outright reversal. Against all expectations, France appears to be uncustomarily integrationist in the area of film. Paris cinemas still show over three hundred different movies every week from as many as thirty different countries, and the original language version of every film that opens is always available in at least some Parisian theaters. In the land of the melting pot, in contrast, access to foreign film has steadily declined in recent years to the point that it has now become severely limited even in New York and virtually nonexistent elsewhere. Art cinemas and revival houses continue to close as the number of theater chains and multiplexes specializing in domestic blockbusters multiplies. Hollywood's growing fondness for "le remake" over the same period of time suggests that pre-assimilation into native products is fast becoming a requirement for foreign films to enter American cinemas. In other ways as well, the remake practice points to the contradictory dynamics of Franco-American cultural relations at present. In a recurrent pattern, the parallels that quickly emerge from any comparison between France and the United

States turn out to be the breeding place of cross-cultural conflict as often as they lead to common ground.

Thus, on the one hand, France, a country convinced of its cultural superiority and (therefore) of its duty to disseminate French culture worldwide in the guise of *civilisation* itself, nonetheless readily portrays itself at home as the victim of "American cultural imperialism."[6] The United States, which has its own sense of global destiny—one that, thanks to Hollywood, now includes culture in its once primarily political and economic outreach—holds unchallengeable sway over the international film market, and yet claims, in its turn, to be the target of "inexcusable discrimination" as a result of France's state-supported system of quotas and subsidies (Valenti). Moreover, even as Hollywood diffuses its images throughout the world, some of them unquestionably point to a startling lack of originality and creative talent within the American movie industry, of which the current obsession with remaking French films is only one of many examples. Thus Hollywood's new passion for borrowing from the French might suggest an aesthetic and cultural crisis exactly parallel to that which preoccupies France.

On the other hand, the United States and France, who rank first and second among the film-producing nations of the world, no doubt constantly seek ways to extend their influence within a market that is increasingly characterized by transnational filmmaking. In this context, far from epitomizing creative sterility, might not the remake rather bear witness to Hollywood's openness to new ideas, including the foreign; and should we not welcome such an apparent deviation from the political and cultural isolationism of America during the Reagan and post-Reagan years? Viewed from France, could remakes not be similarly interpreted as one sign of a newly successful strategy for the internationalization of French cinema? Having penetrated, albeit indirectly, the largest and most important of foreign markets, could France not eventually expect to develop an audience for its own films within the United States? Indeed, David Ansen expresses just such a hope: "Perhaps, as Hollywood continues to retread and recycle, we'll develop a renewed appetite for foreign flavors" ("Oscar" 87). From this perspective, the American remake would ultimately prove to be a path to the preservation, rather than the destruction, of France's native culture; and, in the meantime, the sale of remake rights to Hollywood would continue to help finance French filmmaking.

Here opinions differ once again, for even if the sale of distribution rights initially brings home less revenue, all future income from a U.S. release subsequently accrues in France. To the extent, however, that French filmmakers "have been increasingly enraged by the American habit of doing remakes" (Cohen, "Aux Armes"), their outrage has far more to do with culture (once again) than with economics, or, to put it perhaps more accurately, with the competing interests of *la civilisation française* and the profit-driven culture of

America. Hollywood producers typically justify their extreme reluctance to distribute foreign-language films in the United States on the grounds that the American moviegoing public dislikes subtitles only slightly less than dubbing, which it supposedly loathes. Phil Barlow of Disney Studios puts it most bluntly: "There has never been a really successful foreign film that wasn't a fluke" (qtd. in Young 17). Clearly, the definition of "really successful" is already problematic, especially in a comparative context. A film such as *Trois Hommes et un couffin*, for example, which in the eyes of the French was a runaway hit in the U.S., can nonetheless expect to be beaten at the box office by its own remake within a matter of days, even if the latter is ultimately not "really successful."[7]

Moreover, the French have begun to point out that no one will ever know what size audience dubbed foreign films might actually attract in the United States as long as Hollywood continues to refuse to distribute them. René Cleitman and other French producers openly denounce both a practice they see as a form of de facto protectionism and the illusion that sustains it: "Americans have discovered therein a fantastic way of protecting their market, on the pretext that their audience was hostile to dubbing, which has absolutely not been proven" ("L'Europe" 104). Still worse, however, is the refusal to release French films at all, even in their subtitled version, a possibility that Touchstone Pictures seems to have turned into a policy in the case of those movies it plans to remake. "So clever French comedies end up being used as animated scripts," as Josh Young puts it (17). In this context, French complaints that what amounts to a "theft of ideas" endangers France's very identity seem less paranoid and Ellen Pall's particularly depressing assessment— that the Americanization of French films translates foreign-language hits for an audience that not only will not read subtitles or tolerate dubbing but cannot "even, perhaps, make the imaginative leap into life in another country"— seems less implausible.

In a recent interview, Daniel Toscan du Plantier, president of Unifrance Film International, speaks somewhat more optimistically about the cultural crisis that separates France and the United States: "We're the two countries obsessed by movies, the two nations where film is at the heart of the national consciousness. So we should be able to find an accommodation, provided we accept that cinema is politics, and one image for the world is politically unacceptable" (qtd. in Cohen, "Aux Armes"). It is tempting to cite the practice of the remake as ideally suited to respond to this desire for cultural plurality, since the reproduction of a film always results, by definition, in two sets of visual images. Cultural commentators, whether French or foreign, generally agree that what Richard Bernstein calls "that form that we particularly associate with a special French genius," that is, "the movies" (182), both represents *la différence* of Frenchness itself and differs in obvious ways from the films of any other nation. This distinctiveness should be especially evident in the case of Hollywood, whose cinema has historically served as a contrasting context within which French filmmakers have been able to articulate their own originality (see, for example, Flitterman-Lewis and Forbes). This belief in the specificity of French cinema resurfaces repeatedly in discussions of American remakes of French films, where it provides the most common explanation for the equally widespread opinion that the Hollywood version is always inferior to the original on which it is based. Molly Haskell, for example, reverses Phil Barlow's judgment, quoted above, but she speaks with equal authority: "I don't think there was ever a case where the remake was better" (qtd. in Young 17).

At the same time, however, those who assert the absolute difference of all French cinema, including that of the very popular comedies on which most recent American remakes have been based, characteristically stop at the level of assertion without ever proceeding to any specific analysis or providing any concrete examples.[8] Indeed, Richard Roud's comments, in his now classic study of French cinema, are curiously reminiscent of a frequently quoted "definition" of pornography: "I know it when I see it." Although Roud finds it "perhaps as difficult to define what is different about 'the' French cinema as it is to describe 'a' France," he nonetheless confidently assumes the existence of a common "feeling" that "we all know what a French film is like" (15). Toscan du Plantier, currently one of the staunchest defenders of French cinematic and cultural specificity, does not fare much better. In a particularly telling statement, the French producer asserts that France, in contrast to the United States, is "driven by intangible values. That difference is clear in the movies we make" (qtd. in Cohen, "Aux Armes"). One can readily agree on the intangibility of both such values and the means of their cinematic expression, since no further explanation or illustration is forthcoming. The reviews of Vincent Canby, the *New York Times* film critic who has been relentless in his repeated critiques of American remakes, may be most revealing. In the first place, Canby remains vague even in very specific contexts. In a discussion, for example, of Francis Veber's remake (*Three Fugitives*) of an original film of his own (*Les Fugitifs*), which was never released in the United States, Canby (not otherwise noted for any tendency toward Derridean poststructuralism) appears to be able to discern the presence of Frenchness by its very absence. Thus he complains that the actors in the American film (Martin Short and Nick Nolte replace Pierre Richard and Gérard Depardieu) seem to give "a dim facsimile of a French performance that looks familiar, even though we haven't seen it yet." Similarly, in the case of the remake of *The Man with One Red Shoe*, Canby criticizes Tom Hanks for not being "Pierre Richard, who is as emblematic of France as the Eiffel Tower," and the American film as a whole for not being funny "mostly because French films are French" ("Movies Lost").

In short, the problem with American remakes of French films comes down to the most basic of tautologies: French films are French and American films are not. One wonders, in that case, what precisely they *are*, since they somehow seem to be "not French" without necessarily remaining—or becoming—American either. Paradoxically, while Hollywood remakes are condemned for their inferiority to—and thus, for their difference from—the French films on which they are modeled, they are simultaneously accused of not being different *enough*. This judgment is implicit in Molly Haskell's widely shared attribution of the "remake craze" itself to Hollywood's "poverty of ideas" (Young 17). Josh Young makes the paradox explicit and reproduces it within a single sentence in his puzzling assessment of Veber, who, in directing *Three Fugitives*, "tried to stick closely to his original film, causing the remake to stumble over cultural differences" (17). Finally, Canby too illustrates the same apparent contradiction. If French films ultimately elude their American imitators by virtue of their quintessential Frenchness, the latter nonetheless must come dangerously close to succeeding, since "idiosyncratic alien films are [being] remade, American-style, without being effectively reconceived." Canby now faults Hollywood remakes for being too similar to their foreign predecessors to retain any cultural identity of their own; they become "stateless reproductions, so slick they seem machine tooled" ("Movies Lost"). In short, to restate the opening sentence of this paragraph, the problem with American remakes of French films comes down to the most basic of tautologies: American remakes are remakes and therefore highly imitative; they accomplish precisely what they set out to do.

To resume, Hollywood remakes of original French films have been written into any—or all—of the following scripts: either they embody American culture and its dominance and so threaten to erase any trace of foreign influence that they might encounter along their imperialist path, or they represent foolish and futile attempts to reproduce a foreign model whose cultural and aesthetic specificity—and, especially, superiority—make it, by definition, inimitable. In the most optimistic of scenarios, these films produce a carbon copy or a literal translation of a French original, in which case the remake not only has no discernible cultural identity of its own but is presumably gratuitous as well. What all of these positions have in common is a curious but consistent tendency to privilege one culture over another and, as a result, to focus on the *same* to the exclusion of the *different*. Roger Cohen takes us back to our starting point and points the way forward: "Another look at remakes would probably not be a bad thing, given the arguments that have divided Paris and Hollywood of late. After all, the premise of a remake is that French and American sensibilities are incompatible, their ways of enjoying movies irreconcilable" ("Aux Armes"). Cohen reminds us that cross-cultural differences and conflict exist—witness Euro Disney—and that similar things, like Michelin guidebooks, only look identical from a distance and in the absence of actual comparison.

In the pages that follow, I propose to take "another look at remakes." Although movies necessarily figure prominently in a project that is grounded in detailed textual analysis, this is not—or not only—a book about film but rather—or also—a book about culture. As the French producer Marin Karmitz noted in 1989 in relation to the use of the English language in European films, "What we are facing is not a crisis of cinema but a crisis of culture" (Canby, "Ici Se Habla"). The editors of a special issue of *CinémAction* devoted to remakes and adaptations attribute the failure of many remakes to the fact that national cinemas "incarnate and reflect the mentality of the country: what's at stake is a cultural problem, that of the consubstantiality of cinema with a culture" (Protopopoff & Serceau 106). I will look at culture, in the words of James Clifford "as an assemblage of texts to be interpreted" (38) and at national cultures, in the words of Mel van Elteren, as processes "constituted in and through their relations to each other" (65).

In *The Great Cat Massacre and Other Episodes in French Cultural History*, Robert Darnton suggests that his inquiry into "the unmapped territory known in France as 'l'histoire des mentalités,'" a "genre that has not yet received a name in English," might simply be called "cultural history," since it treats our own native and contemporary civilization as anthropologists treat foreign cultures. "Frenchness exists," asserts Darnton (61), with a conciseness of expression appropriate to the apparent enormity of the affirmation. Moreover, a discovery that emerges from the analysis of prerevolutionary French folktales concludes with a series of even bolder assertions about the persistence of Frenchness over time, especially in the realm of popular culture and in the cinema in particular: "It became a master theme of French culture in general, at its most sophisticated as well as its most popular . . . The theme still lives in films . . . It survives in ordinary language . . . It has passed from the ancient peasantry into everyone's everyday life" (64–65). To the extent that the distinctive cultural style or world view identified as "Frenchness" represents "a defense strategy" rather than the "formula for conquering the world" characteristic of "its Anglo-Saxon opposite" (62), Darnton's view of national identity is able to account for the contemporary conflict that incites France to protect its national film industry from the perceived domination of Hollywood.

Such a pattern of consistency and repetition is hardly surprising. The term *culture* itself is related through its Indo-European root (*kwel*) to revolving and cyclical movement; and books devoted to the study of cultural specificity within a specific national context appear to represent a subgenre of cultural studies to which the notion of the "remake" is virtually endemic. As in the case of Darnton, such studies tend to be explicitly comparative in nature.

Since France and the United States have traditionally provided each other with a contrasting context that has allowed each to articulate its own particular notion of culture, interest in "Frenchness" and in "Americanness" tend to go hand in hand. Raymonde Carroll's *Cultural Misunderstandings: The Franco-American Experience* (1988) is motivated by the desire to understand the origin of "some frequent cultural misunderstandings which occur between the French and Americans in several important areas of interpersonal relationships" (1). Less personally motivated, Kuisel's *Seducing the French* (1993) initially explores "Gallic attitudes toward America" as a way to comprehend "how French people think and feel about themselves" (ix); in the process he discovers that he is writing a book as much about the United States as about France. The discursive analysis that informs Jean-Philippe Mathy's *Extrême-Occident: French Intellectuals and America* (1993) is similarly intercultural.

Even those writers who mean to focus exclusively or predominantly on a single national culture almost always end up establishing at least an implicitly comparative context by virtue of their own biculturality. Just as France and America have served each other as definitional others, so has this cross-cultural interest been reflected in the lives and work of particular individuals. Indeed, the example of Alexis de Tocqueville, whose *Democracy in America* inaugurated a tradition of French Americanists, continues to haunt his successors, most recently, Hervé Varenne in *Americans Together* (1977). The American equivalent, though less specific and personal in its many incarnations, is no less powerful. The "tale of entry," which Victor Crapanzano classifies as "in its own right, a genre or subgenre of ethnography" (69) because it recurs so frequently and in so standard a form in anthropological writing, has in literature and film most often taken the form of "the American in Paris." Robert Daly's *Portraits of France* (1991), Richard Bernstein's *Fragile Glory: A Portrait of France and the French* (1990), Theodore Zeldin's *The French* (1983), and James Corbett's *Through French Windows: An Introduction to France in the Nineties* (1994) are all the work of American or, in the case of Zeldin, British observers of a foreign culture. Indeed, however astute their understanding of France and however successful their work has been in French translation, they write in English for an English-speaking public. The introduction to even the most scholarly and rigorously theoretical of these works, Mathy's *Extrême-Occident*, "end[s] on a more confessional note": "As a Frenchman living in the United States, I could not deny that my study reflects a personal experience of uprooting and acculturation" (14). Moreover, *On Becoming American* (1988), which recounts the process of cultural metamorphosis that transformed its writer, born Sanche de Gramont and author of an earlier book entitled *The French*, into Ted Morgan, might best be identified as a personal "remake."

Double Takes

The works I have cited above represent an even larger phenomenon in contemporary cultural studies. Notably, autobiographers and novelists have joined anthropologists, journalists, and cultural historians in exploring national identity from a cross-cultural perspective. In this case too, there is an earlier tradition, marked by such classic examples as Pierre Daninos's *Les Carnets du Major W. Marmaduke Thompson: Découverte de la France et les Français* (1959), that has been recently revived. Framed by Franco-American negotiations over Disneyland, Linda Ashour's *Speaking in Tongues* (1988) navigates between southern France and the American South; Diane Johnson's *Le Divorce*, a finalist for the 1996 National Book Award for fiction, offers a new version of the American in a Paris that now includes Euro Disney. Peter Mayle's wide-ranging fascination with Provence (as explored in *A Year in Provence* [1990], *Toujours Provence* [1991], and *Choosing Cézanne* [1997]) is shared by Nicholas Delbanco (*Running in Place: Scenes from the South of France* [1989]) in the area of travel writing and by Francine Pascal (*If Wishes Were Horses* [1994]) in that of the novel. Similarly, on this side of the ocean, Philippe Labro explores southern culture in the fictional *L'Etudiant étranger* (1986) and travels through the far West in *Un Eté dans l'ouest* (1988); here, the traditional "tale of entry" is told in reverse as that of "the Parisian in America." What is significant, however, is that regardless of the date or the genre of the work in question and regardless of the nationality of the writer or the language in which he or she writes, all of these works not only confirm Darnton's conviction that something exists that can be called "Frenchness" and "Americanness," but also fundamentally agree about the particular traits that each category includes. What Elwood Hartman notes in 1979, in the conclusion to a review article that provides a useful and valid synthesis of studies resulting in "A Profile of French National Character," remains true today: "[I]t is evident that great similarities exist in the findings of all observers, regardless of their own nationality, point in time, or research methods" (59).

At the same time, of course, even if such abstractions as "Frenchness" and Americanness" represent a sense of identity in which some Americans and certainly most French people deeply believe (Kuisel xii), they are artificial constructions that greatly oversimplify the reality of either nation. One way to move beyond this level of generalization is to study how national cultures are embodied in concrete practices. Almost all cultural historians suggest, like Darnton, that forms of popular culture, including movies, can serve as important sources of information, although very few cite specific examples and none explore film in any depth nor in a specifically comparative context. Thus, Mathy locates "the ideological power of American civilization in the movie theater" (88) but excludes popular culture and the mass media from his book's concerns (13). At the same time, the history of film continues to be written largely in terms of national cinemas, even as films themselves tend increasingly to be transnational hybrids; similarly, the study of film continues to focus on the work of a select group of highly respected auteurs, whose films are internationally known, to the exclusion of mainstream directors whose appeal is likely to be both broader and more specifically national. *French Film: Texts and Contexts* (1990), edited by Susan Hayward and Ginette Vincendeau, provides an interesting case in point. The book is designed to bridge the gap between French and film studies on the argument that the reduction of French cinema within the latter to the work of a few "masters" and to the category of "European art cinema" has "lost sight of the films' cultural specificity and has tended to obscure important differences between films as well as directors and to make European/French cinema appear simply as Hollywood's 'other'" (1). Yet, paradoxically, all of the essays included in the collection focus on films that are "central texts within the canon of French cinema" and "mainstream cinema is largely absent" (2).

Even if film provides only one more example of the many different contexts in which France and the United States act as definitional others, it is an example of particular significance in light of Plantier's perceptive identification of the United States and France as "the two countries obsessed by movies, the two nations where film is at the heart of the national consciousness" (qtd. in Cohen, "Aux Armes"). The number of French auteurs who figure among the small group of internationally known and respected directors to which I refer above helps explain why contemporary concern with the preservation of "Frenchness" has increasingly focused on the threat that Hollywood represents not only to the autonomy and the originality of France's film industry but also to the very integrity of a French national identity. Similarly, Hollywood's current fascination with remaking French films not only heightens the longstanding fear that the United States lacks a distinctive cultural identity of its own, but also contributes to more recent concerns that the American commitment to multiculturalism has provoked a crisis of national identity similar to that of the French.

Although Hollywood's passion for remaking French films has been widely recognized, little critical discussion has yet taken place outside the limited context of the popular press. As we have seen, movie reviewers typically focus on American remakes with little or no reference to their French models, often because the critics themselves have never seen the original films. Moreover, to the extent that such analysis has been comparative in nature, it has largely served to assess the relative aesthetic merit of the two films rather than to identify potential areas of national differences or similarities that such cross-cultural comparison is uniquely suited to reveal. Finally, even as reviewers commonly assert the superiority of the French original (even unseen), they also affirm the essential similarities of the two versions of the film. Thus, as Jim Collins and the other editors of *Film Theory Goes to the Movies* noted in a different context: "The analysis of contemporary movies has, for the most part, been left to the world of popular reviewing—a system that is based on sound-bite value judgements, which precludes consideration of the cultural significance of these texts" (1). In a discussion of the general methodological difficulties of cultural analysis, Carroll notes the following:

> The challenge consists in uncovering how "texts" which belong to the same culture but which appear to be different . . . can affirm the same truth, can be two equally valid expressions of the same cultural proposition; or else how "texts" which belong to different cultures but which we suppose to be identical in the name of the universality of human sentiments (friendship, love, family, etc.) can express different cultural propositions and even contradictory truths. (*Cultural* 143)

Although Carroll has very different "texts" in mind, the films under consideration here can clearly rise to this challenge particularly well. As the essays to come will show, the careful, in-depth comparison of French films and their American remakes reveals that in many cases significant differences exist between the two versions of the "same" film; moreover, the successive comparison of a series of paired originals and remakes establishes a broader context in which patterns of divergence begin to emerge, which gradually serve to distinguish those differences and similarities that may be specifically cultural in nature from those attributable to other factors.

In *Amérique* Jean Baudrillard uses the vocabulary of film to construct an analogy between contemporary French and American culture: "American is the original version of modernity. We are the dubbed or subtitled version" (qtd. in Kuisel 223). This apparent subversion of notions of primacy or origin is characteristic of postmodernist theory and practice, many insights of which also inform this book; in this domain, I am particularly indebted to the work of Linda Hutcheon and Jim Collins. Like film itself, which as an art form mediates between the once separate domains of serious literature and mass entertainment, postmodernism bridges the gap between the elite and the popular and privileges the latter—a confusion at the heart of the debate over both Euro Disney and the GATT. Postmodernism also contests notions of "origin" and "originality" and their presumed authenticity in the face of the copy or the reproduction.

Indeed, postmodernist interest in such forms as parody and such techniques as intertexuality privileges the same practice of repetition with a difference that characterizes the remake phenomenon. Given the significant difference that we will at times encounter between films that share the same name, it will be difficult to argue for any connection between "original" and "originality." Determining origin can be similarly contradictory and confusing.

Certainly *Breathless* is conceived as a remake of *A Bout de souffle*, but the French film is already a (re)construction of conventions and characters cast off from a group of Hollywood movies known by the French term *film noir*. *I Want to Go Home* not only borrows from French film culture but also incorporates explicit intertextual references to American musical comedies; moreover, the "original" version of this French movie was filmed entirely in English. Is *Three Men and a Baby* a remake of *Trois Hommes et un couffin* or are both films remakes of *The Three Godfathers* and, if so, of which version? As John Ellis has noted, "national cinemas that see themselves as developing a style distinct from that of American cinema" nonetheless tend to retain significant features of Hollywood film when they make mainstream entertainment movies (23–24). In this context, postmodernism's emphasis on notions of "difference" and of "culture" as plural, multiple, and provisional provides an appropriate framework in which to study contemporary Franco-American differences as well. Indeed, to the extent that postmodernist art constitutes a "bricolage" of disparate cultural phenomena (Collins, *Uncommon Cultures* 145) in which "the production of meaning depends upon a direct engagement with the 'already said'" (141), the remake could be perceived as the epitome of contemporary postmodernist culture.

Feminist theory has figured so largely within both film studies and cultural studies that it hardly seems necessary to announce the influential role that it will play in these pages. As Nancy K. Miller, for example, noted some years ago, "feminist criticism, through its emphasis on the cultural and social narratives of gender, belongs at the heart of the cultural studies project" (72). Carroll draws upon the changes in gender roles associated in both France and the United States with a feminist "revolution" to illustrate precisely the distinction between the social and the cultural: "One cannot deny that change has occurred. But on further study, it quickly becomes apparent that each of these revolutions happened in a different way, according to the culture of the revolutionaries. The incomprehension of French feminism by American feminists is equaled only by the incomprehension of American feminism by French feminists" (*Cultural* 138). Because relationships between men and women, narratives of romance and parenting, and the gendered nature of human behavior all figure so prominently in the texts that I will examine here—as a result, no doubt, of the increasing centrality of feminist thought within popular culture and mainstream media that marks the twentieth century—the comparison of French and American versions of these stories can be expected to reveal significant areas of difference with great clarity. In the case of both nations, moreover, the analogies between national discourses of culture and those of gender are particularly revelatory. Thus, France's historic belief in its cultural distinctiveness reaches from the realm of civilization into that of gender and of sexual relations. "Vive la différence" continues to inform the attitudes and the behavior of both men and women in a country where feminist reform has never included the goal of erasing differences traditionally perceived to distinguish the sexes. In the United States, in contrast, the same desire to eradicate—or, at least, to deny—differences of origin and class that has produced the vision of the "melting pot" and the myth of America as resolutely middle class has also led to a feminist movement designed to challenge the notion of gender-specific jobs and roles, whether in the workplace or in the home.[9]

Although Carroll's charge of mutual "incomprehension" in the domain of cross-cultural feminism is surely exaggerated and disregards some twenty years of feminist scholarship designed to bridge the gap (at least of understanding if not of agreement), it is true that the relationship *between* gender and culture has often been ignored. Despite what Kuisel describes as "a flood of books about French nationalism" to appear in the last decade (4), virtually all of this work has been conceived within the theoretical framework established by Benedict Anderson in his highly influential *Imagined Communities: Reflections on the Origin and Spread of Nationalism*, first published in 1983. In reporting on the symposium on "Gender, Nationalisms and National Identities" that was held at Bellagio, Italy, in July 1992, Catherine Hall concurs with my view that Anderson "has done much to set the terms of debate on nations and nationalisms" and goes on to note his lack of interest in questions of gender and sexuality: "Feminists who comb his book for inspiration on ways of thinking about the particular relation of women or men to the nation, or nationalism to feminism, will find little joy" (97–98). In fact, although almost every aspect of Anderson's discussion of nation—the importance of military experience, the devotion to the "fatherland" and to the "mother tongue," the trope of woman as nation—clearly relates to the roles of men and women, he seems to be unconscious of the gendered implications of his own argument and even of his own words. Hall draws the logical conclusion: "Indeed, 'national identity' and what is meant by that has become a hot topic. How national identity might relate to gender, however, is a less central subject" (97; see also Parker et al.).

At the same time, however, feminist criticism and theory have also tended to ignore cultural differences in the organization of gender relations and roles; and to the extent that feminist study has focused almost exclusively on women and women's issues, feminism has arguably neglected gender as well, particularly in relation to men and the construction of masculinity. In keeping with more recent developments in feminist theory, the cross-cultural comparison of analogous narratives of gender appears to provide a promising methodology and context for the exploration not only of culture and/or gender but also, more significantly, of their complex interaction. Though this is clearly a long-term project, the approach that I have adopted here can help reveal the immediate benefits of questioning Western ideology's favorite story of identity by insisting on the fact and the richness of cultural diversity. Such attention to difference similarly addresses contemporary feminism's urgent need to remake the traditional tale of gender dichotomization as an internally pluralistic discourse.

In the specific area of feminist film theory, the work of Laura Mulvey, first outlined in 1975 in "Visual Pleasure and Narrative Cinema," has been even more influential than that of Anderson within cultural studies. Mulvey's psychoanalytical approach, however, shared until very recently by almost all contemporary theorists of film, including most feminists, has paid little attention to the culturally specific context in which films are created and take on meaning. Lucy Fischer's *Shot/Countershot: Film Tradition and Women's Cinema* (1989) provides an excellent example of this oversight. Although Fischer adopts an explicitly comparative approach, grounded in the conviction that feminist films are best understood as "'remakes' of the mainstream canon" (327), her actual juxtaposition of "women's films" with classic texts directed by men raises significant methodological concerns. In addition to her highly questionable, if not uncommon, practice of conflating "feminism" with "women," Fischer pairs works from different national traditions on the basis of shared thematic or stylistic features, and her analysis clearly rests on the assumption that differences of language and cultural context are not worthy even of mention, let alone consideration.

Moreover, the universalist assumptions of psychoanalytical criticism, even as they position the image of Woman at the center of film as an art form, may paradoxically also lead theorists to ignore gender itself as a historical and cultural construct. This may help explain the curious absence of any French contribution to "The Spectatrix," a special issue that *Camera Obscura* devoted in 1989 to contemporary multicultural responses to Mulvey's seminal essay in the still relatively radical belief that "different geographical contexts often illuminate the extent to which theory is inflected by national and cultural determinations" (Bergstrom & Doane 14). Many, even most, of the essays included frequently refer to the work of such Freudian theorists as Christian Metz and Raymond Bellour as well as citing that of Freud and Lacan directly. In this context, as the editors note: "The most surprising omission is undoubtedly France, considering the immeasurable impact of French film theory internationally. However, there is a distinct absence of film theory written in France that is concerned with feminist issues, nor has there been any effort to publish translations of influential work from the anglophone or German-speaking world" (Bergstrom & Doane 22).

In arguing for comparativism, Fischer also notes that "to say that feminist studies should take a comparative approach is not to indicate what the precise nature of that comparison might be" (*Shot/Countershot* 7). By limiting

Double Takes

my comparative base to two specific cultural contexts and pairing texts explicitly conceived to be in intertextual and cross-cultural dialogue, I believe that I can contribute to the evolution of cultural studies, film studies, and gender studies toward increased attentiveness and greater inclusiveness in all three areas: culture, cinema, and gender. At the same time, my work remains heavily indebted to the critical and theoretical insights of many others, and particularly those, no doubt, whom I have had and will continue to have occasion to critique. Notably, I will draw upon Mulvey's work in the area of what the editors of "The Spectatrix" (*Camera Obscura* 20–21) now define "as a category in its own right, gaze theory" (Bergstrom & Doane 19), which focuses on the construction of the spectator as a gendered subject and on film as an inherently voyeuristic medium and the realm of male fantasy. I will also refer often to feminist strategies of "reading against the grain" or what Charlotte Brunsdon has called the "re-making of classical popular cultural texts" (qtd. in Bergstrom & Doane 21) on the example inaugurated by Pam Cook and Claire Johnston, who first argued for the significance of textual ruptures or ideological disjunctures within mainstream cinema. I am similarly indebted to the ongoing debate over realism that has taken place within feminist film theory and which has resulted in multiple analyses, in the work of Fischer, Ellis, and many others, of the dominant discourse of heterosexual romance and of the editing and narrative strategies that support it.

Narrative structure in general will also be among my central concerns, since it figures so importantly in the understanding of both the individual works that I will analyze here, often characterized by patterns of internal repetition, and of their relationship to comparable texts. Darnton's notion of "culture-as-language" (260) points as well to my continued interest throughout the pages to come in the pedagogy that underlies the study of a foreign language and culture. Alice Kaplan describes the dilemma facing American students of French, caught between the desire for originality and the need for imitation, in terms that echo the concerns of this project: "They can't believe that language isn't theirs to remake" (135). French film is often studied within the context of foreign language departments, and Collins and his coeditors suggest in *Film Theory Goes to the Movies* that it is time to reconsider "the pedagogical dimensions of the practice of film theory, that pedagogical function becoming a theoretical issue in and of itself now that the study of popular culture is inseparable from the ongoing debate over the politics of education" (6). The practice and theory of translation, many of whose standard procedures in the case of French and English are analogous to strategies used in remaking films, will also play a role in the pages to come. In a discussion of Hollywood's recent passion for remakes, Paul Arthur notes that "the process of theme and variation is endemic to commercial film making." By chance, he also cites Euro Disney as evidence that American popular culture has become a "global lingua franca." Many others would concur with Prince Charles that "the universal language is bad English and much of that can be heard at Euro Disney" (Corliss, "Voilà" 83).

Robert Darnton argues that even if his version of cultural history resists traditional standards of evidence ("World views cannot be pinned down with 'proof'"), it is sufficient to analyze texts attentively and compare them systematically to reach an understanding of cultural difference (261). Because I also believe that critical theory must be closely tied to the analysis of textual practice(s), I have sought in this introduction to provide nothing more than a general framework for the analyses to come. To repeat, in a new context, what Elaine Showalter once said about women's writing: "No theory, however suggestive, can be a substitute for the close and extensive knowledge of [cultural] texts which constitutes our essential subject" ("Feminist" 205). Moreover, in a statement that I will have occasion to recall more than once, Michel Serceau, one of the editors of *CinémAction*'s special issue on remakes and adaptations, cautions against both defining "a remake" too narrowly (6) and constructing "a theory of the remake" too hastily (9). This is advice that I have attempted to take very seriously. Although my methodology always remains in some sense comparative, I have also sought to vary the kind of comparisons I use and to multiply the contexts in which they take place in order to explore more fully cross-cultural differences and similarities between France and the United States. What results is less the continuous development characteristic of a sequence of chapters than a structure of recurrence and repetition, no doubt better suited to a study of remakes, that unites a series of interrelated essays. Written, as Darnton says, to "essay" ideas (262), the texts to come, like their introduction, privilege integration over assimilation. Thus, in the event that Euro Disney's presence throughout these pages has sometimes seemed once again to position the amusement park somewhere it doesn't belong, be forewarned that this is unlikely to be the last text to show up in what may initially appear to be the wrong place.

My opening essay on Alain Resnais's *I Want to Go Home* (1989), written by the American cartoonist Jules Feiffer, reintroduces a number of general methodological concerns and addresses them in a specific context. In one of the first English-language films to be able to claim French nationality, Resnais turns the comic strip into an insightful tool of cross-cultural analysis that mediates between American visual culture and French literary culture. Full of self-reflective visual jokes and structured like a postmodernist treasure house of intertextual references, *I Want to Go Home* includes literal remakes of some of the films it cites, notably Vincente Minnelli's *An American in Paris* (1959) and Jean Renoir's *The Rules of the Game* (1939). In remaking Jean-Luc Godard's *A Bout de souffle*, the subject of my second chapter, Jim McBride also turns to the culture of the American comic book to complement the cinematic self-referentiality that characterizes his original French model. The comparison between these two new versions of cross-cultural romance focuses attention on the relationship between gender and culture, as McBride transforms a conflict between lovers of different nationalities into a crisis within American masculinity.

The analysis of Coline Serreau's *Trois Hommes et un couffin* (1985) and Leonard Nimoy's *Three Men and a Baby* (1988) confirms the importance of narrative structure and of the historical and theoretical context of feminism(s) to an understanding of the differences between French films and their American remakes. The comparative study of Serreau's and Nimoy's films also establishes particular patterns of change that will, in subsequent analyses, prove to be recurrent, notably, a shift in genre from "feminine" French realism to "masculine" American farce and the dependence of both original and remake on internally repetitive motifs. *Three Men and a Little Lady* (1990), Emile Ardolino's Franco-American co-production, also constitutes a curious bicultural hybrid that mediates between Serreau's original French film and Nimoy's American remake. The discussion in my fourth chapter of *French in Action*, Pierre Capretz's video textbook, which provides yet another version of cross-cultural romance and of the adventures of an American in Paris, addresses the degree to which the teaching of French (language, literature, and culture) determines how Americans view France. As the site of a national educational debate over curricular reform in general, and over sexism and ethnocentrism in the study of foreign languages in particular, *French in Action* also further clarifies the role played by visual media and by postmodernist textuality in constructing discourses of culture and gender. This discussion highlights the role that the remake phenomenon could play in pushing the pedagogical goals of foreign language study well beyond its traditional boundaries.

The comparison of Jean-Charles Tacchella's *Cousin, Cousine* (1975) and Joel Schumacher's *Cousins* (1989) foregrounds the ethical and the aesthetic implications of both marital and cinematic "infidelity." In contrast to Serreau's and Nimoy's versions of *Three Men*, which reveal how the narratives of mothering, masculinity, and misogyny can be differently written within different cultures, the divergent discourses of gender in *Cousin, Cousine* and its remake function essentially to point to broader areas of Franco-American cultural differences. Parallel narratives of adultery serve in turn to illustrate a particular understanding of freedom, which underlies French national identity, and to inform a cultural thematics of happiness, which is of equal importance to an American sense of cultural specificity. The subsequent analysis of François Truffaut's *L'Homme qui aimait les femmes* (1977) and Blake Edwards's *The Man Who Loved Women* (1983) introduces still further complexity into an understanding of the interaction of gender and culture. Those scenes retained by Edwards tend to present gender stereotypes perceived as

Disneyland comes home to Paris. Subway poster, November 1995, author's photo.

universal and therefore transcultural; in contrast, those episodes that Edwards either omits or adds focus on gender as a culturally specific social and historical construction. Mediated by Yvonne Rainer's *The Man Who Envied Women* (1985), Truffaut's and Edwards's films also allow the relationship between classical narrative cinema and contemporary film theory to be explored. The three films together provide textbook illustrations of theoretical concerns about the centrality of the look, the visual objectification of women by a cinematic gaze coded as "male," the use of psychoanalysis as a critical tool, and the ideological significance of textual moments of narrative rupture.

Finally, the broad discussion of the final essay emphasizes the general importance of comedy within French national cinema, as well as in Hollywood, and returns to a number of general methodological and theoretical concerns, including the importance of comparison itself, which were raised in previous essays. In contrast to the general argument of the book as a whole, the evident fact that not all Hollywood remakes of French films effectively reconceive them and reveal interesting cultural differences is discussed in relation to such paired works as Luc Besson's *La Femme Nikita* (199) and John Badham's *Point of No Return* (1993), since remade as a popular television series, and Edouard Molinaro's *La Cage aux folles* (1978) and Mike Nichols's *The Birdcage* (1996). A more general discussion of Francis Veber's cross-cultural work confirms the significance and the divergent manifestations of the homoerotic and homophobic subtext that consistently underlie Franco-American cinematic explorations of masculinity.

Roger Cohen bases the recommendation to take "another look at re-makes," which I have chosen to follow, on a premise that he and I find virtu-ally self-evident, although, as we have already seen, it does not appear to be widely shared: cultural differences—ones both visible and worth seeing—separate Hollywood's remakes from the French films on which they are based. As I follow Cohen's advice, however, I will want to challenge his as-sumption that the space thus opened up between France and the United States reflects incompatibilities so fundamental as to be irreconcilable. The very idea of a "remake"—the word is the same in French and English—ar-gues against this view. Official French hostility to the cultural invasiveness of the United States (and vice versa) is at least balanced—and often out-weighed—by the general public's infatuation with the products of that inva-sion, hence Victoria de Grazia's useful advice: "To avoid old debates, we might accept that American cinema is 'good,' like French wine; the problem is to determine how the myth of its goodness was constructed and spread" (87). To put it succinctly, Euro Disney is also *at home* in France. "*La preuve*" (your evidence), as the French would say? In a recent subway campaign (No-vember 1995) promoting the amusement park, Euro Disney is nowhere to be seen—nor, for that matter, is Marne-la-Vallée. We are invited, quite simply, to visit "Disneyland Paris."[10]

Comic Strips and Cultural Stereotypes

Alain Resnais's *I Want to Go Home*

I have deliberately chosen to devote the opening essay of a comparative study of French and American culture not only to a single film, Alain Resnais's *I Want to Go Home* (1989), but also to one that is no doubt relatively unknown even to readers well acquainted with contemporary French cinema. To my knowledge, the film was never released in the United States and is only available on videotape in a dubbed version, even though Resnais figures prominently among those French directors who enjoy international reputations and the film in question has both English as its primary language and American culture as its principal subject. The inability of such a film to find a U.S. distributor, despite its evident accessibility and interest, clearly provides support for the French view that America's reputed antipathy to foreign films is less a fact of the moviegoing public than a fiction of the movie-making industry. Certainly the latter has everything to gain, since such a myth simultaneously protects American-made movies, eliminates foreign competition, and justifies Hollywood's current obsession with remaking the French films. As Richard Roud points out, however, this also means that the American public has only a limited and stereotypical knowledge of French film, largely determined by the choices—negative as well as positive—of U.S. distributors: "Thus our view of the French cinema has been conditioned as much by what we have *not* seen as by what we have" (15).

By chance, the conception and initial planning phase of *I Want to Go Home* roughly coincide with the period during which Disney was negotiating a contract to build an amusement park in Europe. But if Euro Disney eventually found a home, however controversial and apparently incongruous, at Marne-la-Vallée, Resnais's film, despite its title, can never expect to be really at home anywhere. Disneyland Paris disorients; *I Want to Go Home* profoundly dislocates. Some of Resnais's best-known films have been the result of an unusually close collaboration between director and scriptwriter; and certainly the choice of such novelists as Marguerite Duras (*Hiroshima, mon amour*) and Alain Robbe-Grillet (*L'Année dernière à Marienbad*) was neither obvious nor conventional at the time. Still, even in this context, the assigning of the screenplay to Jules Feiffer, an American better known as a cartoonist than a playwright, who speaks virtually no French, is surprising. As one reviewer notes, in a statement that seems more descriptive than critical: "Resnais' profoundly European artistic sensibility is alien to Feiffer's loose caricatural style" (Len. 32). Moreover, although *I Want to Go Home* was filmed in France with a French production crew, the casting intermingles French and Americans—both actors and the characters they play—in approximately equal numbers; and all of them speak English most of the time (the French included) and French some of the time (Americans included). Since 1989, the same year the Euro Disney contract was signed, English-language films have been able to claim French nationality; and *Home* was one of thirty such projects that year, out of a total of ninety, to take advantage of the new government regulations. In fact, the movie exists in two equally curious versions, whose relationship replicates that of "model" and "copy" in the case of remakes and points to the difficulty of determining either origin or originality within postmodernist culture. Resnais's "original" film has an English sound track and French subtitles; "la version française" consists of a French film made in English that has been dubbed (back) into French.

According to François Thomas, whose *L'Atelier d'Alain Resnais* recounts in detail the filming of *I Want to Go Home*, only financial restraints prevented the director from constructing two different sets for every scene in order to reflect the contradictory viewpoints of his two American protagonists (293). For his own count, Thomas repeatedly speculates on the cross-cultural distinctions that he believes inform the entire project. He notes, for example, that Feiffer's script "can give rise to two different films depending on whether the director is American or French" (289). Similarly, every scene and the film as a whole allow for alternative interpretations as either funny or painful depending on the nationality of the character(s) with whom one chooses to identify at any given moment (301). Perhaps this tension accounts for the radically dissimilar reactions of reviewers, who do not appear to be talking about the same film. For *Cahiers du cinéma*, *I Want to Go Home* is nothing less than "a cerebral adventure" and an "allegory of melancholy" that "touches something essential—and ineffable" (Mazabrard 56). *Variety*, in contrast, reports on "a stillborn satiric comedy" that "leaves an aftertaste of perplexed dissatisfaction and faint embarrassment" (Len. 32). Last, if not least, Resnais's film has one additional distinguishing feature that furthers its capacity for perpetual disorientation. *I Want to Go Home* combines animation and live action;

Joey and Hepp Cat arrive in Paris. *I Want to Go Home* combines animation and live action as cartoon characters in balloons pop up periodically to comment on the behavior of their human counterparts. Copyright © 1989, France 2 Cinema.

cartoon characters in balloons pop up periodically to comment on the behavior of their human counterparts.

As a film that transgresses a number of boundaries—between national and international, native and foreign, art and popular entertainment—*I Want to Go Home* is of considerable methodological significance as well. Although, as I have noted, Robert Darnton saw his early work in "l'histoire des mentalités" as leading into the "unmapped territory" of a genre that "ha[d] not yet received a name in English" (3), with increasing frequency more recent inquiries into cultural difference describe their interests and approaches as parallel, if not identical, to those of contemporary anthropology and ethnography. In this context, Resnais's film, despite its title plea, best qualifies as a travelogue, and one, moreover, that draws together three paradigmatic tales taken from three different fields of inquiry. *I Want to Go Home* includes, at one and the same time, the "tale of entry," whose importance within anthropology has led Victor Crapanzano to grant it the status of a "subgenre" of ethnographic writing (69); its literary equivalent, the narrative of the "innocent abroad"; and finally, that version of the same story that may be specific to film, the "American in Paris." Moreover, the alternate use of a female and a male hero in *Home*'s own internal repetition of these three superimposed plots opens up the possibility that the filmic narrative will also reveal something of interest about the interaction of gender and culture.

Darnton's work on fairy tales long ago convinced me of the usefulness of the comparative analysis of alternate versions of the "same" text in order to identify cultural differences. Hence my interest in American remakes of recent French films, to which *I Want to Go Home* bears at once a somewhat idiosyncratic and a potentially revealing relationship. The central and explicit concern of Resnais's film with Franco-American differences in language, culture, and national identity offers within a single film the kind of cross-cultural analysis that usually emerges only from comparing two or more films. Thus the structure of *Home* enables me to forgo comparison in this particular case, even as it justifies the extensive use I will subsequently make of this method of analysis. As we will see, remakes are also one of the explicit thematic concerns of *I Want to Go Home*. In addition, Resnais alludes, often quite specifically, to a number of other films within his own. Indeed, the intertexuality of *Home* is at times so marked that Resnais can be seen to "remake" at least certain sequences of some of the films he cites.

I Want to Go Home recounts the experiences—always interrelated, frequently at odds, and ultimately convergent—of two Americans in Paris. Elsie Wellman (Laura Benson) joyously pulls up roots and sets off to pursue graduate study at the Sorbonne. Two years later, at the invitation of an art gallery whose current exhibit features his work as a cartoonist, Joey (Joe E.) Wellman (Adolph Green), accompanied by his longtime companion Lena (Linda Lavin), reluctantly follows in his daughter's footsteps. Coincidence, in the form of Christian Gauthier (Gérard Depardieu), a noted French scholar who turns out to be both the inaccessible director of Elsie's thesis and Joey's most ardent fan, eventually reunites the estranged pair during a weekend at Gauthier's mother's home in the country. This event includes a costume party, where the guests dress like their favorite comic strip characters, which results in a series of revelations and reversals that convince Elsie to head home to Cleveland and Joey to stay in France.

When *I Want to Go Home* opened at the Venice Film Festival, *Variety* called it a "Franco-American hayride" that "lines up stick figures and half-baked sentimental or farcical situations" (Len. 32, 38). I am quite willing to agree with this assessment, provided that we go on to acknowledge that it is neither the result of an unfortunate accident nor some kind of unintentional error but, rather, precisely the point. The narrative structure of the film, which is almost as simplistic, schematic, and stereotypical in its realization as in my summary, suits to perfection a work clearly conceived as the filmic equivalent of a comic strip—and so conceived, I would suggest, because this is in fact a particularly appropriate form in which to explore constructions of national identity. Resnais's central concern with cultural difference and specificity logically results in a visual representation, both humorous and satirical, in which the distinctive features of his subjects are deliberately exaggerated or distorted or both, just as in the cartoon or the caricature. As Richard F. Kuisel points out, cross-cultural perceptions, especially those that remain relatively constant over time, as in the case of France and America, have been and continue to be highly patterned, characterized by stereotyped thinking that "tends toward simplification to the point of caricature" (9). The *bande dessinée* aspect of *I Want to Go Home* could also be interpreted as a reasonable visual representation of what Benedict Anderson, whose *Imagined Communities* has become the common reference point of other contemporary studies of nationalism, sees as the essentially fabricated and artificial quality of any notion of nation or national identity.

Resnais casts the cartoonist himself as the comic lead in the stereotypical plot of the unhappy tourist who has the extraordinary misfortune to encounter—in rapid succession, at the briefest of intervals, and always in a highly exaggerated form—the greatest possible number of a foreign culture's most characteristic pitfalls. In this Franco-American version of what may well be a universal story, Joey Wellman, a native of Cleveland, struggles to survive in the hostile environment of a France reduced to Paris and to a house somewhere in the country. (I would like to think that *Cahiers du cinéma* is right to identify the site as Normandy on the amusing—and not implausible—grounds that "débarquement oblige" [Mazabrard 54], but in fact the exact setting is never specified within the film itself.) An excursion that simply takes us into "la France profonde" also makes sense, however, since Paris too is interestingly void of its characteristic symbols—an art gallery at the Place des Vosges and an office inside the Collège de France are the closest we get to anything that might qualify as a national monument, let alone a tourist attraction. Thus the emphasis of the film is on Joey's encounter with French and Parisian culture, complete with obnoxious cab drivers, who will neither tell you where you are ("I'm not a guide. I'm a taxi driver. You can't really expect to have everything for a hundred francs, now can you?") nor take you where you want to go; unrecognizable food that omits "le breakfast" and emphasizes the "organic" in a very different sense than in the United States; pay phones whose rejection of money (even the frivolous and confusing local variety) differentiates them from virtually everything and everyone else in Paris ("At least in Cleveland, when you don't eat something, it doesn't cost a fortune"); a bewildering bureaucratic structure run by unreliable and irresponsible public officials; and an apparently mad population who alternate between outrageous flattery and open insult and whose only consistency lies in the stubborn refusal to speak English—all the while submerged in a near-impenetrable fog of cigarette smoke.

Double Takes

Resnais complements this American's-eye view of the French—or, rather, this Frenchman's view of an American's view of the French (or maybe both, given the collaborative nature of the project)—with an equally stereotypical self-portrait of Christian Gauthier, Wellman's cross-cultural counterpart. Gauthier revels in juggling the many and paradoxical demands forced upon him by his double life as a committed *bon vivant* and a revered scholar and teacher. Rarely able to find time for his official academic responsibilities, Gauthier takes his officious duties as "un emmerdeur intellectuel" (an intellectual gadfly) very seriously indeed. He devotes his eloquence and his charm to transforming his irrepressible sociability and his appetite for sexual conquest into something a bit more noble—the inability to disappoint his friends, whatever the personal cost: "My most important work is still in progress, forever unfinished. But why? Because I'm irreplaceable, that's why. It's hell for a man to be as irreplaceable as I am. That's the cross I have to bear." With his customary energy and good humor, Gauthier insists that at heart he is nonetheless "un triste" (melancholic): "I've told you everything there was to know about Gauthier—*un triste et un emmerdeur intellectuel.*" Ever contradictory and ever resourceful ("Here's what we're going to do" is his answer to every and to everyone's problems), Resnais's Frenchman epitomizes "the System D," *la débrouillardise* (the ability to get by, to find a way around obstacles)—that is, what in the eyes of many constitutes Frenchness itself (see, for example, Zeldin 186–87).[1]

The choice of Gérard Depardieu to play this role is hardly insignificant. Ginette Vincendeau, whose work on Jean Gabin focuses on how a given actor can at a particular historical moment come to represent current conceptions of "Frenchness," both within and beyond France, has recently turned her attention to Depardieu, who she believes has become "as much an international icon as Maurice Chevalier used to be, especially since *Green Card* (1990)" (343). Certainly, within the corpus of films that gets distributed in the United States, Depardieu has become virtually synonymous with French cinema itself—to the point that I suspect American audiences might well challenge the authenticity of any film *sans* Depardieu that claimed to be French. (Perhaps this is why he shows up unexpectedly in a tiny cameo role in Jean Rappeneau's recent *Le Hussard sur le toit* [1995], the most expensive French film ever made and a project apparently conceived in part for the purpose of appealing to an American public.) Surprisingly, Vincendeau never mentions *I Want to Go Home*, although Resnais's film appeared a year before *Green Card* and Feiffer's final script was completed some three years earlier. Yet *Home* already assumes the inseparability of Depardieu and French culture to the point that it can function as a self-reflexive visual joke. As Elsie, en route to Paris, waxes ecstatic over the great French writers whose books are spread out before her, the camera gradually moves in to show us Depardieu's photo on the back of the one she is holding, Christian Gauthier's *Les Enigmes de Flaubert*: "Oh Racine, here I am. Molière, your shore draws near. Apollinaire, do you hear me? You would understand me, Jean-Paul. Oh Simone, so would you . . . Oh Flaubert . . . My thesis director. Oh Christian Gauthier, successor to all of them, . . . *la crème de la crème de la Sorbonne*." For Resnais, the selection of his leading American actor was similarly significant. (Thomas reports that the first two contracts signed, well before the completion of the script, were those of Green and Depardieu [291].) Adolph Green and his partner Betty Camden have written either the lyrics or the script for over fifteen musical comedies, including *Singing in the Rain* and *New York, New York*; the soundtrack of *Home* includes three of his songs. Toward the end of the film, Green's association with American popular culture is highlighted in a self-referential scene, to which I will return, that is comparable to the one featuring Depardieu.[2]

In a description that is less inexact than incomplete, *Variety* characterizes Depardieu's role as "a dead end, never growing beyond the cultural stereotype" (Len. 38). Let me repeat that I too see *I Want to Go Home* as a kind of cross-cultural comic strip. I will argue, however, that this is only one dimension of the film and that Resnais simultaneously pursues an analysis of cultural identity and difference that far exceeds the boundaries of caricature. As I have discussed in the introductory chapter to this book, scholars generally agree both that nations construct their sense of identity through a dialectical relationship with those defined as "other," and that France and the United States constitute one clear example of such interaction. No doubt few of us need to consult either books or specialists to know that French attitudes toward Americans—and vice versa—are often ambivalent, if not simply contradictory. Each maintains a classic love/hate relationship with the other. To some extent, the well-known refrain "I Love France/I Hate The French" may be only the American version of a script that has been dubbed into so many languages that any hope of recovering the *version originale* has long been lost. (Even in English, there are clearly variants: "I love France/I Hate Parisians," for example, or "I Hate Paris/I Love Châteaux," and so on.) Still, the history of Franco-American relations since World War II suggests that the United States can fairly claim the rights to at least the modern remake of this perhaps more universal tale. The Francophone version of this difficult liaison dates from the same period; and although the French too have a number of rivals, they have devoted themselves to both pro- and anti-Americanism with a passion worthy of an exclusive commitment. In the Francocentric rendition of "I Love America/I Hate America" or, as the French would say, "Je t'aime moi non plus," official Frenchdom deplores "American cultural imperialism" as a threat to the very existence of France as an independent nation and a distinctive culture, even as the general public continues to give the products of this foreign invasion a relatively warm welcome.

Double Takes

Resnais uses the metaphor of the divided family to articulate and to emphasize the fundamentally dialectical nature of this kind of cultural conflict. Elsie counters her father's exaggerated fears of French culture with an infatuation that is every bit as disproportionate, and which, in contrast to the American tendency to distinguish between feelings about the country and its citizens (so ingrained that even Joey pays it some heed), takes the extravagant form of attempting her own cultural reincarnation as a French native. This process logically requires that she shed all signs of the vulgar materialism and anti-intellectualism associated with middle-class America. Already during the flight to Paris, between "Simone" and "Flaubert" in the ode to Gauthier quoted above, Elsie explains precisely what still separates her from them: "I am fleeing from the self-importance of all the closed-minded boors of Cleveland chic. I am fleeing toward a culture where it isn't ridiculous to think during dinner parties." Two years later, she is still struggling: "I wandered about like a lost soul all night long to prove to myself that I'm neither vulgar nor provincial, that I don't have a middle-class mind. *I* don't wear polyester. *I* don't read comic books. I refuse, as Flaubert would say, to sell my soul. In short, I don't belong to Cleveland, that godforsaken place." The Gauthier family is similarly divided. Gauthier's generous insistence on sharing whoever currently qualifies as the object of his overwhelming affection for Americans and their culture ("My mother has never seen a crazy American cartoonist," he tells Joey on the way to the country; "you will be my gift to her") is received by his family as a horrible imposition and a trial by boredom. As Gauthier's mother Isabelle (Micheline Presle) suggests upon receipt of her son's latest "gift": "You never come to see me without bringing me an entire army. And why is it always the American army?"

In *I Want to Go Home*, Resnais turns the comic strip into a particularly insightful tool of cultural analysis by establishing a double equation between American and "low" or popular culture, on the one hand, and between French and "high" or elite culture, on the other. As we have seen, Kuisel and others predict that issues of culture, and in particular Hollywood and American mass culture as a threat to the "true" culture of France (hence the conflict over Euro Disney) will increasingly be the focus of French resistance to "Americanization" in the nineties: "The basis of anti-Americanism is cultural and pivots on the notion of protecting and disseminating *civilisation*" (236). Kuisel's sense of *civilisation* would make Gauthier its near-perfect embodiment; the word connotes, for example, a humanistic education; a style of life equated with good food, wine, and *le bon goût*; and a philosophical stance that is at once skeptical, tragic, and realistic (235–36). Interestingly, however, it is not the French professor but the American student who views France less as a specific cultural domain than as the very seat of *civilisation* itself. Even if modern France has had to abandon most of the reality—if not yet all of the rhetoric—of the *mission civilisatrice* that historically defined its national identity and determined its international role, Elsie's faith is still intact. Indeed, in her desire to become more French than the French themselves, she voluntarily surrenders to France's cultural missionaries on their own soil. Elsie's elitist notion of civilization is embodied in a literary canon of "master works," dominated by the neoclassical writers of the seventeenth century—Racine, Molière, Pascal— and by the nineteenth-century novelist Flaubert, the subject of Gauthier's book and of Elsie's own thesis.[3] The prominence thus accorded to a great stylist, whose prose has given rise to countless *explications de textes*, reflects the particular importance that Elsie accords to the verbal text, to written language, in her sense of *civilisation*. What she repeatedly laments about her father is nothing less than his (cultural) illiteracy: "He hasn't read a single one of Flaubert's books. 'Mickey Mouse' is the only book he ever gave me."

The response to Elsie's complaint comes appropriately from Sally Catt, the comic strip character Wellman once created for his daughter and who, to Elsie's dismay, accompanies her to France. As Sally Catt explains what constitutes culture for Joey, she is successively transformed on screen into each of the cartoon figures she names: "His culture consists of Garfield, Charlie Brown, Snoopy, and Mickey Mouse." *I Want to Go Home* immediately establishes this opposition between a French literary culture and an American visual culture in the opening sequence of the film. Resnais's camera tracks through the dark airplane, past the intent faces of the other passengers, who are all clearly engrossed in the movie being shown, the projection of which provides the scene's only source of light, until the camera turns to discover a single reading lamp still lit and then moves in to reveal Elsie and finally, in close-up, the French books spread out before her. Resnais uses the comic strip, at the opposite end of the hierarchical scale of cultural art forms from Flaubert, to mediate between American culture as a whole and the Hollywood film industry, whose paradoxical ability to dominate the international market with a reportedly mediocre product makes it the ideal example of "American cultural imperialism." (Although we never see the in-flight film, the series of explosions we hear on the sound track, accompanied visually by the smile of a delighted child, certainly suggests an American action-adventure movie.)

Even Gauthier, the *bande dessinée* collector and connoisseur who has earlier condemned a proposal to transfer Joey's Hepp Catt to the screen ("Look at Pépé—animation destroyed a creation of genius"), appears at one point to equate the comic strip with the animated cartoon.[4] In an effort to prove Wellman worthy of the attention of his family and friends, Gauthier coerces Joey into a public performance of his ability to draw—not his own cartoon characters, however, but those of Walt Disney and Warner Brothers. The comic strip also functions as a metaphor for the poor quality of American movies, dismissed as a whole through the paradigmatic example of Steven Spielberg, who "doesn't make films; he makes comic books," according to Harry Dempsey (John Ashton), ex-Hollywood director and Wellman's rival for the position of Gauthier's current favorite American genius, who now films only remakes himself—in exile. Harry chooses the vernissage of the American cartoon exhibit and a position in front of a huge reproduction of Hepp Catt to pronounce the definitive death of American culture: "Shit. America has no more culture. Our art is dead, our theater is dead, our music is dead, our films are dead . . . I'm as dead as this lousy cartoon . . . Nobody reads this guy any more. He's dead."

Apart from its mediating functions, however, Resnais grants the comic strip considerable significance in its own right. As a form of entertainment associated, at least in part, with children, it tends to connote the naïve, the simplistic, the innocent—it is humorous but harmless. More generally, it strives for accessibility, epitomizes dailiness, and appears most often in an eminently disposable consumer product. In short, the comic strip offers as perfect an embodiment of the stereotypical traits of the American character and culture as the "civilizing mission" does of Frenchness. Gauthier's words upon first meeting Joey convey this message in an explicitly comparative context:

> You're so much at ease [*si bien dans votre peau*], so real, you Americans, while we're so secretive, so cynical. I can't bear our cynicism any more—and neither can you, that goes without saying. Even though you're no longer a young man, your work radiates all the innocence of the American emigrant—the dreamer, what sustains hope, what Hollywood has achieved.

The fact that it is an American (Elsie) who believes most strongly in the standard French view of Frenchness and a native of France (Gauthier) who most enthusiastically embraces certain traits and values defined as characteristically American suggests the complexity with which Resnais treats issues of national identity and of cross-cultural relationships. Notably, *I Want to Go Home* approaches the question of cultural expansionism or imperialism with a healthy dose of amusement and skepticism. Perhaps the best single example is the ironic reversal of reality that Harry's remakes represent, both in terms of national origin and of aesthetic value. In perfect contradiction to actual practice, Harry directs French remakes of Hollywood films; moreover, they are well received critically. As Gauthier tells Joey, "Harry is a great director, a genius . . . Who can forget the remakes of *High Noon*, *Public Enemy*, or *To Have and Have Not*? Unforgettable." Nor is Harry himself at all modest about his success: "Hollywood loathes me. And why? Because my remakes are better—that's why." Frankly, to the extent that French culture has been and is undergoing a process commonly called "Americanization," I have always suspected that the French themselves act as the principal agents in what might be more accurately described as the "Frenchification" or perhaps the "Gallicization" of a newly colonized foreign culture. Such a strategy is perfectly consistent with what I described earlier as a French preference for assimilation over integration in culture as well as in politics. (As Elsie's experience suggests, the *mission civilisatrice* may simply have moved its base of operations back to the home office—less as a result of a reduction *in* than a redistribution *of* the candidates available for conversion.)[5]

Resnais provides a concrete example of the process of assimilation that can occur when France's civilizing mission meets American cultural imperialism. The French justify their interest in America's cartoon culture by literally remaking it as "art"—by blowing it up to portrait size and repositioning it on the wall of a gallery. (Given the importance here of both place and the kind of critical discourse that accompanies it, one is inevitably reminded of the Michelin guide to Euro Disney.) Joey's original assessment of the projected exhibit is therefore in some sense both exact and inexact: "You have to be absolutely insane to send people to an art gallery to see cartoons. The French won't understand a thing." In fact, it is less that the French will not understand at all than that they will no doubt understand somewhat differently. Despite the prevalence of a certain official discourse that differentiates French from American culture in ways that simply replicate traditional distinctions between "high" and "low" culture, and thus essentially support a pro-French or an anti-American agenda, the results of assimilation actually strike me as slightly more subtle and interesting. It follows logically from this cross-cultural contrast that French culture, that is, what is recognized within France *as* culture—what becomes culture by virtue of being *in* France—will, by definition, always belong to the realm of "high" or "true" culture, even in the absence of a comparative context: hence Jerry Lewis and, more recently, Mickey Rourke (via Michael Cimino) (see Levy and Stanley); increasingly Euro Disney; and certainly the cartoon, animated or not and regardless of national origin. Richard Bernstein is one of many cultural commentators to single out the *bande dessinée* as the "most popular cultural form in France" (223); Astérix and Obélix appropriately dominate the cover of *Time*'s special issue on "The New France" (July 15, 1991). Gauthier's library contains an admirable collection of the works of "artists" such as Al Capp, Will Eisner, Roy Crane, Robert Kreb, Art Spiegelmann, and . . . Joey Wellman ("No one has ever taken me for an artist—it's incredible"). In response to Harry's (American) disdain for comic strips and animated cartoons, Gauthier's friend Terry (Geraldine Chaplin) praises Disney's "great tragic vision" and Gauthier himself not only defends Spielberg but radically raises the cinematic stakes in the process: "But why banish the comic strip? Orson Welles himself acknowledged Milton Caniff's influence on *Citizen Kane*."[6]

Double Takes

This tendency to identify a cultural entity (an American comic strip) as specifically French only when it can be reconceptualized nonspecifically as part of a general category (Art) supports the relatively common association of Frenchness with a propensity for abstract thought (as does France's preferred self-representation in the supranational form of "civilization"). In contrast, the same process seems to function in U.S. culture in reverse. Americans claim a phenomenon as cultural (that is, as representative of *American* culture) to the extent that it *resists* generalization and can be reconceptualized *more* specifically as a personalized, individualized, even psychologized event (see, for example, Nostrand). In the final scene of *I Want to Go Home*, Joey, who is allowed to have the last word, suddenly reveals to Isabelle Gauthier his own understanding of typically American behavior: "If you find that I talk about myself too much, like all Americans do, I want you to kick me out. If I make too many confidences that are too personal, like all Americans do too, if I reveal too much about myself, if I'm too sincere, just kick me out, without any explanation." *What* Joey says may be even less revealing than *how* he says it; his "I" immediately assumes personal responsibility for traits explicitly—and repeatedly—introduced as culturally determined.[7] Similarly, in the scene in which the film's title and thematics become most closely united, Joey uses the particularistic thinking that determines the pattern of his own perceptions to gain some understanding of a very different world view: "I want to go home—is that so hard to understand? Yes. I'll tell you why, because I figured it out. Because here the whole point is that everything is meant to be hard to understand—including my own daughter, including my girlfriend, including the people who say they're my friends."[8] Howard L. Nostrand maintains that Americans, who are uncomfortable in the presence of abstraction, always demand examples (469). Joey's behavior suggests that Americans will, if necessary, provide their own examples, even their own selves as examples.[9]

In general, the American narrative within *I Want to Go Home* constantly superimposes two parallel story lines, one specifically cultural, one individual (and consequently, in this case, culturally specific). At the same time that Joey, the miserable American tourist, exhibits a wide range of highly stereotypical behavior that can only be classified as sociocultural, everything he says and does is also a direct response to a personal relationship—his estrangement from his daughter—and to the psychological anguish he feels as a result. Notably, the comic strip that promotes Wellman to the position of international artist—and therefore of representative American—simultaneously reconciles father and daughter. Elsie's decision to return to America has as much to do with the resolution of her conflict with her father ("I'm going home—I'm not mad at you anymore") as it does with her disengagement from French culture. Moreover, the particular way in which she subsequently reclaims her national identity sanctions her sense of belonging to a culture in which the personal and the psychological matter: "What a surprise. I'm an American and I want to be happy. So I'm going home in order to be happy, because I'm not happy here."

I Want to Go Home not only reveals how the private acts of individuals simultaneously reflect a culturally informed sense of both self and the world, but also explores the effect that constructions of national identity can have on the personal lives of ordinary people. Any recent analysis of Frenchness inevitably brings to mind the sometimes virulent polemic that currently surrounds this issue. The increasingly visible presence of an Arab population born in France of immigrant parents has lately renewed interest in the question of what it means to be French—a question "posed," in Bernstein's words, "as though the very survival of the French nation were at stake" (161). Bernstein argues that the general public supports a position that to some extent mediates between the conflicting views that Frenchness depends on shared knowledge of a common culture or that it depends on natural ties of blood or racial similarity: "The assumption, shared by many who do not otherwise associate with the far right, is, essentially, that the French identity is something, not that you have exactly to be born with, but that at least has to be inculcated early on in life" (112).

The uncharacteristic awkwardness with which Bernstein states this idea, due in large part to the number of qualifiers that its expression evidently requires, offers an intriguing and no doubt accurate reflection of both the difficulty of attempting to reconcile contradictory beliefs and the imprecision of the notion of Frenchness that results from the effort. It also seems appropriate that language should call attention to itself in this particular context, since language and national identity are, of course, frequently conflated in France. On the one hand, French, like any other language, is certainly available to be learned, potentially with native (or near-native) fluency. On the other hand, the inevitable duality of linguistic interaction, by virtue of which every language is simultaneously native and foreign, somehow seems to break down in France, where native speakers often appear unable to accept "foreign French." A convincing argument can be made that it is more difficult in France than elsewhere for a foreigner to be (mis)taken for a native speaker, not only because the standards are exceptionally high and because the French delight in their ability to detect "imposters," but also because they engage in certain practices that might be characterized as "protectionist." Although the French frequently lament the declining importance of their language (an effect largely attributed to an increase in speakers of English) and actively support policies that encourage the teaching of French worldwide, back home they nonetheless regularly thwart the efforts of foreigners to speak (and therefore to learn and to perfect) their language by insistently responding to them in an English that they often command far less well than the foreigners do French.[10]

Double Takes

I Want to Go Home includes just such an incident. Elsie, understandably frustrated at showing up yet again for an appointment that Gauthier has once more canceled, finds her rightful expression of outrage transformed into public humiliation. Gauthier's secretary first responds by switching into English, as if Elsie were suddenly unable to understand French, and then proceeds to correct her French.[11] In other ways, too, Resnais uses Elsie's experience in France to work out an answer to the very question that Frenchness raises for Bernstein: "Can a foreigner become French and be regarded by those born French as just as French as they?" (112). During the weekend in the country, Elsie overhears a conversation that not only shatters her illusions of personal competence in "Frenchness" but also attacks her very pretensions as ridiculous. Moreover, Gauthier's scorn, provoked by Elsie's stated hope in an earlier scene to speak French "well enough to pass for a Frenchwoman," explicitly links language and national identity: "[That] stuck-up girl? Oh no. The mixed-up Americans who come over here and ape French people are nothing but dissidents, traitors. We should put them all on a plane that takes them straight back to Cleveland, Minneapolis, or New York."

What happens to Elsie serves as a *mise en abyme*, a mirror image of the filmic experience as a whole, structured around a similarly painful conversation meant to be overheard by its own audience. Initially, as in the opening sequence of *Home* in which Elsie, en route to Paris, thinks aloud, we are more amused than surprised at the sound of her heavily accented and anglicized classroom French. But what we overhear in the next scene, and what the film subsequently reiterates every time she opens her mouth, is the incredible (indeed, I would argue, impossible) fact that after two full years of complete and uninterrupted immersion in the language and the culture of France, the quality of Elsie's spoken French has not improved in the slightest. In fact, although it would be difficult under these conditions to prove conclusively that her linguistic facility actually *decreases* in the course of the film, this pattern would be entirely consistent with the foreignness of French for Elsie; and eventually an undeniable change does occur. In the final conversation that she attempts in France, subsequent to her decision to go home, Elsie's French has already "left" her (literally) incomprehensible and very nearly speechless—she first can't remember the word *tranquille* and then she can't pronounce it! Resnais's linguistic fantasy suggests that the language of France, like its national identity, is "something, not that you have exactly to be born with, but that at least has to be inculcated early on in life" (Bernstein 112).

To digress briefly into the realm of domestic policy, longstanding assumptions in France about language and national identity are clearly being confounded of late by the presence of a new generation who may be of Arab descent and whose parents may have been immigrants, but who are themselves native-born French citizens who speak French as their native language. Margot Hornblower reports that "the children of France's former colonies are confronting their one-time masters with a basic identity question: 'To be French, must one be named Marcel rather than Muhammed?'" (27). Interestingly, by formulating the question in terms of naming, Hornblower to some extent leaves intact the historic inseparability of nationality and language.[12] The real issue, of course, is the growing number of French-speaking French who are neither white nor of European background. In Richard Bernstein's words, "race relations and ethnic conflicts" are the "central domestic problems" that France must face today and in the future (151). Although race relations surely constitute one of America's "central domestic problems" as well, the multiculturalism of the United States puts a slightly different twist on the question of naming. Precisely because racial difference has historically been more problematic than ethnicity, the recent preference that many Black Americans have expressed for the term *African Americans* is a potentially ingenious strategy. Even if you cannot change the attitudes that some of your fellow citizens hold, you can reposition yourself in relation to those attitudes.

Although France professes to export a universal *civilisation*, which therefore presumably abandons its French nationality at the country's borders, the Frenchness that circulates internally would appear to be not just *special* (distinctive) but even *especial* (exceptional). Bernstein uses the appropriately self-reflexive term *franco-français* (Franco-French) to sum up the belief that "only the French can really understand the French," that they are "incomprehensible to the rest of the world" (11). Joey, as we know, reaches a similar conclusion: "Here that's the whole point. Everything is meant to be hard to understand." But, ironically, in that case the same cachet of Franco-Frenchness that confers prestige on such homemade products as French films simultaneously increases the chances that they will have to be remade abroad, since in this context the French seem to take pride in the very impossibility of successful cultural exportation. In contrast to the internal process of assimilation that I have called "Frenchification," "Americanization" names a cross-cultural activity. "Americanness" may lend itself to such transplantation to the extent that a nation sustained by successive waves of immigrants periodically reproduces within its own boundaries the relationship that the country as a whole bears to foreign nations. In any event it is the very existence of such cultural diversity at home that some critics believe explains the success of American films abroad.

It is no doubt time to recall that the film I have been talking about up until now is *la version française*, the dubbed version of *I Want to Go Home*. (In point of fact, one should really distinguish between two different French versions of the film—the original one made by a French director and produced in France and the one that was subsequently dubbed into the French language.) One of the reasons I am comfortable usng the dubbed version is the

Double Takes

inaccessibility of the original version; neither the Paris Vidéothèque nor even the Phonothèque at the Bibliothèque Nationale was able to locate a copy. There, like everywhere else—in video stores in France and Canada, on cable television in Quebec, in foreign-film catalogues in the U.S.—only the dubbed version is available. Moreover, although sound and image are not particularly well synchronized, in most cases the movements of the actors' mouths seem to conform to the French words they are speaking. In most cases, again, not only does it make narrative sense that the American characters should speak French but on several occasions the fact that they do so is specifically justified (in French) within the film. Take, for example, Lena's first words to Joey: "We're going to Paris. We're going to try to speak French"; Gauthier's initial expression of concern for Joey: "Can you follow what I'm saying . . . Nonsense, you're following me perfectly"; Elsa's first words to her father: "Now I get bawled out in French"; and Joey's response to his daughter: "In that case you must deliver a fine speech for me in French." In addition, as one would expect, the Americans speak French with an accent, make errors in pronunciation and grammar, throw in words in English, and so on.

Were it not in fact for the testimony of François Thomas, who professes that Resnais himself always spoke English on the set (304); of *Variety*, which refers to Depardieu's "first English-speaking part" (Len. 38); and of *Cahiers du cinéma*, which explicitly states that the entire film is subtitled in French (Mazabrard 55); I would frankly have serious doubts that any version other than the one I have been able to see ever existed. Still, let us try to imagine for a moment a screening of the original film in its native country: every actor, regardless of national origin, speaks English while French-speaking audiences read subtitles. As spectators, we would be put in the position that Joey occupies (in the dubbed version of the film) and share the confusion and the frustration he feels as a result of his inability to understand and to communicate. Colette Mazabrard's reaction seems to confirm this hypothesis: "This France becomes a foreign land for us (the entire film is in English, subtitled in French). Like the American in the film, who is lost in a foreign language, we experience a strangeness made up of familiarity (due to the caricatures) and of anxiety (we can't identify, we fall by the wayside)" (55).[13] What Mazabrard calls "the experience of disorientation [*dépaysement*]" is also what she identifies as both "the originality" and the "inspired modernity" of *I Want to Go Home* (55–56). Certainly Resnais's film (in both versions) foregrounds the internationalism and the dominance of the English language that many filmmakers increasingly see as the future of contemporary cinema. Notably, in the very same article in which Vincent Canby—citing none other than Marin Karmitz, the producer of *Home*—expresses serious concern over the disappearance of national cinemas, increasingly sacrificed to transnational projects filmed in an "all-purpose" English, he nonetheless singles out Resnais and

Karmitz's projected film for praise precisely because "language is the heart of it" ("Ici Se Habla").

The climactic episode of *I Want to Go Home* (filmed entirely in English, subtitled in French) offers us a microcosm of the original version of Resnais's film as well as a final virtuoso exploration of American cultural assumptions. Joey's visit to the country so exacerbates his desire to go home that he finally abandons the relatively familiar (if still often confusing and not entirely friendly) world of the Gauthier estate to set out alone and on foot. He resurfaces in the following scene as the center of attention of a crowd of puzzled villagers whose assistance he seeks to help him accomplish his goal. Joey's attempts to effect cross-cultural communication provide a detailed catalogue of what Americans regard both as the specific language(s) of their own culture and (therefore) as universally comprehensible. His most conventional efforts are also his least successful. For example, on the assumption that "everyone understands dollars," he offers money, only to discover the worthlessness of any commodity in the absence of a common understanding of the purpose of the exchange. Similarly, Joey subsequently cites his own personal and cultural history as if it automatically attested to a shared history and a common memory: "I fought in World War II. I did things for you in *Stars and Stripes*. I drew cartoons while you were occupied—against the Nazis. We were Allies." In this case, Joey not only recalls a past many French would prefer to forget but he also selects what may well be the event most directly responsible for shaping the modern world views of France and the United States in dramatically different ways.

For the most part, however, Joey depends on Hollywood, principal exporter of Americanness, to provide him with a common language. He first lists the names of American actors ("I'm an American citizen. The United States. Humphrey Bogart, Henry Fonda, John Wayne"), an exercise that initially appears to succeed, since it leads to a series of conversational exchanges with another individual. But Joey's interlocutor turns out to be functioning not within American film culture but within a kind of French theater of the absurd; he responds to Joey's pleas for help by reciting isolated bits of (very basic) film dialogue that he has committed to memory ("J'ai vu des films. Je peux dire 'Hands up. Number one, two, three. Oh wonderful. How are you?'"). Ironically, Joey's subsequent lament—"In World War II movies, all the French speak American"—identifies the conversational "reality" of this very fiction as he has just experienced it. Joey next tries singing lines from the "golden oldies," notably the show tunes of Cole Porter. Since a musical refrain at least lends itself to ready imitation, Joey (alias Adolph Green in this scene) and the French villagers are soon united in a choral performance, punctuated by encouraging shouts of "You've Got It." This renewed dependence on an essentially formulaic language does nothing to further Joey's original purpose, but the scene nonetheless provides the key transition that will finally allow him to succeed.

What began as a quest for a *means* of communication has resulted in the redefinition of the very *goal* of communication. Joey no longer desires either self-expression or the exchange of ideas; rather, in keeping with the etymological meaning of communication, he now seeks only to establish a connection, a common bond, between himself and others. His success is confirmed in the following scene when Elsie finally discovers her father in the local café. Actively engaged in drawing and distributing his cartoon characters to the delighted villagers, Joey announces that he has "made a few friends." In direct contrast then to the exclusive nature of France's largely literary and linguistic culture, the strength of Americanness appears to reside in the cross-cultural accessibility of its visual imagery. For Jean-Philippe Mathy, this difference figures importantly in French anti-Americanism:

> French high culture is dominated by the word, the signifier, by style, formalism, and formality, it is filled with anguish over the question of language as an adequate representation of reality . . . Nothing could be more distasteful to its more prominent representatives than American popular culture, with its pragmatic use of language and its fascination for the image and the visual. (253)

This would explain why Joey's sketches prove far more popular in the local café than in the salon of Isabelle Gauthier's mansion, despite (or perhaps because of) her son's belief that Joey's special talent lies in his ability "to have made all of us believe we could create comic strips." This collaboration finds an appropriate echo in Joey's own discovery that cross-cultural communication requires a mutual willingness to compromise and to adapt. His subsequent decision to prolong his stay in France is then every bit as fitting a conclusion to his new understanding of American cultural interaction as is Elsie's departure to her full realization of the meaning of Frenchness. *Home*, the most important word in the American language according to Ted Morgan (a.k.a. Sanche de Gramont—in America you can change your name), is less a place than an idea, that of "feeling comfortable wherever you are" (253–54).

Although Joey finds his cartoons to be a better stimulation to cross-cultural communication than his allusions to Hollywood musicals, *I Want to Go Home* also speaks a number of different filmic languages fluently. Resnais is well known not only for "his lifelong passion for comic books" (Len. 32) but, like most New Wave directors, for his extensive knowledge of film as well. *Home* is a postmodernist treasure house of intertexual references, only a few of which I will mention here; since I am also quite sure that there are others of which I am not even aware, treasure *hunt* might be the more accurate term. I find Mazabrard's description evocative in this context: "*I Want to Go*

Home opens up all kinds of paths, each of which in turn either becomes an impasse or is simply abandoned . . . and creates the impression of thousands of little cerebral deaths" (54). As we have seen, both Depardieu and Green peer out from behind the characters they play to invoke entire national cinemas; and certainly *Home* is self-referential within Resnais's own corpus. Indeed, according to *Cahiers du cinéma*, it sometimes seems to be a "remake" of *La Vie est un roman* (1982) "so glaring are the similarities" (Jousse and Saada). Certainly the two films share a similar (con)fusion of reality and fantasy, and the country manor, magically animated in the final shot of *Home* to expand up and out into a Fantasyland castle, directly evokes the setting of Resnais's earlier film.

Although Adolph Green, in an interview with *Cahiers du cinéma*, rejects the suggestion that *I Want to Go Home* is "un peu le remake" of *An American in Paris* ("No. I don't think there's any connection between those two films" [Jousse and Saada 61]), Resnais's film clearly recalls Vincente Minnelli's 1951 Academy Award winner in a number of ways. To begin with, *An American in Paris* is precisely one of those (post–)World War II films in which all the French speak English; in this case, they are all thoroughly familiar with American musical comedy as well. Jerry's (Gene Kelly) opening monologue on the advantages of being an artist in Paris recalls, with the same touch of ironic self-awareness, the experience of both Joey and Harry in Resnais's film ("Back home everyone said I had no talent. They may be saying the same thing here but it sounds better in French"). On the other hand, Jerry's hostile reaction to "one of those third-year girls" (whose French is far worse than Elsie's) is more reminiscent of Gauthier ("They're officious and dull. They're always making profound observations they've overheard"). In general, Minnelli's film also includes fantasy sequences; actors and characters who speak English or French as a foreign language; people who are hurt by conversations they overhear; a costume ball; a coloration strong in reds and blues; and so on. Up until the final editing of *I Want to Go Home*, Resnais had planned for his film to be framed by two appearances of Hepp Catt singing "I'll Build a Stairway to Paradise," the central production number of *An American in Paris*; in the final cut, it is Joey, dressed as Hepp Catt, who sings a few bars as he descends the staircase at the beginning of the masquerade party. Joey's final "You've Got It" medley with the local villagers is no doubt also reminiscent of Jerry's rendition of "I Got Rhythm" with the children of Paris. On the other hand, given the richly postmodernist intertextuality of *Home*, this might (also) be a reference to *My Fair Lady* . . .

Although *I Want to Go Home* clearly reminds *Cahiers du cinéma* critics of several other movies, they curiously omit the one film of which *Home* is unquestionably "un peu le remake": Jean Renoir's *La Règle du jeu* (*The Rules of the Game*) (1939).[14] Resnais has recalled his first viewing of Renoir's film as

Double Takes

"the most astounding experience that cinema has ever given me . . . Everything was upside down, all my ideas about film had been challenged"; and he adds: "Since then, I've seen it at least fifteen times—like most filmmakers of my generation" (Rafferty 83). It is no doubt as a result of such influence that even though Renoir is often considered "the most French of French filmmakers" (Betton 13) and *La Règle du jeu* "a film that could only have been made in France" (Roud 27), both director and film also figure among the most frequently quoted in the history of cinema. This may account for what to my knowledge is the most recent and surely the most curious reference to date: the reappearance of the opening sequence of *La Règle du jeu* at the beginning of *The Naked Gun*, David Zucker's 1987 spoof of spy movies. On the other hand, Resnais himself turns perhaps the single most significant episode of Renoir's film into the cinematic equivalent of an American comic strip.

The *bal masqué*, which concludes the hunting party at the end of Renoir's film, resurfaces at a comparable dramatic moment and with similar thematic importance in the masquerade party that Gauthier organizes to entertain his weekend guests. Although Resnais certainly exaggerates the farcical dimension of the original scene and virtually eliminates the tragedy in which Renoir's sense of the comic culminates, the party sequences in both films clearly represent versions of the same phenomenon: the breakdown of social order and the increasingly chaotic world that unfolds as a result. Moreover, Resnais adapts some of Renoir's most distinctive stylistic techniques—notably, a searching camera; the visual isolation of individual characters; and a fragmentary structure, punctuated by abrupt spatial transitions—to repeat his predecessor's message (see also Thomas 324).

Still, the primary importance of all such similarities may ultimately lie in their ability to accentuate the fundamental difference between the two films in both the nature of the social order and in the reasons for its breakdown. In accordance with his reputation as a "Franco-French" filmmaker, Renoir's concern in 1939 lies with social class, particularly as embodied in the *ancienne noblesse*, one exemplary form in which the notion of Frenchness as a virtually inborn and inherited right to exceptional status was once expressed. *La Règle du jeu* depicts a dying society whose strength and survival depend on rigid distinctions of class, now increasingly threatened by the inevitable consequences of post-revolutionary democratization. Renoir portrays this conflict through the structural parallelism of the intersecting worlds of servants and masters, whose potential for violent collision explodes under cover of the *bal masqué*.

In contrast, Resnais's modernized or "Americanized" remake of Renoir's French original recasts a cultural politics of isolationism and homogeneity in the role of the outmoded social order, now increasingly under attack by the pervasive internationalization of the modern world, which makes cross-cultural contacts and influences virtually inevitable. Resnais consequently replaces the identifications that cut across class boundaries in *La Règle du jeu* with examples of Franco-American communication and communality. Not surprisingly, this intercultural mingling results in an exchange of attributes more ironic than tragic as the characters in *I Want to Go Home*, despite their national representativeness, begin to resemble each other. In many ways, Gauthier makes a better "American" than Joey does; he is, for example, far more energetic, friendly, outgoing, and generous. On the other hand, Joey, the American, shows an extraordinary *méfiance* (distrust) of anything foreign and generalizes *à la française* about the French as a nation and a people. Joey is also eminently *grogneux*, that is, constantly complaining and critical of everything and everyone he encounters; and Mme Gauthier recognizes in him the same *triste* (melancholic) quality that figures so importantly in her son's sense of his own Frenchness: "You are the saddest American I have ever seen. With all the Americans that Christian brings me, I have never seen such extraordinary melancholy."

The respective endings of the masquerade parties in Renoir's and Resnais's films reemphasize and reinforce the overall differences that distinguish *La Règle du jeu* and *I Want to Go Home*. Renoir's film closes with the reestablishment of the status quo so that *La Règle du jeu* asserts a final time one possible version of Frenchness: the inherent value of Order; the valorization of group coherence over individual desire; the respect for a social hierarchy that assigns particular people to distinctive places. As one of the Marquis de la Chesnaye's (Marcel Dalio) guests says about his host in the final words of the film: "He has class—that's increasingly rare nowadays." Although Resnais opts for an equally consistent and therefore very different conclusion, at the same time, the ending of *I Want to Go Home* also reveals an interesting similarity to *La Règle du jeu*'s own alternative ending, as revised by Renoir himself in response to the hostile reactions of contemporary audiences. In Renoir's auto-remake, the film concludes with the dual expulsion of Octave (Jean Renoir) and Marceau (Julien Carette), the two parallel characters from the worlds of master and servant whose exceptional aptitude for social mobility exposes the vulnerability of the class demarcations on which traditional social hierarchy depends. Similarly, in Resnais's contemporary remake, the party ends with Joey's departure, explicitly motivated by his wish to go home; and the film ends when Elsie, whose desire for integration threatens the integrity of French cultural identity, carries out the wish she inherits from her father. Thus, *I Want to Go Home* simultaneously returns to the United States and to Resnais's particular version of Americanness: the valorization of individual choice and personal happiness over group conformity and coherence, and the preference for open-ended temporal and spatial structures, even at the risk of creating disorder.

In one sense, Resnais, like Elsie, also actualizes what he inherits as an

unrealized possibility, indeed, one that Renoir himself finally—and definitively—eliminates. The conception of André Jurieu (Roland Toutain), the single character who cannot be absorbed into the social order of *La Règle du jeu*
and who must die as a result, suggests that there may be some general tendency in France to attach to the outsider *within* French culture certain traits
that the French otherwise tend to associate with a "foreignness" specific to
America. As a record-breaking aviator, Jurieu represents modern technology
and the individual self-realization of the isolated and independent hero;
moreover, he consistently displays a childlike (and sometimes child*ish*) disre-
spect and disregard for social conventions, particularly when they conflict
with his own personal desires and happiness. Yet, precisely at the moment
when he finally convinces Christine de la Chesnaye (Nora Grégor) to leave
her husband and run away with him, Jurieu abruptly remembers that "there
are rules." In part, this ability to mediate between the contradictory roles of
romantic rebel and staunch defender of social propriety simply—and, in the
case of Jurieu, appropriately—brings us back to where Americanness and
Frenchness intersect. At the same time, however, the fact that Jurieu reverses
direction at (and as a result of) an interchange that Renoir specifically figures
as cross-*gendered* raises new questions about the "identity" of men whose differences cut across classes, cultures, and the conventions of both.

Like Renoir, Resnais makes adultery and seduction the principal motor of
dramatic action and the immediate cause of the breakdown of social order.
Both directors structure their masquerade parties around the searches of husbands or lovers for their missing and potentially unfaithful wives or companions; in both cases, the chase ultimately erupts in violence. Here, too, the
shift from class to culture, which disrupts the overall continuity of the two
films, is evident. The simultaneous pursuit of mistress and servant in *La Règle
du jeu* becomes Gauthier's triumph over two American rivals (Harry and
Joey), whose wife and lover he successively seduces. More important, however, Resnais echoes Renoir's narrative of gender only in the single episode
that he specifically sets out to remake; elsewhere, he substitutes the particular relationship between parent and child for that between men and women
in general. As a result, Renoir's exploration of the traditional opposition
between a "female" nature (associated with the disruptive forces of individual
desire) and a "male" culture (associated with the order imposed by societal
structures and conventions) becomes in Resnais's film a more direct and constantly surprising examination of the interaction between gender and culture.

From the beginning, *I Want to Go Home* defines both French and
American culture as not only "male," but also explicitly, even literally, patriarchal. En route to Paris, Elsie already engenders her choice between American
popular or visual culture and French elite or literary culture in the respective
forms of her own father, the cartoonist, and Gauthier, the Flaubert scholar,

who functions in her imagination as a paternal substitute. What Elsie clearly craves from Gauthier is the attention and affection she believes that her own father has denied her since childhood: "You're going to talk to me, you're going to give me your opinion, aren't you? Please, Christian, be patient with little Elsie, be nice." Similarly, as she tells Joey in her "fine speech in French," what Elsie rejects as the provinciality of Cleveland culture is her own paternal heritage: "I struggled for two years to prove to myself that I wasn't your daughter"; the fact that Sally Catt speaks in Adolph Green's voice serves as a constant reminder of this association.

In any conventional version of this cross-cultural narrative of gender, we might reasonably expect one of two possible outcomes. The "American story" would reunite the repentant child with the forgiving father, and they would head home together to live happily ever after. The reconciliation of father and daughter does, of course, take place in *I Want to Go Home,* but only as a result of the reversal of their positions. Female/child and male/parent exchange authority and power as Joey seeks not only Elsie's forgiveness for his past behavior but also, more important, her permission to change in the future: "I've never been anywhere before. I don't know if I'm ready to go home yet. Could I stay, Elsie? Would you be mad if I stayed?" Thus the daughter also engenders the model that the father strives to imitate.

The "French remake" of the same cross-cultural encounter challenges our expectations even more directly, precisely to the extent that they are aroused in the first place by film's own generic conventions. Film history provides multiple examples of American schoolgirls whose encounters with older French men result in either seduction or love; indeed, this is one of the most common paths to the kind of dramatic cultural integration that Elsie strives to attain. Many spectators will therefore wish to interpret Elsie's obsession with Gauthier as a prelude to their romantic involvement, since even Gauthier's own mother does so initially. But Resnais once again reverses traditional gender and generational roles. Not Elsie but her father ultimately acts out the female role in the conventional romance plot. However complex his motivation for remaining in France, Joey literally "stays" with the Frenchwoman who seduces him.

In a final surprise, it turns out that Elsie is not in search of a father (or a mentor or a lover) at all; rather, she needs a *mother*, whom she unexpectedly discovers in the person of Isabelle Gauthier (and whose subsequent romantic involvement with Elsie's father confirms her right to this maternal role). In clear contrast to Joey and to her own son, Isabelle Gauthier immediately perceives Elsie's estrangement as simultaneously cultural ("Is being an American as serious as all that?") and personal ("Is it so very tiresome to be the daughter of a great man?"); and she reestablishes connection through communication ("You talk to me. No one has ever talked to me like you did," affirms Elsie).

Double Takes

Significantly, Mme Gauthier chooses this particular moment to reveal that she and Elsie share a common language—English, that is, Elsie's *mother* tongue.

The final scene of *I Want to Go Home* contains a number of internal repetitions and revisions of previous episodes. Resnais's film comes full circle to close in once again on Elsie, again in transit between France and the United States but now en route home. The interior monologue, which marked Elsie's personal and cultural isolation in the opening sequence of *Home*, is now replaced by communication, as Elsie and Lena reaffirm the bonding of women, once again on the figurative model of mother and daughter. This reconciliation, facilitated by Joey's temporary absence ("He'll be back," affirms Elsie, "we all come back"), might appear to require the absence of men; in fact, it would be more appropriate to say that Lena and Elsie are reunited *at the expense of* men. The women's reunion is marked by the curious moment at which Elsie, who has suddenly broken into uncontrollable laughter, shares the joke with Lena. Elsie's outburst is provoked by the passenger seated next to her, not, significantly, by anything he says or does, but by the simple fact of his being who he is: "Get this, he's a cartoonist!" In point of fact, he is a *French male cartoonist*, on his way to New York in search of success, currently engaged in reading Will Eisner's essay *Comics and Sequential Art*—in short, a composite portrait of all the men encountered in the course of the film. In some sense, then, Resnais leaves us with what we might call a final feminist remake of the comic strip. *I Want to Go Home* culminates in its only example of female laughter, presented as a collective force that mocks men across cultures and their culture across boundaries. On the other hand, Elsie, whose own in-flight reading consists of *The Art of Will Eisner*, also presumably laughs in the face of this unexpected encounter with her own cross-cultural double.

Jim McBride's "Breathless in L.A."

Remaking Jean-Luc Godard's Narrative of Gender

Although cross-cultural comparison and gender differences figure importantly within *I Want to Go Home*, the significance of the relationship between gender and culture in Resnais's film became particularly evident in juxtaposing that film with Renoir's *La Règle du jeu*. How opportune, then, that *Home* should itself mediate, if indirectly and unintentionally, between another French film, Jean-Luc Godard's *A Bout de souffle* (1959), and its American remake, Jim McBride's *Breathless* (1983). The ethnographer Michael M. J. Fischer argues that the "bifocality" that determines the perspective of cultural criticism should be understood to mean "two or more" cultures in juxtaposition: "Successful cross-cultural comparison requires at least a third case to avoid simplistic better-worse judgments, to foster multiple axes of comparison, and to evoke a sense of the larger universes in which cultures are situated" (199). A "third case" may be especially useful to introduce this particular pairing, since few critics have resisted the temptation to view Godard and McBride in terms of "better-worse judgments." As one of the inaugural films of the French New Wave (along with Resnais's own *Hiroshima, mon amour*), *A Bout de souffle* enjoys a status very nearly equivalent to that of *La Règle du jeu*; yet the influence of American comic strips and animated cartoons functions as importantly in McBride's revision of Godard as it does in Resnais's of Renoir. Moreover, if the Hollywood remake of yet another French version of "the American in Paris," one that once again incorporates playful intertextual allusions to American movies, is strongly reminiscent of *I Want to Go Home*, McBride's and Godard's films also multiply the available "axes of comparison" by viewing cultures, both native and foreign, from two distinct national perspectives. As a result, this cross-cultural comparison promises to evoke a sense of the larger international context in which specific film cultures are located.

Double Takes

The quarter century that separates *Breathless* from *A Bout de souffle* might seem consistent with the apparent folly of ever attempting such a remake at all. In retrospect, however, the project appears less anomalous than inevitable, so appropriately does this particular example of the Franco-American remake configure the central problematics of what has since become an increasingly common cinematic practice. John Ellis argues that film's distinctive status as both an art form and a popular entertainment (a tension no doubt exemplified, for many, by the two versions of *Breathless*) results in a dominant "narrative image" based on "repetition with a difference"; thus every individual film strives to be "at once unique and similar" (34). Because Hollywood provides the model that enables us to perceive films as similar, that is, as *films*, the complementary claim to uniqueness has frequently originated in a given film's specific national identity or, as we saw in the Introduction, in its claims to such an identity. Certainly this has been the case in France, where, in Louis Delluc's celebrated formulation: "The French cinema must be *cinema*; the French cinema must be *French*" (qtd. in Flitterman-Lewis 27).

Delluc's imperative of the 1920s explicitly informed the period of the French New Wave in the late 1950s and early 1960s as well. The designation "New Wave" links a highly diverse group of young filmmakers, perhaps best characterized, as the name implies, by a spirit of youthful innovation; indeed, the term was originally coined in 1958 by the journalist Françoise Giroud to describe an entire generation. In a narrower sense, it has come to identify directors such as Godard (and, for most critics, Resnais), many of whom began their careers as film critics for *Cahiers du cinéma*. Thus, they brought a knowledge of film history and theory to a filmmaking practice associated with certain thematic interests and experimental techniques, including a strong focus on narrative. In particular, New Wave directors were influenced by the notion of film authorship, which sought patterns of formal and thematic consistency within the corpus of individual directors, and the concept of genre, based on the conformity of individual films to a shared set of cinematic conventions. It is this combined focus on the individual and the culturally inscribed, together with the *Cahiers*'s critics' early and ongoing fascination with Hollywood, that leads Sandy Flitterman-Lewis to the following conclusion:

> It is important . . . to understand the work of New Wave directors from the perspective of the dominant Hollywood narrative model, for the dual imperatives of Louis Delluc's maxim regain their force in this third moment of national cinematic identity. It is in this sense that the films of the New Wave can be seen as continued attempts both to establish the main codes of classical American cinema and to subvert, undermine, and rework them. (31)

The parallel preoccupation of French New Wave filmmakers with auteur and genre theory turned Delluc's underlying notion of specificity into the explicit informing principle of their own cinematic production, as, significantly, in the case of Godard and *A Bout de souffle*: "What I wanted was to take a conventional story and *remake*, but differently, everything the cinema had done" (qtd. in Marie 206, my emphasis). As Godard's own word choice so aptly implies, New Wave cinema's fascination with self-referential allusion and citation may find its ultimate logical conclusion in the self-reflexivity now literalized in the current remake phenomenon.

Moreover, the patterns of similarity and difference most characteristic of the connections between the two versions of *Breathless* foreground precisely what Ellis calls the "pervasive sexualization" of classic film narrative—the focus on relations between men and women, on the plot of heterosexual romance—that is largely responsible for the impression that film creates of repeating variants of the same old story (67–68). The involvement between a man and a woman of different nationalities structures both Godard's original and McBride's remake, and the most immediately evident difference between the two films results from the simultaneous reversal of national and sexual identity that inevitably focuses our attention not only on gender as well as culture but also on the relationship between gender and culture. Indeed, it is this exemplary illustration of bifocality or "reciprocity of perspectives" (M. Fischer 199) that stands out in the minds of French film critics. Daniel Protopopoff, in a special issue of *CinémAction* devoted to remakes (October 1989), suggests that "what is worth retaining" from the comparison of the two versions of *Breathless* is "an inversion of the respective situations of the characters" (123). For Alain Philippon, who begins his review of *Breathless* in *Cahiers du cinéma* by characterizing *A Bout de souffle* as "the film that a priori has everything to prevent a remake," finds the only imaginable explanation for McBride's movie in "a scriptwriting temptation: he was French, she was American (version 1), he would be American and she French (version 2)" (43).

It seems curious, then, that mainstream American reviewers tend to be particularly troubled—a reaction that turns out to be particularly revealing—by this very relationship between the two films. Consider, for example, the following excerpts from two otherwise very different reviews of McBride's film by the *New York Times*' Vincent Canby and *New York*'s David Denby:

> Reversing the nationalities in "Breathless"—making this the story of an American gangster and a French girl, rather than the reverse situation to be found in Jean-Luc Godard's classic—was a bold move. It may even have been in some ways an ill-advised one, since the finished product's borrowed existential urgency goes largely unexplained. (Canby, "It Takes More")

Double Takes

> Reversing the nationalities of the main characters, for instance, robs the story of any sense. Why does Jesse want a French girl? French girls in Los Angeles don't mean anything comparable to what American girls meant in Paris. Does she represent class or glamour or culture for him? Not as far as we can see. She's there only because this movie is a reverse angle on Godard's *Breathless*, not because she belongs with this particular man. (Denby 80)

The similarity of language and approach that characterizes these parallel passages coincides with Canby's and Denby's apparent internalization of a process of reversal very like the one on which they comment. What each announces as essentially an issue of culture ("reversing the nationalities") actually introduces a discussion in which gender becomes an equal concern—and even, precisely to the extent that its importance goes unacknowledged, an overriding one.

For both critics, the meaning of gender and culture tends to divide along traditional male and female lines. Whereas "Jesse" or "an American gangster" is immediately individualized, at least to some extent, "a French girl" is consistently reduced to her national and sexual identity. At the same time, however, these identities seem to cancel each other out, since the woman's cultural insignificance is either casually assumed (that is, existentialism becomes inexplicable in the absence of a French *man*) or actively asserted. Lest we dismiss this latter strategy as the result of some strange ethnocentric bias on Denby's part, his parallel discussion of "American girls" in Paris, whose cultural importance he takes for granted, offers us a different example of essentially the same thing. Not only does Denby portray culture as feminized to the extent that it is objectified and denigrated, but he also continues to deny agency and subjectivity to Godard's female lead in the process. The "American college girl abroad" figures importantly in the "obsession" of (presumably male) Parisian intellectuals who, in the late fifties, "fell in love with . . . the consumer products of a mass culture" (79). Thus the "worthless girl" (79) in *A Bout de souffle* essentially serves to enhance the stature of the male hero; in contrast, the pursuit of a "French architecture student at U.C.L.A." makes his unfortunate counterpart in *Breathless* "look like a jerk half the time" (78). Clearly then, despite what Denby keeps repeating in the passage quoted above, the real source of his irritation lies less with the nationality of women than with the gender of men. Indeed, his discomfort stems from the very difference between Godard's original and McBride's remake that is most often singled out by reviewers: the change that appears to have taken place in the central *male* character.

Although Denby and Canby appropriately present the reversal of nationalities in *A Bout de souffle* and *Breathless* as a problem of narrative, both subsequently reveal a tendency to conceptualize "*the* story" as a fixed formal abstraction, a kind of supranational ur-narrative in which characters can apparently be recast without significantly altering either their individual roles or the basic structure of the plot (however detrimental the effect may be on the perceived merit of the film as a whole). In the original French version of this scenario, the critics who reviewed Godard's film at the time of its release emphasized either the relative unimportance of the story line, or its utter banality, or both. Indeed, critical opinion alternately describes *A Bout de souffle* as a film that either lends itself to an (apparently American) remake—Marcel Martin, for example, speaks of "a story that could take place on Broadway as easily as on the Champs-Elysées" (201)—or already *is* one itself—according to Georges Sadoul, "[the story] has been floating around for twenty years in American, French, Italian, and British movies. Yet another recasting of our good old *Quai des brumes*" (207). Although Jim McBride similarly calls upon the repetitiveness of cinematic narrative to justify his own imitation of Godard, he also usefully reminds us that the same story need not be (re)told in the same way: "We have at our disposal a limited number of stories that can be made into films and that are worth telling again and again. *A Bout de souffle* is one of them. But they must be told to each generation in a new way" (Frank & Krohn 66).

The basic plot is invariable: a petty car thief kills a traffic cop, tries to convince a woman to flee with him, and ends up being shot by the police as a result of her betrayal. Nonetheless, Godard's and McBride's respective films not only tell two fundamentally different stories but also assign the leading role to a character for whom gender difference is at least as "fundamental" as that of national origin. Curiously, the juxtaposition of the descriptions that accompany the video versions of the two films reflect precisely this difference in perspective. In the passage from the French original to the American remake, the intellectual dilemma of a central female character has been rewritten as the action-adventure story of a leading male actor:

> *A Bout de souffle*: Patricia, a dazzling American student, navigates in 1950s' Paris between an intellectual world and adventure with Michel, a handsome, romantic hoodlum whose heart she has managed to capture . . .

> *Breathless*: Richard Gere stars as a drifter one step ahead of the law . . . Set in contemporary Los Angeles, *Breathless* tells the story of Gere, who accidentally shoots and kills a cop and takes cover in the home of a former flame . . .

In general, when *A Bout de souffle* and *Breathless* are viewed from within the particular comparative context that each creates for the other, they reveal a series of interrelated changes that mediate between gender and culture and between female and male.

Double Takes

Within this framework, *A Bout de souffle* might best be described as a generalized narrative of gender. Such a reading may appear unconventional but certainly not surprising, given the attention that Godard has consistently paid throughout his career to broad issues of ideology and representation, particularly as they relate to sexual politics. This interpretation can perhaps be illustrated both sufficiently and most efficiently by an episode positioned at the structural and thematic center of Godard's film, the significance of which is further enhanced by its conspicuous absence from McBride's remake, which includes neither the original scene nor any vaguely comparable equivalent. The sequence in question, the press conference held by the writer Parvulesco (played, significantly, by the filmmaker Jean-Pierre Melville) at which Patricia (Jean Seberg) figures as the most visible and insistent of the journalists present, mediates the film in multiple ways. What Parvulesco and Patricia "mutually see" in each other in the course of this inter-view is the fact of sexual difference, the opposition between men and women that determines the view of the world articulated by Rainer Maria Rilke and confirmed by Parvulesco: "Modern life will increasingly separate man and woman." Parvulesco presents culture as clearly subordinate to gender, despite his initial assertion that "no connection exists between the French woman and the American woman." In fact, national identity introduces difference into the general structure of male/female relations but it does not in itself alter that general structure: "The American woman dominates man; the French woman doesn't dominate him yet." (For Parvulesco, as for Denby, "man" clearly belongs to a generic category that overrides all cultural particularity.) More specifically, this scene not only constitutes a *mise en abyme* of the central narrative that Patricia and Michel (Jean-Paul Belmondo) act out in the course of the film, but also, through Parvulesco, interprets and evaluates their particular version of the story in advance. Asked to judge the relative morality of "a woman who betrays or a man who abandons," Parvulesco ironically selects the woman as "the most moral." Similarly, having asserted that "love is the only thing in which one can believe in our day and age," he subsequently notes that "feelings are a luxury in which few women indulge."

It is entirely appropriate that the paradigmatic scene at the center of *A Bout de souffle* should take the form of a conversation between a man and a woman—particularly one in which the woman's role, as defined by her profession, consists in soliciting knowledge from a male authority. "All speech," according to Elaine Showalter, "is necessarily talk about gender" ("Introduction" 1). Michel Marie, who singles out the dialogue in *A Bout de souffle* as Godard's "most fundamental innovation" (208) and sums up the film as "a tragedy of language and of the impossibility of communication" (211), nonetheless entirely overlooks what may best represent its "revolutionary use of language" (208). Although Patricia's status as an outsider, like Elsie's in

Resnais's *I Want to Go Home* (another "tragedy" of language and miscommunication), is marked by her American accent and the foreignness of her French, Godard explicitly subordinates culture to gender and (re)makes the problem of cross-cultural communication into a metaphor for the relationship of men and women. Just as the semantic range of the word "intercourse" mediates between the acts of "communication" and "coitus" (according to Parvulesco, "eroticism is a form of love and love is a form of eroticism"), Patricia repeatedly—and alternately—refuses to have sex with Michel and fails to understand what he says. The two central characters in *A Bout de souffle* cannot communicate; as man and woman, they have nothing "in common," by definition.

The final conversation between Patricia and Michel, positioned immediately after her announcement that she has betrayed him to the police, takes the form of an internal remake of the interview sequence at the heart of the film. The gap between (female) questions and (male) answers, already evident in the earlier scene, now opens still wider to produce an exchange of contrasting remarks that is structured contrapuntally rather than dialogically, literally at cross purposes. We are prepared for this fundamental breakdown in communication by the couple's parting words the previous evening, which seem designed to illustrate Showalter's theory of the inseparability of gender and language. When Patricia addresses Michel in words that clearly recall those cited by Parvulesco ("modern life will increasingly separate man and woman"), the difference of *her* repetition introduces a grammatical error into the masculine original, which Michel, in the film's only example of this particular version of *his* linguistic superiority, quickly corrects:

Patricia: On est forcé de se sépare. [We are forced to separate.]
Michel: er.
Patricia: se séparer.

The emphasis that Michel places on first- and second-person pronouns in the course of the couple's subsequent exercise in mis(sed)communication—for example, "When we talked, I talked about me and you about you; you should have talked about me and I about you"—encodes the difference of gender, usually evident only in the third-person singular forms of personal pronouns, in the very structure of conversation itself. The distance between "I" and "you" has consistently functioned as a signifier not of mutuality but of the fundamental opposition between men and women. Indeed, it structures the film as a whole, which unfolds in the space between Michel's first words—"Je suis con"—and his last ones—"C'est vraiment déguelasse." At the precise moment when Michel is unquestionably talking about Patricia, her inability to understand, first, him ("What did he say?") and, then, his words

Double Takes

("What does 'déguelasse' mean?") confirms the impossibility of cross-gender communication. The only response to Patricia's final questions comes in the form of a revision that transforms one man's personal opinion into a collective attitude shared by men as a group. The police officer, who speaks with the voice of authority, repeats Michel's general complaint as a gender-specific insult that targets Patricia directly as a woman: "Il a dit: *vous êtes* vraiment *une déguelasse*" (my emphasis). This linguistic accord that establishes male association, enabling them to converse across the usual boundaries of law and order, specifically re-en-genders the difference between "right" and "wrong" as a conflict between men and women.[1]

Although the character defined as the outsider still plays the leading role in McBride's remake of A Bout de souffle, foreignness is no longer equated with femaleness. Monica (Valérie Kaprisky), the French woman, appears thoroughly Americanized, and the traditional national values that her words and behavior consistently reflect—pragmatism, realism, commitment to work and career, ambition, foresightedness—become particularly evident in the face of their rejection by Jesse (Richard Gere), the American male who stars opposite her. Moreover, to the extent that language continues to encode difference, Jesse's habit of alternating between Spanish and his native language rather than Monica's perfectly fluent and correct, if (slightly) Gallic-accented English, again designates him, not her, as the foreigner. Indeed, Monica imitates her cultural counterpart (her last name, Poiccard, clearly alludes to Michel Poicard, Godard's hero) in using a French word, *taré*, to characterize Jesse, whose meaning (crazy, jerk, disgusting person) she must subsequently explain to him.

Ironically, Godard emphasizes cross-cultural differences between a French man and an American woman for the ultimate purpose of describing a gender conflict of a nature potentially both universal and permanent. In fact, the very discourse of cultural difference is itself sexualized within Godard's film: every time Patricia generalizes about the French ("Les Français disent toujours . . ."), Michel counters with several generalizations about women ("Les femmes ne veulent jamais . . . ," "Les femmes, c'est toujours . . . ," and so on). Similarly, what she introduces as a conversation about the reputed beauty of a specific foreign place (Mexico), he quickly transforms into a monologue about the relative physical attractiveness of women of different nationalities ("Swedish women are uglier than Parisian women. Lausanne and Geneva are the only cities where all the girls are fifteens on a scale of twenty"). In contrast to Godard, McBride stresses the personal relationship between a particular man and woman, whose difference of nationality is essentially insignificant, in order to illustrate an intracultural conflict specific to American masculinity.

Significantly, McBride's remake respects the formal structure of A Bout de souffle. Although the central sequence of Breathless differs radically in content from that of Godard's model, it does function as a *mise en abyme* that enables the film to reflect internally on itself. Similarly, both versions of the film make equally evident the parallel importance of the discourses of gender and culture, however much their conceptualization or function may vary. The male/female interview that identifies the war between the sexes as Godard's primary interest is replaced in *Breathless* by an argument between two American males that establishes a conflict within American masculinity as McBride's central concern. Jesse and a young boy quarrel over the interpretation of the Silver Surfer, a comic book character. In other words, they disagree about precisely what leads to cross-cultural male bonding in Resnais's *I Want to Go Home*, where a huge statue of Spiderman, another Marvel Comics superhero, visually dominates the art gallery sequence (see Thomas 308). American cartoons, which become representative of high culture in the Parisian art world of Resnais's film, but which also materialize on screen to counsel the Cleveland cartoonist and his daughter, again serve as a real-life model for the American hero of McBride's movie.

Curiously, the fan letters that Marvel published in response to the inaugural issue of *The Silver Surfer* both reproduce and bridge this tension between art and popular culture (and echo the disagreement at the center of *Breathless* as well). The fans, all male, who write primarily to express either admiration for or disapproval of the hero's values and behavior, nonetheless also evaluate, without exception and clearly on the basis of knowledge, the quality of the art work and the relative strengths of different illustrators. Moreover, they also seem to be relatively sophisticated about narrative and genre as well. One unhappy reader, for example, identifies the banality of the very plot structure that has been most influential in Hollywood cinema with the conventions of the comic book: "Ol' SS goes the way of all Marvel heroes by getting a certified, grade A, Mighty Marvel *romantic hang-up*! . . . There's nothing wrong with such a plot, despite the overuse of the 'Creeping Zombieism' theme, but the bathos seemed to be laid on with a shovel." Another, who describes the plot as "a regular Lee masterpiece," focuses his analytical attention on design: "John handles the art pretty well, but good old Jack Kirby, who first drew the S.S. does it better." A third, who describes the first issue as "perhaps the most excellent story to appear in a Marvel comic," finds the art to be "likewise excellent. John did a great job of penciling. Joe Sinnott did a fine inking job." Although these and other readers also worry that turning the adventures of the Surfer into a regular series may have an adverse effect on artistic and narrative quality, their collective fascination with this character, whom still another reader describes as "a compilation of the most golden fantasies of all my most beautiful dreams," may help explain why the Silver Surfer debuted in January 1998, thirty years after he first appeared in a Marvel comic book, as the hero of a weekly television series. As *TV Guide* (15 March 1997) noted in announcing the program: "Never a mainstream taste, the Surfer has always had a rabid cult following. Surf's up!" (54).

Here, too, *I Want to Go Home* mediates between *A Bout de souffle* and *Breathless*. Ellis characterizes Hollywood's dominant narrative image as "a mass of references to other films" (31), and it is especially through their choices of cultural referents that Godard's and McBride's films reveal themselves to be "at once unique and similar" (Ellis 34). *A Bout de souffle* is highly self-conscious about its relationship to American film (see Andrew), as evidenced, for example, by the famous shot/countershot sequence that juxtaposes close-ups of Michel and Humphrey Bogart. The film posters we glimpse (*Vivre dangereusement jusqu'au bout* [*Live Fast, Die Young*], *Plus dure sera la chute* [*The Harder They Fall*]) as well as Michel's characteristic gestures (the perpetual cigarette and the finger drawn across the lips in homage to Bogart) all connect Godard's protagonist to the strong, tough hero of a certain American cinema of the thirties and forties—by chance, precisely that which Harry is busy remaking in *I Want to Go Home*. McBride, in contrast to Godard but in keeping with Resnais, uses the comic strip as a kind of shorthand, both for American popular culture as a whole, and for the animated cartoon as metaphor for Hollywood, in particular. According to McBride, references to the Silver Surfer took on an increasingly important role during the filming of *Breathless* as they came to serve as a diegetic marker of the film's intentions: "I wanted it to look like a cartoon, and I think that we succeeded. . . . It's the universe of this film. I began with the idea that I was going to make a film in the style of Hollywood, but I didn't really understand what that was. For me, it meant larger than life and less complicated than reality, two-dimensional" (Frank & Krohn 65). Or, as Monica tells Jesse, "You're like one of those rides at Disneyland."

In Jesse's eyes, the Silver Surfer, who functions throughout the film as his alter ego, is an authentic hero, albeit misunderstood, who endures the senseless chaos and self-destructive violence of life on earth because "he wants to help people out." Jesse's identification with a self-sacrificial Christ figure from another galaxy both underscores the "alienation" of his own character and mitigates the meaningless act of violence he himself commits. The same behavior causes the boy to dismiss the Surfer as a "jerk," both because he remains on earth when he has the "power cosmic" to escape at will ("Only a jerk would stay when he could go"), and especially because he stays to save people who not only don't want his help but who "are always after him, like the cops and the marines—he's a jerk." Thus, like Parvulesco, his counterpart in Godard's film, the boy both announces and cynically evaluates the central action of *Breathless* in advance.

The opposing views of heroism, which clearly underlie this difference of

opinion, mediate McBride's cinematic exploration of the currently fragmented state of contemporary masculinity. On the one hand, the boy favors
a traditional conception that equates heroism with the self-imposed isolation
and independent action of the superior man—what we might call the Humphrey Bogart model of manhood. Jesse, on the other hand, supports the philosophy summed up in the Silver Surfer's own somewhat unlikely motto,
"Love is the power supreme." Thus Jesse initially enters Monica's world as
the modern equivalent of the knight in shining armor, determined to protect
a damsel no longer in any danger ("The Silver Surfer saves those in distress,"
shouts Jesse, as he disrupts her oral exam). Appropriately, in the only specifically filmic reference within *Breathless*, McBride replaces Bogart with Errol
Flynn, the ultimate swashbuckler.[2] Subsequently, however, Jesse demonstrates a sensitivity and a capacity for commitment and responsibility worthy
of the so-called feminist "New Man." Notably, Jesse welcomes the news that
Monica may be pregnant with immediate and total enthusiasm: "Yeah—a
muchacho." Here, as is often the case in *Breathless*, Jesse's use of Spanish at
once recalls the American remake's relationship to its original foreign-
language model (particularly since Godard's hero also sprinkles his conversation with Italian words, although far less consistently) and simultaneously
reflects the distance that separates the two films. Michel so thoroughly dismisses Patricia's identical announcement as both her error and her problem
("You should have been more careful") that it definitively disappears from *A
Bout de souffle*.

In continued imitation of Godard, McBride reproduces the central conversation of his own film on the level of the individual couple and in a form
directly analogous to the situation of the two protagonists. Questioned by
Monica, Jesse describes the Silver Surfer as "a spacelost freak, looking for
love," who must leave his girlfriend to "soar alone." When Monica asks why,
Jesse answers evasively: "It's a long story." His subsequent assertion, obviously
as pertinent to his own circumstances as to those of the Silver Surfer, that "he
and his girlfriend are trapped in two different galaxies" might be interpreted
as the reprise of an even longer and still more conventional narrative, the
same old story of the irreconcilable differences between men and women that
Godard already (re)tells. In the case of his own particular version of this story,
however, Jesse never doubts that "Love *is* the power supreme." Thus, in an
internal duplication of McBride's own task as director, Jesse systematically
sets out to remake virtually everything that occurs in the film, much of it borrowed from Godard, in terms of the love story that he is determined to create
for Monica and himself.

For example, Jesse reworks both the tale of seduction and the crime plot,
which provide the core dramatic structure of the film(s). He reinterprets

Double Takes

Monica's initial assertion that he is "crazy" to mean "I love you," and offers all subsequent signs of his often very strange behavior as further evidence of his love. Similarly, he tells Monica that *desperado* means "desperate for [her]." When she complains that "You Americans, all you think about is sex," in an elision of nationality and gender that supports the film's specific cultural focus on masculinity, Jesse immediately reverses the terms: "Sex? I'm in love with you. And you love me too—you'll see." Thus Jesse's version of being on the lam translates into "Let's go to Mexico and have a baby." Nor can we simply dismiss this narrative emplotment as Jesse's subjective delusion, for all of the (male) friends to whom he appeals for help, despite their full awareness that he has killed a policeman, nonetheless repeatedly identify his real problem as his love for Monica. (In similar circumstances, in contrast, Michel reverses the terms in describing his dilemma: "I'm in a hell of a lot more trouble than I am in love.")

Jesse's determination to rewrite everything to conform to his personal love story applies even to Godard's narrative of ideas, the story of existentialism, which underlies the original version—and the originality—of *A Bout de souffle*.[3] In the American remake, Jesse's response to the Faulknerian dilemma posed by Monica between "grief or nothing" constitutes part of an internally repetitive sequence. As a result, the meaning of Jesse's choice, which he consciously "remakes" at this point—"*Like I told you*, baby, it's all or nothing with me" (my emphasis)—originates not in the similar words pronounced in an earlier film (though to a very different purpose), but in Jesse's own prior expression of unconditional love for Monica. Indeed, Jesse understands "nothing" as an inseparable part of the fixed expression "all or nothing," which represents his refusal to compromise, especially when it comes to love. Michel's choice, in contrast, which Godard translates by the Sartrean term *le néant* (nothingness or nonexistence), confirms his own obsession with death. In a 1960 interview in *Le Monde*, Godard explained *A Bout de souffle* in precisely this way: "I told the story of an American woman and a French man. It can't work out between them because he thinks about death and she doesn't" (Baby 197). In this context, McBride's remake might be interpreted not simply as further evidence of a frequently cited cultural divergence—the reputed indifference of Americans to the reality of death—but as an ironic reflection of the inability of many native speakers of English to hear, let alone to reproduce, the phonetic distinction between the French words for death (*la mort*) and for love (*l'amour*). By the time the exchange recurs a third time in *Breathless*, in the version I am about to quote, it has taken on an explicitly self-referential dimension that is particularly appropriate to Jesse's effort to remake reality and his own life story to conform to the most common of narrative structures, the storybook—perhaps I should say *comic-book*—romance:

Monica: Yeah—you, me, the baby, a grass house, the sea—everything else goes away.

Jesse: Ain't nothing else—that's it. Love is the power supreme. That's the whole story, baby.

In terms of the specific language of film itself—or, alternatively, of film itself as a specific language—the different idioms spoken by Godard and McBride continue to effect a "translation" between French and English. In keeping with Delluc's two parallel criteria for the French cinema, Godard's original project, as we know, already accounts for both cinematic identity ("What I wanted was to take a conventional story") and national specificity ("and remake, but differently, everything the cinema had done"). In the first instance, Godard respects the very definition of film, originally established in Hollywood but long since accepted as an international norm, as a particular kind of *narrative* medium. In the second case, in keeping with the tendency to associate the specificity of Frenchness with that of the French language, a connection we encountered earlier in Resnais's *I Want to Go Home*, Godard's most obvious innovations in *A Bout de souffle* result from the stylistic virtuosity of his camera, which makes form at least as important as content. Indeed, it is precisely this combination of banality and originality that causes reviewers such as Vincent Canby to question McBride's sanity in trying to remake, on the one hand, a film whose "story is not important, being not much different from those of dozens of other movies," and, on the other hand, a film that "remains important for the way it questioned the look, sound, and methods of all narrative films that had gone before" ("Stomach"). This tendency to privilege what Richard Roud, for example, calls "plastic values" in *Rediscovering French Film* (15) and Susan Hayward and Ginette Vincendeau categorize as "description" in *French Film: Texts and Contexts* (3) is identified in the introductions to both critical works as a defining characteristic of French film, in explicit opposition to the preference of American film for "narration."

E. Ann Kaplan, Lucy Fischer, and many other feminist film theorists point out that the coupling of Hollywood's dominant narrative model with the story of heterosexual romance is further reinforced by the presence of certain stylistic devices—notably, continuity editing, classical framing and composition (such as two-shots), and plot linearity—that are specifically designed to make the world on camera appear realistic or "natural" (L. Fischer, *Shot/Countershot* 243). In contrast, a film such as *A Bout de souffle*, which is filled with self-referential allusions and intertextual quotations, foregrounds film's status as a conscious work of art and thus exposes the conventionality of the codes on which it traditionally draws. In particular, Godard makes extensive use of the jump cut, not only the very antithesis of the continuity and the linearity on which classical Hollywood realism depends, but, even more importantly, the

Double Takes

Godard's self-referential allusions foreground film's status as a conscious work of art; Patricia's (Jean Seberg) direct stare into the camera challenges the conventional codes of gendered behavior that govern mainstream American cinema. *A Bout de souffle.* Courtesy of the Stills Archive, Museum of Modern Art, New York.

stylistic equivalent of the emotional and narrative disconnectedness that characterizes his representation of the heterosexual couple. Similarly, the shot/countershot sequences, which frequently isolate Michel and Patricia in separate frames; the juxtaposition of reverse angle shots, which destabilize the couple even when both partners appear in the same frame; and the mid-to-long shots, which keep the lovers at a distance, provide continuous visual support for the oppositional structure that determines the relationship between men and women in Godard's film. Appropriately, the final montage of close-ups of Patricia staring directly into the camera simultaneously disrupts the usual direction of the cinematic gaze and refuses the narrative (en)closure that in conventional cinema marks the woman's containment within the romantic plot of the heterosexual couple (L. Fischer, *Shot/Countershot* 245). Unlike McBride's Monica, who equates freedom *with* Jesse ("I feel so free with you"), Patricia repeatedly asserts her desire to be "free *from* men" (my emphasis).

In the American remake of Godard's highly idiomatic French original, McBride reinscribes his predecessor's challenge to the narrative conventions of Hollywood cinema within his own national context. Far from undermining the traditional role of narrativity by replacing or displacing the dominance of the story, McBride rather exaggerates its importance, so that *Breathless*, like a comic strip, becomes profusely, indeed excessively, dependent on dramatic convention. The American film therefore remains as consciously self-reflexive as its French counterpart, but McBride substitutes genre-coded sequences, incorporated in their entirety, for the multiplicity of specific allusions and citations that characterize Godard's system of cinematic references.[4] For example, McBride clearly bases the episode in which Jesse delivers a stolen car to a prospective buyer on the identical scene in *A Bout de souffle* ("une Américaine" becomes "a little foreign job" to respect the specific cultural referents of gender). Subsequently, however, McBride vastly expands his version—not, I would argue, because the sequence has taken on either a different function or a greater importance within the context of his own film, but because it has, if anything, become newly autonomous. McBride quickly deviates from extradiegetic imitation of Godard to intradiegetic repetition. The narrative conventions that govern the formulaic fight scene require the internal reproduction of the same: the American movie hero must triumph more often and more violently over more attacks from a greater number of potentially stronger opponents.

A similar narrative excess emphasizes the conventionality of the chase sequence that McBride adds to the brief game of hide and seek that Godard's lovers play with the police. *Breathless* once again offers less its own particular version of this scene than a generic model, complete with variants, of what has become a standard but essential element of the action-adventure story. McBride's heroes, for example, alternately flee both on foot and in a car; and an episode initially encoded in dramatic form has its own internal comic sequel. (In flight from the police, Monica and Jesse literally run into a street gang from whom they escape by warning them of the imminent arrival of the police.) In keeping with the paradoxical convention that requires "repetition with a difference," the director of *Breathless* also updates the chase scene with a relatively original race down the ramps of a parking garage. Throughout *Breathless*, as we know, McBride incorporates episodes of the cosmic adventures of the Silver Surfer; and Jesse's parallel identification with Jerry Lee Lewis produces a series of what might well be characterized as mini-music videos.

McBride's innovations in the area of cinematographic style and technique conform to his parallel interests in film as a narrative medium and a love story. Instead of jump cuts, which not only disrupt visual and narrative continuity in *A Bout de souffle* but also figure sexual and gender conflict, McBride's prefers intercutting between concurrent sequences of action, which involve Monica and Jesse individually; this both assures the coherence of the narrative and reflects the connectedness of the couple. Similarly, whereas Godard constantly shifts the angle from which he films his two antagonists, McBride's camera periodically moves around his protagonists to encircle the lovers in a visual embrace.

An addiction to love stories has been most often associated, particularly in Hollywood, with women. (Even in *A Bout de souffle*, when Patricia unexpectedly wishes that her romance with Michel might equal the passion of Romeo and Juliet, he dismisses her desire as "bien des idées de filles, ça.") This may explain what some reviewers see as the "feminization" of both narrative and hero in McBride's remake. *Newsweek*'s David Ansen, for example, paradoxically describes Jesse as "a macho, funny-sad update of all those tragic heroines of the past who lived all for love, and the world well lost" ("Lovers" 54). The frequency with which male critics object to the filming of Richard Gere's body as an erotic object is, I suspect, similarly motivated, if less openly acknowledged, by the displacement of a technique usually reserved for the female anatomy rather than by anything inherently objectionable in either the shots themselves or how McBride uses them (see, for example, Denby). If the hero of *Breathless* indeed relates a story that has special appeal for a female audience, this would also provide one explanation for the fact that Jesse's romantic retelling of events progressively overcomes Monica's strong initial preference for reality over fiction.

McBride depends primarily on the highly appropriate strategy of the internal remake, marked by exact intratextual repetition, to record Monica's entrance into the world of Jesse's fantasies. The process begins at the moment when their voices unite in a choral recitation of the comic-book passage that relates the Silver Surfer's love for his girlfriend. Subsequently, Monica behaves in ways that can be described in the identical terms that she originally applies to Jesse. Notably, he repeats her global opinion of him—"You're crazy, but I like it"—as she imitates his previous actions by initiating sexual intercourse in circumstances that make the act unexpected and inappropriate and thus dangerous and exciting. In keeping with the allusion to Nora Ephron's

Sleepless in Seattle (1993), which is embedded in the title of this chapter, Monica and Jesse make love to the accompaniment and in imitation of the actors whose movie romance is projected in larger-than-life-size images on the screen behind which the heroes of *Breathless* hide from the police. Monica's Hollywood double describes her ideal man in terms that clearly identify Jesse as his identical twin: "I want a guy with spirit and guts, a guy who can laugh at anything or do anything, a guy who can win the world for me." Of particular significance, however, as evidenced by the fact that we hear it twice, is the line of dialogue ("I don't want to be afraid of love or anything else") that Monica borrows from the actress in the film within the film and repeats as part of her own conversation with Jesse. Monica's scripted words prepare her final acceptance of the role that Jesse has reserved for her in his narrative of romance ("Love is the power supreme. That's the whole story").

In continued imitation of Godard's *A Bout de souffle*, *Breathless* concludes with a post-betrayal sequence that structures the final confrontation between the two lovers as an internal duplication of the film's central episode; in fact, McBride's finale functions as a virtual microcosm of the entire film. On the other hand, the betrayal itself, which in its original form confirms the gulf of difference that separates men from women in Godard's world, now opens up a gap that rather reveals the difference between the French and the American versions of the same film. In the specific context of McBride's remake, Monica's betrayal really "doesn't make any sense," as Jesse himself points out within the film, nor, for that matter, does Jesse's own behavior—either here, where he strikes her, or in the moment immediately prior to her betrayal when his totally uncharacteristic display of distraction and impatience forces Monica to ask him to (re)tell his favorite story: "Tell me you love me." It is almost as if McBride's apparent desire to end at least where Godard begins temporarily causes him to confuse translation, the cross-cultural movement of the language of film, with betrayal, the abandonment of one's own national identity. But regardless of what motivates contradiction in this particular instance, it does confirm the significance of textual rupture in reading mainstream cinema, one of the principal tenets of feminist film theory since Claire Johnston first outlined what Janet Bergstrom calls "the rupture thesis" in the late 1960s (81). Johnston argued that "the apparent formal coherence" of many Hollywood films is, in fact, "riddled with cracks," which occasionally split open under the pressure of internal ideological tensions (qtd. in Bergstrom 81). In the case of *Breathless*, our overall awareness of narrative coherence is unquestionably heightened by virtue of its temporary disruption, particularly since McBride immediately reestablishes the primacy of the love story that makes his version of *Breathless* distinctive.

In contrast, then, to the lovers' climactic *dialogue de sourds* that logically completes their misalliance in *A Bout de souffle*, McBride's film ends with a pseudo-conversation—in fact, a monologue—in which the male hero reasserts his control over the narrative process as a whole and his preference for the plot of romance in particular. Jesse continues to repeat, as he has throughout the film, that Monica loves him; and his unshakeable faith in that love continues to determine his actions. Thus, as he leaves Monica to keep his appointment with Berrutti (Gary Goodrow), both his parting words ("We can still make it, darling") and the purpose he successfully accomplishes (to get the money they need to escape) confirm that he acts only out of love and on behalf of the couple. At the parallel moment in the French film, Godard first passes in silence over Michel's original reason for meeting Berrutti (Henry-Jacques Huet), since the lovers no longer plan to escape together, and then substitutes a revised motive—Michel now risks his life for the sole purpose of warning his friend—which confirms the solidarity that unites men in opposition to women's treachery.

The ways in which Godard and McBride bring both their films and the lives of their male heroes to an end again reveals their common concern for narrative logic, internal consistency, and (albeit unconsciously) national identity. At the close of *Breathless*, Monica says, for the first and only time in the film, "I love you, Jesse," as she runs *toward* him. Her ultimate confirmation of his emplotment of romantic love allows him to die as the hero she has finally recognized in him: Jesse is shot only after he picks up his own gun and turns to fire directly at the police. Michel's death, in contrast, occurs as he runs *away* from Patricia. He is shot in the back, in a metaphoric repetition of her act of betrayal that clearly charges Patricia—and not the police—with his murder. The stylization of Michel's hesitant, meandering, apparently endless run, which no doubt reflects his disinterest in life itself, makes it seem as if he is being filmed in slow motion. Jesse, in contrast, in imitation of Jerry Lee Lewis, dances and sings his way—"You leave me . . . breathless"—into the final freeze-frame of the film. McBride remade the ending of his *Breathless* after advance projections of the film were unpopular with spectators. "I think that it [the addition of the song and the dance] changes the film completely," he notes without exaggeration. Indeed, McBride turns the original French hero's obsession with death into nothing less than a celebration of life, simultaneously confirming America's famous optimism and yet another, perhaps the most important, of Hollywood's narrative conventions: the happy ending: "I wanted to make a film that would be full of life, I wanted the character of Jesse to be full of life . . . He wants to go on living, it's worth it" (Frank & Krohn 66). Ironically, by radically revising the conclusion to *A Bout de souffle*, McBride does in some sense end up where Godard began, since François Truffaud's original screenplay proposed a far happier ending: Michel drives off with Berrutti, shouting back insults at Patricia, which she fails to understand.

The interview with Jim McBride, which appeared in *Cahiers du cinéma* (August 1983) at the time of the release of the American version of *Breathless*, provides a fascinating account of how he came to direct a remake of Godard's *A Bout de souffle*. The *Cahiers du cinéma* journalists are obviously torn. On the one hand, they are eager to treat McBride as a cult hero and a representative martyr of American independent filmmaking. They present his early career, characterized by his inability either to complete films or to distribute those he was able to complete, as a microcosm of Hollywood's relationship to filmmaking "on its margins" (Frank & Krohn 33). On the other hand, the French critics are also clearly shocked by McBride's ready admission (in the same issue of *Cahiers* in which his remake is panned) that he initially saw Godard's New Wave classic as little more than a marketable property. After struggling for eight years to begin a new career in Hollywood, McBride finally came up with the idea of remaking *A Bout de souffle*, a project he describes as "a rather cynical idea, in some sense, a purely pragmatic one" (Frank & Krohn 64). Thus, in his introduction to the interview, Serge Toubiana rewrites his original version of the horror story of the vampirism of independent filmmakers by Hollywood: "[I]t is coupled in Jim McBride's case with a rather sad story of vampirism between Hollywood and Europe (*A bout de souffle*, a film bled to death), Hollywood coming full circle and reclaiming the substance—emptied, commercialized—that the New Wave folks had cleverly pinched from America (out of love for American auteurs and for America herself) at the end of the fifties" (Frank & Krohn 33).

What else might help us understand how McBride came to remake Godard's discourse of gender and, in particular, his inscription of the heterosexual couple? To some extent, *A Bout de souffle* and *Breathless* offer new evidence in support of the broader structural and conceptual differences between Frenchness and Americanness that already began to emerge from the internal cross-cultural comparison within Resnais's *I Want to Go Home*. Notably, in keeping with what Howard Nostrand defines as French "intellectuality," which tends "to deduce the details from a central, generating idea," the specific case history of Godard's two lovers remains clearly secondary and subordinate to a generalized exploration of the relationship between men and women. McBride, who offers us instead only a single concrete example of the abstract problematic of the couple, illustrates the particularism frequently seen to be more characteristic of an American way of thinking (Nostrand 469).

Raymonde Carroll's discussion of the couple in *Cultural Misunderstandings* (58–70), an investigation into the effects that Franco-American differences have on interpersonal relationships, offers us a particularly strong argument for attributing the difference between Godard's *A Bout de souffle* and McBride's *Breathless* to the specificity of national context. Confirming general cultural patterns of difference noted by Bernstein, Kuisel, and others, Carroll argues that Americans define romantic involvement between a man and a woman primarily in individual and private terms, whereas the French perceive the couple as essentially a social category. Moreover, though men and women of both nations value egalitarian relationships, the French seek only reciprocity or complementarity where Americans expect mutuality; consequently, only the latter equate affective ties with harmony. Carroll thus maintains that the stability of the American couple requires not only that each partner constantly support the other but that each specifically encourage the other to realize his or her ideal self-image—to wit, Monica and Jesse. The French, on the other hand, equate a couple whose partners always agree with indifference, the very opposite of passion—hence, Patricia and Michel.

In a final example of the correspondence between Carroll's understanding of Franco-American culture and that which informs *A Bout de souffle* and *Breathless*, she distinguishes between France, where men and women in love "speak" their relationship, and the United States, where the couple demonstrates unity and closeness by the visual image its partners present to the outside world. In part, of course, this difference conforms to a general tendency, evident in *I Want to Go Home* and the controversy over GATT, to define French culture as predominantly literary and linguistic and its American counterpart as essentially visual. (Note that Patricia goes to Paris to become a writer; and Monica comes to Los Angeles to study architecture.) Thus, despite Godard's interest in visual experimentation, the longest scene in *A Bout de souffle* takes place in a hotel room where Patricia and Michel engage in precisely the kind of verbal exchange that Carroll considers characteristic of the discourse of the Francophone couple: they mock, contradict, and criticize each other, and they consistently take opposite positions on every issue they discuss. In contrast, although conversational sequences retain their centrality in *Breathless*, McBride eliminates the linguistic hierarchy that structures the relationship between the lovers in the French film and substitutes a series of narrative and visual strategies that insist on the spatial proximity and the metaphoric resemblance of the American movie couple.

In conclusion, I want to point out one further and particularly fascinating instance of parallelism between Godard's film and McBride's remake. The narrative whose full realization results in *Breathless* is, in fact, already embedded in schematic and anecdotal form in *A Bout de souffle*, where it is even internally repetitive. (One is curiously reminded of the resemblance between the ending of Resnais's *I Want to Go Home* and the alternative ending that was temporarily imposed upon Renoir's *La Règle du jeu*.) On two different occasions, Michel (re)tells Patricia a story he read in the newspaper, which is interestingly analogous in structure to dialectical argument: (1) (Thesis:) A bus driver steals money and claims to be a rich producer in order to convince the woman he loves to run away with him; (2) (Antithesis:) They blow all their money in a three-day spree on the coast; (3) (Synthesis:) The woman stays with her lover and becomes his partner in crime.[5] A conclusion that Patricia clearly regards (much as Monica initially does) as a complete non sequitur, in terms of both narrative coherence and plausible female behavior, seems merely paradoxical to Michel, who (like Jesse) admires the woman's fidelity as at once "unusual" and "normal" (that is, proper, appropriate).

In this tiny mirror that *A Bout de souffle* holds up to allow *Breathless* to see its own future image, Godard identifies Los Angeles as a logical setting for this exemplary story of faithful lovers and associates the hero's success with the authority he borrows from the (American) entertainment industry. Indeed, he outlines the very narrative model that David Ansen, for example, cites to explain the differences of both origin and focus that distinguish McBride's film from Godard's: "'Breathless' owes more to the Hollywood tradition of lovers-on-the-run films . . . than to the original" ("Lovers"). By chance, in the latest American tribute to a French film classic, whose unexpected location rivals in strangeness the reappearance of Renoir's *La Règle du jeu* within Zucker's crime spoof (or of Euro Disney in a Michelin guidebook), a Spring 1990 issue of *Vogue* magazine (362–75) features a fashion layout in which supermodel Christy Turlington and a male counterpart ("another boxer turned actor—Stéphane Ferrara"), carefully dressed and posed to resemble Seberg and Belmondo, recreate the roles of Patricia and Michel in a remade version of *A Bout de souffle*, which *Vogue* depicts as "the story of two lovers on a crime spree" (365).

Three Takes On Motherhood, Masculinity, and Marriage

Serreau's Original, Nimoy's Remake, and Ardolino's Sequel

Although *Three Men and a Baby*, Leonard Nimoy's 1988 re-vision of Coline Serreau's *Trois Hommes et un couffin* (1985), clearly did not inaugurate the current trend of American remakes of French comedies, it did focus the attention of film critics of both nationalities on the phenomenon. That different reviewers (see, for example, Boujet; Canby, "Bachelor Fathers"; Mordore; and Pertié) all typically focus on questions of cultural difference and specificity is hardly surprising; such concerns are inherent in the very concept of the "remake," as indicated by the bilingualism of the word itself. Moreover, despite parallel—and often contradictory—claims to the originary and original nature of their own cultural product, reviewers on both sides of the Atlantic reveal a common awareness that one particularly key difference and/or specificity is at issue. Though each film had commercial success in its country of conception, neither film was fully able to duplicate this audience appeal in the country of its model or copy. However paradoxically, this situation seems to reflect the simultaneous presence and absence of significant cross-cultural interests.

Yet, at the same time, Nimoy's and Serreau's films can also claim another potentially important source of distinction that has remained invisible in the popular press. Alone among contemporary Franco-American intercultural repetitions (such as *L'Homme qui aimait les femmes/The Man Who Loved Women; Cousin, Cousine/Cousins; Les Fugitifs/Three Fugitives; La Femme Nikita/Point of No Return*), this one involved a directorial substitution that altered not only nationality but sex as well.[1] "Substitution" is indeed the appropriate term in this context, since Touchstone Studios initially hired Serreau, who both wrote and directed *Trois Hommes et un couffin,* to remake her own film. Subsequent to her withdrawal for "health reasons" shortly before shooting was scheduled to begin (Mancini 33), she was replaced by Nimoy, who directed *Three Men and a Baby* from a script that James Orr and Jim Cruickshank "based on" Serreau's original screenplay.[2] Thus, the press's failure to consider simultaneously the possible significance of gender and culture seems a somewhat curious oversight in this case, particularly since the importance of the former is also clearly encoded in the very titles of the two films.

Within the realm of academic criticism, however, I am not the first person to view *Trois Hommes* and its remake as fertile ground on which to explore gender and culture. In contemporaneous issues of *Contemporary French Civilization* and *Camera Obscura,* Raymonde Carroll and Tania Modleski use the respective insights of cultural anthropology and feminist theory to inform readings of Serreau's and Nimoy's films. Their discussions reflect and reconfirm—as does my own—the potential value of the "remake"; indeed, given the filmic texts under consideration, such a critical repetition seems highly appropriate, if not inevitable. Moreover, although I frequently concur in Carroll's and Modleski's contextual assumptions and often agree with their specific textual interpretations, I find their conclusions limited by methodological approaches that are exclusive—and mutually so. The tendency they share to privilege one film over the other and, more important, to focus exclusively on *either* gender *or* culture in many ways duplicates the critical approach that characterizes the popular press.

Thus, as Carroll engages in a careful comparative analysis of *Trois Hommes* and *Three Men* that accentuates cultural difference and specificity, she inevitably brings to light distinctions between the two directors' conceptualizations of sexual identity and gender roles. Her very narrow understanding of gender, however, as both separate from and subordinate to culture, means that Carroll's exposure of what she calls the "invisible verities" of culture effectively renders the evidence of gender invisible in its turn. For example, not only does her stated focus on "cultural presuppositions" explicitly preclude any attention to such issues as cinematic specificity or narrative structure ("Film" 347), but in a cross-cultural discussion of interpersonal relations that includes the categories of friends, the couple, parents and children, adults and babies, and men and women, she regards gender as irrelevant to all but the very last ("Film" 358).

Yet, when gender is finally seen to be at issue, as in the case of Modleski's feminist analysis, it tends in its own turn to become the only issue, blocking any parallel attention to cultural or linguistic difference. If Modleski's strongly psychoanalytical approach leads almost inevitably toward a privileging of gender issues, it tends just as inevitably to repeat the cultural blindness that characterizes traditional Freudian psychoanalysis. Carroll and Modleski might each be said to practice a particular form of imperialism characteristic of her own cultural origins.[3] Where Carroll reiterates the dominance of national identity à la française, Modleski (like Joey, in Resnais's I Want to Go Home) reinscribes a typically American belief that our relationship to others is one of fundamental resemblance. Her assumption that Serreau's and Nimoy's films are essentially indistinguishable leads her to reduce the French film to an infrequent reference point in an analysis that focuses almost exclusively on the American remake and within which Trois Hommes is always "more" or "less," "better" or "worse" than Three Men—but never significantly "different from" it. To the extent that Modleski's analysis still depends upon a comparative context, it too is determined on the basis of gender, not culture: the substitution of a male for a female baby in another American film, John Ford's Three Godfathers (1946).

In fact, in another interesting example of the complexities of determining origin and originality, several critics mention Ford's Three Godfathers, a Western in which three outlaws sacrifice themselves to save an infant found in the desert, in relation to Serreau's Trois Hommes et un couffin. Notably, in the course of reviewing Nimoy's remake, Louis Skorecki of Libération cites Ford as the real model for Serreau's film and thus as evidence of America's ignorance of its own cinematic heritage, especially since Three Godfathers, based on a novel by Peter B. Kyne, was first filmed in 1936 by Richard Belslawski. Certainly the two films, both Christmas parables, reveal fascinating differences within American culture. In Belslawski's original, for example, the baby is clearly perceived to need a mother, and a murderer buys redemption by "delivering" the child to the "virgin" mother whose fiancé he has killed earlier in the film. In Ford's remake, in contrast, the dying mother delegates her maternal authority to the three outlaws collectively, and the film subsequently becomes a kind of "paternity" battle among the three godfathers and eventually the sheriff. On the other hand, neither film has much direct relevance to Trois Hommes or Three Men.

By focusing respectively on context and text, on a cultural "container" and a textual "contained," Carroll and Modleski reenact the very transformation encoded in the titles of Trois Hommes et un couffin and Three Men and a Baby. The shift from basket to baby, from container to contained, identifies a linguistic reversal that recurs frequently in the translation of French into English. J. P. Vinay and J. Darbelnet, in their comprehensive study of the comparative stylistics of French and English, argue that this practice, called "modulation," reflects the coexistence of two distinctive world views: one prone to abstraction and generalization, the other to concrete pragmatism. Such differences have no independent or absolute existence; they both surface and take on meaning only in a comparative context. Thus, the "Frenchness" of Serreau's film cannot be fully understood without paying close attention to the "Americanness" of Nimoy's. Similarly, as I noted earlier, my particular theoretical interest in the remake lies in what it reveals not only about culture and/or gender but about the nature of the relationship *between* the two. From this perspective, the parallel versions of *Three Men* offer us an especially appropriate context for exploration—not, of course, because of a fortuitous change in the sex of the director (which, at most, serves only, and only after the fact, as an opportune sign of the gender differences that lie elsewhere)[4] but because of the narrative incoherence that each film reveals independently and which their comparison makes particularly evident.

The basic story is identical in both the French and the American versions: two carefree bachelors are astonished to discover one Sunday morning that the "delivery" they agreed to accept in the temporary absence of their third roommate has apparently turned out to be his baby daughter; subsequently, the three men undergo a radical (if also predictable) change of lifestyle as they learn to care for, protect, and love the newest member of their household. More specifically, however, Serreau posits and Nimoy retains—but with a significant difference—two incompatible plot structures that are respectively en-gendered as masculine and feminine. An initial confusion of two "packages," of heroin and heroine, introduces narrative rivalry between a masculine story of action and adventure, of opposition to law and order, and a "feminine" plot of domesticity, of compliance with societal norms and values. (In French, of course, *heroin* and *heroine*—*l'héroïne* in both cases—are exact homonyms—same sound, same spelling, same etymology, same feminine gender.) Moreover, in the course of confirming narratives of different genders, the two films reveal an alteration of genre as well. The transformation of "feminine" French realism into "masculine" American comedy simultaneously exposes narrative structure as a reflection of world view and makes visible the significance of gender for an understanding of each, both independently and interdependently.[5]

Trois Hommes openly announces its structural incoherence and explicitly identifies it as a problem of narration. Indeed, since the heroin plot has reached full closure early in the film, long before Jacques (André Dussollier) returns, it is in fact the narrative process itself, the *telling* of the story, that reveals (and, in part, creates) a confusion that was not previously apparent. Thus, Jacques's initial inability to comprehend the discourse of "drugs, diapers, babies, and cops," which Michel (Michel Boujenah) and Pierre (Roland Giraud) shout out in chorus, reflects *en abyme* the viewer's first conscious encounter with incompatible plots and genres. Toward the end of the film, an explicit act of internal repetition serves as reminder and reconfirmation that the question of coherence centers on issues of narrative and narrativity. In one of the many scenes of diegetic "remake" that characterize Serreau's narrative structure, Jacques's own attempt to explain the drug plot to the narcotics agent who was himself an eyewitness dissolves once again into verbal chaos.

In the American version of *Three Men*, in contrast, past events are related to Jack (Ted Danson) quickly and clearly. Both the efficiency of the discursive function, now the responsibility of Peter (Tom Selleck) alone, and Peter's respect for traditional dramatic structure support a narrative that is perfectly coherent in content and immediately comprehensible in meaning. In opposition to the French film, where narration introduces confusion into a previously cohesive plot, the American telling of the tale conceals the absence of any preexistent unity of action. Indeed, the possibility of narrative closure, which allows both Jack and the spectator a reassuring impression of understanding and significance, may well depend on its very artifice, since, in fact, Nimoy's film narrates the drug story long before it reaches actual resolution. The continuity of the narrative process thus functions strategically and metaphorically to represent the false integration of two plots that remain essentially separate and distinct.

As feminist film theory has evolved from the germinal work of Laura Mulvey, Pam Cook, and Claire Johnston, one recurrent method of interpretation, as we have seen, has centered on the identification of moments of textual conflict or incoherence at which mainstream cinema invites a reading of its ideological contra-dictions, of what, like Michel and Pierre, it cannot, will not, or dare not express clearly. Seen from this perspective, the "separate but equal" incoherence of narrative structure that characterizes *Trois Hommes* and its remake reveals that the sociohistorical assumptions and desires of a given culture, on the one hand, and a particular inscription of the discourse of gender, on the other, are both closely related and strongly interdependent. Yet, such a reading also suggests that regardless of the cultural specificity of any single "remake" of the story of gender, the misogyny of the message recurs repeatedly: "separate" is not "equal."

The "container" privileged in the title of *Trois Hommes et un couffin* reflects a narrative structure that repeatedly and doubly "contains"—that both includes and confines—a number of scenes and/or women (the two terms are here synonymous). The absence of these passages from the American remake provides a contextual contrast that increases their visibility and underscores their significance in the original. These scenes, internally recurrent, constitute the locus of the discourse of misogyny contained within Serreau's film. (According to Lucy Fischer, most films, in keeping with the codes of classic realism, use the device of narrative closure to represent women's containment within patriarchy [*Shot/Countershot* 245]; in this context, see my earlier discussion of *A Bout de souffle*.) Each episode provides the film's three male heroes with a renewed opportunity both to act on their theoretical determination to exclude women from every aspect of their lives and to justify that position by exposing or denouncing female incompetence or both.

Two scenes should suffice as illustration, particularly since the first might initially seem to contradict the very argument I have just outlined. Pierre and Michel resolve their initial ignorance of childcare by consulting a female pharmacist (Annik Alane) whose very language—characterized by objectivity, categorization, enumeration, hypothesis, and logic—confirms that the source of her authority derives from Science and not from gender. But any tempta- tion to read this passage as an argument for shared parenting, grounded in an assumption of equal access to acquired knowledge, seems hasty in light of its subsequent textual "revision." For the scene in which the men drive off the professional "Second Mommy" (Dominique Lavanant), who defines her own competence in terms of her diplomas and her knowledge of pediatrics, under- mines the authority both of women and of science. Indeed, Pierre's response to the woman's assertion that "medicine is a serious business" (that is, moth- ering cannot be left to men) makes explicit both the relationship between the two parallel episodes and their parallel relationship to narrative itself: "Have you ever heard the story that goes like this—medicine [*la* médecine] is a whore and the female pharmacist [*la* pharmacienne] her pimp?"

Why, we must obviously ask, might a film "made in France" not only seek—actively and on principle—to exclude women from childcare and to prove them to be either indifferent or incompetent mothers, but also reject everything connected to women, including the very associations posited within its own text and which seem most clearly advantageous to its male heroes' desire to parent? One possible explanation originates in the relation- ship between gender and culture. In France, as I noted earlier, the contempo- rary feminist movement has been most visibly defined by a theoretical dis- course of "difference" in which female sexuality has been reclaimed and revalorized but not necessarily redefined. The female language of *écriture féminine* relies on metaphors derived from such "natural" aspects of the ma- ternal experience as pregnancy, birth, and breast-feeding to celebrate the specificity of the female body. This theory has emerged, moreover, within a sociohistorical context in which the official voices of the dominant culture have been actively promoting pro-natalism.[6] I would propose that in such conditions the central ideological task of men who wish to parent consists in providing evidence of both their right and their ability to "mother."

Serreau's film logically inscribes this project as a two-part process. Given the pervasive cultural belief in women's biological "right" to mother, presum- ably internalized by men at least as completely as by women, the first stage requires the exclusion and the condemnation of all "real" women as a neces- sary prerequisite to any convincing assertion of men's own rights. Signifi- cantly, the men's principled commitment to an all-male household is initially expressed not as a general philosophy of misogyny but in terms of the very particularized rejection, both literal and metaphoric, of mothers, including their own: "We'll leave mothers [*les* mères] wherever they are." Moreover, this first necessity is reinforced by a further consequence of the initial cultural premise. For if the maternal role is "naturally" female, then men can prove themselves to be "women" and (therefore) "mothers" only through a process of direct substitution. In Serreau's film, this textual "remake" of men takes place through the feminization of the masculine narrative or, perhaps more accurately, through the incorporation of the men into a narrative already defined as "feminine."[7]

Despite the inability of the men to *tell* their story coherently, the action itself, as I noted above, is perfectly cohesive. In direct contrast to the American film, in which the drug deal becomes the dominant narrative, Serreau brings this masculine plot to rapid resolution in the absence of Jacques, baby Marie's biological father; his return appropriately coincides with the assertion, henceforth unchallenged, of the primacy of the feminine—in this context, the female narrative of mothering. Indeed, the moment at which the narrators themselves begin to make sense is marked by the transition from what "isn't the problem" (the drugs) to what is ("the problem is the baby bottles, the diapers, the shit, and the laundry"). Moreover, in this context, the confusion that initially characterizes the narrative process can now be read as an inevitable result and an accurate reflection of the inseparability of the heroin and the heroine that guarantees the centrality of the feminine plot in Serreau's film. From the time of their delivery until they are returned to the dealers, the drugs are constantly concealed on the baby's body (in the American remake, they are quickly relegated to the diaper pail); thus every episode of the drug plot unfolds in the context of childcare and in the presence of the baby. Indeed, concern for the heroine provides both the sole motivation for the heroes' decision to return the heroin and the only guarantee they offer the drug dealers that they can be trusted. At the moment of repetition, when Jacques himself attempts to explain the structure of the plot, his simulation of pregnancy offers visual support for the explicit identification of biological difference as the source not only of male anxiety but also of narrative confusion. No *male* narrative, argues Jacques, can ever pretend to coherence—short, that is, of undertaking the ultimate "remake" of the original story, the story of our origins:

> If I could somehow remake the world, if I were God, this is what I would do. I would fashion Adam from Eve's rib rather than the other way around. At least that way things would have been clear from the beginning. We wouldn't have been led to believe that someone could be created from our rib. Because nothing is created from our rib. Not ever.

Jacques's subsequent lament about the inferiority of male creativity—"the only things that we can make are buildings, planes, cars"—is echoed much earlier and in a very different context in Nimoy's remake of *Three Men*. Peter's similar analogy—"I'm an architect for Christ sake. I build cities of the future. I put up skyscrapers. I can certainly put a goddam diaper together"—functions not to establish a contrast between the inherent capabilities of men and women, but to justify the extension of men's professional competence into the realm of childcare. Moreover, Mary's biological father expresses his own right and ability to parent in precisely the same terms. Whereas Jacques's potential superiority over Michel and Pierre "naturally" surfaces as a frequent source of anxiety in Serreau's film, the American remake logically (indeed, literally) "reconceives" fatherhood as a question of "performance" rather than procreation. The alteration of Jack's career (in the original, he is a flight attendant) aptly serves to emphasize his redefinition of fatherhood as a social "role": "I'm an actor; I can do a father."

Such a significant textual change reflects the dominant ideology of American feminism, which has consistently emphasized equality rather than difference, gender rather than sex, and societal change over biological destiny.[8] In this cultural context, the transformation of traditional roles that would result in men's active involvement in childcare does not require that they discredit and replace women; it depends rather on women's own denial of any inherent female ability to mother and their subsequent refusal to continue to substitute for fathers. Thus, although Nimoy essentially retains Serreau's structural model of recurrent scenes that focus on different women, agency now lies with the female characters who repeatedly reject motherhood and decline to help the men. As Rebecca (Margaret Colin), for example, denies Peter her assistance in the scene that establishes the pattern, she also dismisses his need ("You're very capable; you'll get through this just fine") and deconstructs his argument, challenging both its premise ("because [she's] a woman") and its conclusions (*she* "automatically know[s] what to do with babies" and *men* "don't know anything about babies"). The explicit repetition of this scene confirms its ideological importance: Jack's own mother (Celeste Holm) counters his pretense that "there's like a biological thing, an instant connection" between her and *his* baby with a similar strategy of simultaneous attack (an injunction to "cut the crap") and support (an assertion that he will make a "fine" father). Since the women's willing abandonment of childcare to men clearly includes their parallel acknowledgment of male competence, it is not surprising that Nimoy's recurrent scenes gradually replace reluctant mothers with committed and adoring fathers (including not only the police detective and the taxi driver, but even, to some extent, the drug dealers themselves). Thus, traditional gender associations are broken down and new ones established at the same time.

Double Takes

But the American film's reflection of different cultural assumptions about gender merely displaces conflict, without in any way eliminating it. Nimoy's narrative structure confirms that men who "mother" need not prove their right and ability to do so; on the contrary, they must now demonstrate not that they are women but rather that they are still men. Thus, Nimoy quickly separates the heroin from the heroine and reverses the relative importance of the two plots. The masculine tale of action and adventure, designed to prove all three men's virility, now structures the film as a whole. That the significance of the story of the drugs lies not in its content but in its form is confirmed by the addition at the end of the remake of a chase scene; the race to and through the airport, totally gratuitous in terms of both plot and character development, serves only to confirm the status of Nimoy's three heroes as virile men of action.

Moreover, if divergent cultural attitudes toward authority partly explain the different ways in which Serreau and Nimoy position their protagonists *within* the narrative of law and order, especially since cinematic representation has played a significant role in shaping such attitudes, here too gender influences how the conventions of genre and ideology take on specific meaning. In aligning themselves with drug dealers, the heroes of *Trois Hommes* may well act in keeping with French film's fondness for the moral ambiguity of the "hors-la-loi," but narrative analogy (reinforced yet again by the constant visual and verbal associations of "heroin" and "heroine") primarily functions in an ironic reversal to identify trafficking in "illegitimate" drugs and the usurpation of motherhood as parallel criminal activities and as equally subversive alternatives to the pharmacists and the police officers whose "legitimate" drug activity identifies them as the cultural representatives of conventional law and order. In general, the protagonists of *Three Men*, who now side with the police, show similar respect for Hollywood's very different ethical code, where the triumph of good over evil often makes the cop the hero. But Nimoy's men also practice their own culturally specific form of usurpation; as their passive support evolves into active participation, they take over the function of the police and solve the crime in their place. Not only do the American fathers receive authorization to parent from the defenders of normative social structures, but they also replace the traditional representatives of author/-ity in order to rewrite the conventional narrative of law and order so that it will incorporate new roles for men.[9]

Still, *Three Men*'s insistent need to prove masculinity leads not to the disappearance of the discourse of misogyny but to its relocation. The titular removal of the baby from the basket metaphorically identifies an all too literal act of "robbing the cradle." The hostility to women that Serreau's Frenchmen direct at the mother resurfaces in Nimoy's film in the representation of the child, suggesting a shift in cultural conceptions of women's "natural" role from the maternal to the sexual; in the American context, misogyny appears to find its best expression in sexual objectification rather than biological destiny. (At the same time, of course, this particular "difference" also reflects a common cross-cultural pattern of the denial of the mother's sexuality.)

In a variety of ways, Nimoy's "baby" realizes the full metaphorical potential of the word itself; explicitly and repeatedly en-gendered as a female, this "baby" simultaneously represents and replaces the woman as sexual object. The concern that Michael (Steve Guttenberg) voices during the initial diaper change—"This is a girl; should we be doing this?"—immediately substitutes an illicit male/female relationship for normal parental/child interaction. Subsequently, in a direct inversion of the structure of the original film, the female narrative of childcare is masculinized and incorporated into a male "tail" of virility and sexual conquest. Peter reads *Sports Illustrated* to Mary; Jack showers with his baby daughter; and throughout Nimoy's film, male "mothering" functions primarily as a sexual turn-on, a highly successful strategy for attracting women. In one scene, Peter's identical rendition of "Goodnight, Sweetheart, Goodnight" serves in quick succession to calm Mary and to arouse Rebecca; and, in general, Nimoy's substitution of such conventional romantic lyrics as "I wanna be Daddy's Girl" and "The moment I met you baby" for the classical score of the French film provides a subtle and suggestive accompaniment for his story of the sexualization of a female infant (see, also, Modleski).

Feminist film theory, however, also posits that textual examples of conflict and incoherence can serve not only to expose mainstream cinema's hidden ideological assumptions but also to uncover the source of a potentially subversive discourse. Might it then be possible to reread the films' double message of misogyny from this perspective? One might argue, for example, that the commitment of Serreau's men to conventional female narrative no doubt results in a certain visual confirmation of the rhythms of domesticity, notably its episodic, interruptible, and repetitive nature. The film is organized around a series of vignettes, each devoted to some aspect of childcare; and this structural representation of fragmentation and repetition seems to respect certain realities of many women's daily labor. Similarly, textual patterns of recurrence create a sense of internal rhyming that recalls narrative structures common in many contemporary female texts of "domestic realism" (see, for example, Aptheker and Juhasz).

On the other hand, change predicated on a simple reversal of gender roles, or on the substitution of one sex for the other in an otherwise unaltered script, seems more likely to confirm than to challenge traditional models of gender. Not surprisingly, then, Serreau's film also uses its male characters to reinscribe some of the most potentially harmful of societal assumptions about appropriate lifestyles for those whose responsibilities include childcare. Notably, *Trois Hommes* reinforces cultural expectations that childcare will be an

79

exclusive occupation, incompatible with any other work and requiring a maternal presence in the home; the film further suggests that the couple is the preferred model for the structure of the family. Indeed, the first third of Serreau's film focuses almost exclusively on the illustration of these beliefs. Caring for Marie constitutes a full-time job for both Pierre and Michel; each totally abandons his regular paid work to take what Pierre explicitly identifies as "maternal leave." While their further rejection of both physical separation and any division of labor might be read as an ironic admission that it takes two men to do the job of one woman, in context it also serves to support the ideology of the couple; for what links all the caretakers (female or male, natural or surrogate) who are denounced in the course of the film as incompetent is their common effort, always unsuccessful, to provide adequate childcare alone.[10]

In contrast, it is precisely the ability to rethink traditional childcare that offers the possibility of a more optimistic reading of Nimoy's discourse of gender. Each of the three American men takes his turn at assuming full responsibility for Mary, and each integrates childcare with a continuing commitment to his usual professional responsibilities. Thus, whereas Serreau's film, whatever its intentions, inevitably encourages us to identify Michel as primary caretaker, precisely because of his proven domestic competence and his metaphorical ability to "work at home," Nimoy gives parallel visual importance to Peter as he visits construction sites with Mary in tow, and to Jack at rehearsals with the baby in a backpack. Such an integration of one's personal and professional life might lead us beyond traditional "mothering," whether masculine or feminine, toward a new definition not only of fathers but of parents, including female ones.

This hypothesis finds support in the contrasting ways in which the two films reach narrative closure. Serreau requires the mother (Philippine Leroy Beaulieu) to acknowledge her own incompetence and to restore the baby to the sole care (however temporary) of the men, whose confident assurance— "for us it's nothing"—confirms their new alignment with the realm of the "natural." Although the association between narrative closure and the "containment" of women is usually a metaphoric one, as in the case of *A Bout de souffle*, *Trois Hommes et un couffin* literalizes this relationship in particularly revealing ways. In the final episode of a dramatic structure that has repeatedly confined women, Serreau's film ends not only with the visual imprisonment of both mother and daughter but with their permanent infantilization as well. In the last two shots of the film, we first see Sylvia (whose smudged makeup, meant to suggest fatigue, in fact gives her the troubling appearance of a battered woman) curled up asleep in Marie's crib, sucking her thumb, and then Marie herself, who is caught in freeze frame just as she begins to take her first steps alone. Nimoy, in contrast, has his fathers alter family structure once again to make room (however marginal) for the mother (Nancy

Travis). At the same time, however, the American film's persistent metamorphosis of French realism into comedy (and often farce), visually reinforced by the heroes' self-referential depiction as life-size comic-strip characters, also consistently questions the seriousness of any appearance of a commitment to change.

Like Joey in Resnais's *I Want to Go Home*, Michael is a cartoonist; moreover, the comic strip character he draws, "Johnny Cool," like the "Silver Surfer" in McBride's *Breathless*, implicitly serves as something of a male role model. Although Michel, Michael's counterpart in Serreau's film, is also described as a "dessinateur," his drawings play no comparable visual function in the French original. Indeed, the contrast between the opening credit sequences of the two films is emblematic of the cross-cultural distinction between art and popular culture that we encountered earlier in Resnais's film. At the beginning of *Trois Hommes et un couffin*, as the camera tracks through the men's apartment, we see a series of paintings of women and children, whose artificially somber and warm coloring and lighting determines that of the contemporary scene as well. *Three Men and a Baby*, in contrast, is framed by sequences in which Michael completes the cartoon murals, which depict scenes from his and his roommates' life, that cover the walls of the entryway to their penthouse.

"The manner in which words are strung together expresses a mode of thought that is as important as the thought itself," notes Vincent Canby, in the course of explicating Marin Karmitz's characterization of the current predilection of French directors for making films in English as "not a crisis of cinema but a crisis of culture" ("Ici Se Habla"). Implicitly, if not intentionally, Canby's words also permit a reading that suggests the important influence that narrative structure ("the manner in which words are strung together") has on world view ("a mode of thought") during the process of reconstruction and reconceptualization that results in the cross-cultural remake. The films of Serreau and Nimoy provide a comparative example that highlights the further complication that gender brings to the contemporary cinematic narrative of "a crisis of culture." By telling the same story differently—to the paradoxical point of both relating two different stories and repeating the same story—*Trois Hommes* and its American remake help reveal the particularly complex ways in which culture and gender interact, in which narrative is simultaneously en-gendered by culture and acculturated by gender.

The introduction to a special issue of *CinémAction*, as I have already noted, warns against the temptation "to construct a theory of the remake too hastily" (M. Serceau 9). In this context, it is no doubt fitting that I initially completed an earlier version of this analysis (Durham, "Taking") only to discover that its subject matter had already been "remade" by the subsequent release of Emile

Double Takes

Ardolino's *Three Men and a Little Lady* in December of 1990. Even the credits announce this latest version of "repetition with a difference" as a particularly curious example of cross-cultural collaboration. Although Touchstone Pictures has clearly marketed *Little Lady* as a sequel to its own (and Nimoy's) *Three Men and a Baby* (promoted, as a result, to the status of "the original"), the film actually reintroduces itself as yet another remake of Serreau's *Trois Hommes et un couffin*. Moreover, this Franco-American co-production (for which Jean-François Lepetit, for example, repeats the role of executive producer that he originally created with *Trois Hommes*) also emerges from a particularly complex process of mediation among a number of contributors who differ by nationality, sex, or both. Were we to reconstruct the credits in the form of a synopsis, we would uncover the rather awkward story of genesis that follows: *Little Lady* was "Directed by" Ardolino from a "Screenplay by" Charlie Peters, which he developed from a "Story by" Sara Parriott and Josann McGibbon, which they "Based on" the film that was "Written by" Serreau. Moreover, although international copyright agreements and/or multinational financial arrangements may well provide a partial explanation for the unusually complicated authorship of *Three Men and a Little Lady*, the contradictory nature of this bicultural (and bigendered) hybrid—the sequel-remake—is also reproduced within the narrative structure of the film where its very complexity significantly furthers our exploration of the interrelationship of gender and culture.

Little Lady begins as a realistic domestic comedy that borrows conventions of both gender and genre from Serreau's *Trois Hommes*. The unexpected phenomenon of a sequel that returns to its own precursor's origins affords an unusual opportunity to reconsider the context in which we initially compared French and American versions of the discourse of gender. In particular, *Little Lady* immediately raises new questions about what I characterized as the relative progressiveness that seemed to distinguish Nimoy's understanding of parental roles and familial structure from their more traditional conceptualization in Serreau's film. Ardolino's sequel suggests that the mere presence of the mother (Nancy Travis) may be sufficient in and of itself to reestablish the "natural" primacy of her role; not only do all three men (also played by the original American actors) significantly alter their earlier behavior by now deferring to Sylvia's authority in any decision that involves Mary (Robin Weisman), but no comparable change occurs in the status of the biological father.

Moreover, in what would appear to be a second direct consequence of the mother's return, her new importance also provokes a systematic attempt to undermine her as a woman that we originally encountered only in *Trois Hommes*. Although Jack, Peter, and Michael continue to share some responsibility for childcare, the only domestic chore still in sight is now performed by Sylvia alone, and it specifically serves to define her difference as one of incompetence: she is a rotten cook and therefore—we can only assume—she cooks relentlessly. Not even Mary will eat what her mother prepares; and the men have developed carefully choreographed movements that allow them to discard Sylvia's food efficiently the moment her back is turned. By positioning Sylvia as the unconscious butt of a joke that all the men in the film take turns sharing with the audience, Ardolino suggests that women's stupidity is rivaled only by their vulnerability, and thus succeeds in justifying both male hypocrisy and the mockery of women as necessary acts of protectiveness.

The move from margin to center that Sylvia makes in the gap between the final visual image of Nimoy's *Three Men* and the opening dialogue of Ardolino's *Little Lady* also heralds the return of the heterosexual couple and the traditional nuclear family. Indeed, our only real glimpse of the four adults' original (in every sense of the word) experiment in cooperative parenting comes in the form of the silent coda with which the sequel begins, and even this series of successively dissolving parallel images serves primarily as a rapid visual transition that takes Mary from infancy to preschool age. Still, what the sequel appears to introduce as an inevitable change in the child (in any child) more accurately reflects a significant revision of the specific discourse of gender, in keeping with the transformation of Nimoy's "baby" into Ardolino's "lady." In fact, the particular semantic richness of these two terms empowers them alone to tell the whole story.

Just as the space between the metaphoric and the literal "baby" leaves room for Nimoy to write his contradictory tale of three men who continue to view women as sexual objects even as they become the responsible fathers of an infant daughter, the multiple meanings of the word *lady* function similarly to structure Ardolino's narrative. As the relationship between the titles of the two films suggests, the heroes' lives now revolve around the mother rather than the baby. As a polite synonym for "woman" as well as a term whose references include "a female head of household," *lady* names both Sylvia's new stature and its primary cause. At the same time, of course, the titular modifier "little" continues to recall both the masculine tendency to associate grown women with young girls (particularly evident in the closing images of Serreau's film) and Sylvia's actual domestic subordination. (Even the culinary tasks that act as the primary means of Sylvia's humiliation may be embedded in *lady*, which derives from the Old English *hlaefdige*, "kneader of bread.") Since the word *lady* further denotes "a woman to whom a man is romantically attached" and also serves as an informal equivalent for "wife," it similarly identifies the essential plot mechanism of *Little Lady*, which has now shifted from the story of parenting to the narrative of romance. Ardolino's already competent fathers must learn to be satisfactory husbands; as a result, they have begun to view women more as potential wives than as temporary sexual partners. Finally, if we interpret the lady of Ardolino's title as a reference to the one generally bestowed upon a British woman of rank, it even announces the particular event that precipitates the central dramatic crisis of the film: Sylvia's decision to return to England to marry Edward (Christopher Cazenove), a wealthy British director and landowner.

Regardless of who is assigned to play the central female part, however, the role itself remains primarily titular in both *Three Men and a Little Lady* and *Three Men and a Baby*. As one might well deduce from the exact repetition of the first words of the titles, the sequel to Nimoy's picture essentially affords Ardolino a renewed opportunity to explore the changing nature of masculinity. In fact, not only are the two American versions of *Three Men* initially indistinguishable by name, but the identical strategy (Sylvia and Mary's imminent departure for England) serves in both films to reveal character and to motivate action. Ardolino's sequel has as its central thematic and dramatic focus the selection of a suitable husband for Sylvia. His identity, however, remains closely associated with Nimoy's earlier concerns about parenting, since whomever Sylvia marries will automatically become Mary's "real" father at the same time. Although paternal love is not in and of itself a sufficient criterion to determine the appropriate spouse, its absence does constitute adequate grounds on which to eliminate a potential husband. Curiously, in this context too, *Little Lady* seems more reminiscent of the French original than of its American remake, for Sylvia's initial choice suggests her own incompetence as a mother. To the extent that she ever takes seriously Edward's professed commitment to fatherhood, Sylvia elects to believe in the self-directed performance of a fellow professional in the theater, despite its inability to convince Mary, its intended audience.

Subsequently, Sylvia is not only oblivious to Edward's plan to put his new daughter in an English boarding school immediately after the wedding, but she refuses to believe Peter and Michael when they expose his scheme; indeed, she goes through with a wedding ceremony that she believes to be authentic. Moreover, when she is finally faced with irrefutable proof, Sylvia's anger expresses the personal insult that she feels as a result of Edward's willingness to lie to her far more than it does any maternal outrage at his treatment of her daughter. Thus Ardolino's Sylvia metaphorically repeats Sylvie's original abandonment of baby Marie in Serreau's film—but this time without the benefit of either necessity or extenuating circumstances. Indeed, in the pivotal scene at the very center of *Little Lady*, in which Peter and Sylvia quarrel violently, his attack on Edward as the wrong father for Mary quickly evolves into the condemnation of Sylvia as an irresponsible mother. For the first and only time in either of the two American films, she is explicitly charged with her "original" crime of child abandonment: "I'm selfish? Well, I didn't leave my baby on a doorstep when she was six months old."

In another example of the Franco-American rapprochement that Nimoy's film seems to mediate between its original model and its own sequel, it is only with *Little Lady* that biological fatherhood becomes in any sense problematic in the American films. Ardolino now systematically sets out to discredit Jack, Mary's natural father, presumably in order to justify his eventual replacement by Peter. In a total reversal of the strategy introduced in Nimoy's film, where Jack's profession serves as the principal means for transforming fatherhood from a biological fact into a social "role" that can be "performed" equally well by all men, his acting career now identifies him as an unsuitable father. Moreover, it also establishes a clear link between Jack, Sylvia, and Edward: the three theatrical professionals are all to some degree denounced as parents. If those who have some "natural" claim on Mary—her biological parents and the man her mother selects as spouse and future father—are, in fact, defined as fundamentally "artificial," then one can logically assume that the opposing premise must also hold true, that is, the "real" father will by definition be an "unnatural" one.

In this context, the fact that Jack's career is less successful and respectable than Sylvia's or Edward's—he acts badly in laxative commercials and B-movies while they direct and perform Shaw and Shakespeare—is clearly to his credit. Unlike Edward, Jack, according to Sylvia, can't "fool" anyone. Still, he periodically reveals a similar tendency to let his work take precedence over his child. That Jack is a fundamentally irresponsible, if entertaining, father is carefully pointed out to us early in the film. Despite persistent pleas and reminders and the importance of the event, Jack nonetheless arrives late for the family's interview with the directors of the primary school to which Mary has applied. More important, when he finally does show up to participate in what has been established as the family's first attempt to assure the community that its highly unusual parenting arrangements will not harm Mary, Jack is not only still costumed and made up as Count Dracula but he continues to play the role. The particular choice of disguise seems specifically designed to undermine the potential privilege of Jack's biological paternity by suggesting that this "blood" relation(ship) is a highly unhealthy one.

At the same time, Jack's portrayal as someone who preys on women is consistent with the reputation he established as a womanizer in *Three Men and a Baby* and could therefore serve the parallel function of exposing his unsuitability as husband as well as father—or rather, in the context of the sequel, his unsuitability as husband and *therefore* as father (the former is now a prerequisite for the latter). In general, however, the discourse of masculinity and sexuality is constructed quite differently in *Little Lady*. In yet another, and even more fascinating, reversal of Nimoy's emplotment of masculinity, in which nurturing fathers had to prove they were still men, in Ardolino's sequel, Jack is further disqualified as a potential husband and father precisely by his discrediting as a "man." The challenge to Jack's virility takes the specific form of an attack on his heterosexuality, the very locus in Nimoy's film of the proof of his heroes' manhood, particularly in the case of Jack, whose exceptional powers of seduction distinguish him from Peter and Michael. At present, however, not only does Jack, unlike Peter and Michael, clearly *not* wish to marry, but he no longer appears to be involved, even casually, with any woman. More important, Jack's appearance is consistently coded as effeminate; another negative consequence of his profession means that we most often see him framed in mirrors, in costume, and heavily made up. In the single most telling sequence, Jack cross-dresses as Chiquita Banana; in the unlikely event that someone might miss the visual allusion to a gay man, the stage manager makes it explicit: "Hey, Fruit of the Loom—you're on."

In direct opposition to Jack, Peter is identified as the right father for Mary and the appropriate husband for Sylvia by both his success in those areas where Jack fails and his failures in those areas where Jack succeeds. Thus, in the love scene he attempts to rehearse with Sylvia in Jack's absence, Peter proves himself an awkward and unwilling actor, precisely because he is not acting: "Jack should be doing this. He's the actor. That was terrible. I was totally unbelievable." In contrast to Nimoy's film, not only has Peter now largely displaced Jack and Michael as primary parent, but the paternal role has expanded in ways that begin to conflate the role of Mary's father with that of Sylvia's husband. Indeed, Peter's dependability—as Sylvia says, "I can always count on you"—seems to make him as promising a husband as he is a successful father. Consistent, moreover, with the logic of the first film, in which Peter is involved in a serious, long-term relationship, we now learn that he was once briefly married. This revelation serves to prove that Peter, unlike Jack, is not a confirmed bachelor and to justify his apparent unwillingness to marry again. Indeed, his very reluctance confirms the importance he attaches to such a commitment.

Yet the roles of father and husband actually turn out to be in competition and even contradiction in *Little Lady*. Jack describes both the stability of the newly patriarchal family Peter has constructed and the dilemma that it creates: "These last five years, with Mary and Sylvia and Michael and me, you have been the glue that kept us together. We depended on you. We made you the father and it worked. It's kept you from admitting how you feel about Sylvia. You love her, don't you?" (Or, as Jack goes on to conclude, more briefly and more characteristically, "It's tough being Papa Bear, isn't it?") Just as Jack and Peter can together legitimately claim to be "Mary's real father," the two men, defined retroactively as "best friends" in Ardolino's sequel, embody different but closely related dimensions of contemporary masculinity. Appropriately, then, Peter and Jack, the latter disguised as a vicar, will both "marry" Sylvia in the concluding scene of *Three Men and A Little Lady*.

Not surprisingly, Jack's version of manhood is the more dated and conventional of the two. Jack epitomizes the phenomenon of male "commitment-phobia," which Barbara Ehrenreich characterizes as "one of the most striking changes of the seventies" in *The Hearts of Men*, her feminist analysis of the evolution of masculinity from the fifties to the eighties (121). Peter, on the other hand, is, if anything, *too* committed and not only to a conception of the role of the head of the family that would seem to preclude any personal attachments on his part. Peter also believes that he represents precisely what women seek in marriage (and in men): "You'd be surprised how practical women are about these things . . . I think women want security." It seems particularly appropriate in this context to have just cited a female scholar's work on masculinity, since both American films emphasize the active role that women have played in redefining societal expectations for men. Thus Sylvia immediately and directly contradicts Peter's assertions about women's desires: "You know what I want? I want a man who'll make a fool of himself over me." (One is reminded of what Monica comes to value in Jesse in Jim McBride's *Breathless*.) In this case, to behave like a "fool" means quite literally that Peter must begin to *talk* (fool, from Late Latin *follis*, windbag, that is, a talkative person), to express himself. As Jack urges, "Just say how you feel," and as Sylvia's mother confirms, Peter must learn to "open up," to become "comfortable with [his] feelings." He must come to understand and to articulate his own emotional needs as a *man* as well as a father and to recognize those of Sylvia as a *woman* as well as a mother. In other words, Peter must grow into the role of the "New Male" (Ehrenreich 127–28). That, by his own admission, it takes Peter five years even "to realize" his "true feelings" for Sylvia and until the final moments of the film to ask her to marry him for his own sake rather than "for Mary's"—"If there were no Mary, I'd still love you . . . Am I making a big enough fool of myself?"—suggests the difficulty of such a transformation.

Still, in keeping with a (remade) fairytale tradition, the prince immediately sets out to prove himself worthy of the princess by the successful completion of the designated task. The second half of Ardolino's film, entirely devoted to Peter's efforts to "make a fool of himself," returns to the action plot that dominates Nimoy's American remake, even as the action itself is now relocated to Europe, as in the French original. Narrative structures, however, continue to reflect changes in the construction of gender. Unlike *Three Men and a Baby*, where the heroes prove their virility by their success in attracting women, Peter is now the unwilling target of a would-be female seducer. The attempt by Miss Lomax (Fiona Shaw) to get Peter to declare and act upon his feelings for her illustrates once again the use of internal plot repetition to establish patterns of gendered behavior. More important, it supports Ehrenreich's argument about the central role that sexuality plays in defining—and redefining—masculinity:

Double Takes

> The qualities now claimed for the authentic male self—sensitivity, emotional lability, a capacity for self-indulgence, even unpredictability—are still, and despite the feminist campaign to the contrary, recognizably "feminine." How much could a man transform himself, in the name of androgynous progress, without ceasing to be . . . "all male," or visibly heterosexual? Sanctions against homosexuality had always defined the outer limit of male rebellion . . . (128)

Although Ehrenreich suggests that such sanctions eased somewhat in the seventies, the period to which she here refers, Ardolino's film would also seem to confirm her fear that the New Right's subsequent backlash against male conformity would restore a moral climate in which accusations of homosexuality could once again be used to control male "rebels" (161). Certainly, Ardolino is as eager to emphasize Peter's heterosexuality as he is to undermine Jack's. The inverse relationship between the two men is further reinforced by the use of the same strategy. Whereas Jack's career consistently serves to feminize him, Peter's profession, used by Nimoy as a metaphor for his competence as a father, is now repeatedly linked to his (hetero)sexual prowess. Early in the film, for example, when Mary suddenly asks Michael and Peter both *if* they have a penis and what it is, Sylvia replies: "Peter, you're the architect. Why don't you explain it to her?" Similarly, when Miss Lomax comes upon Peter gazing out the window at the tent set up for Sylvia's wedding, she suggestively murmurs: "Not so splendid as your mighty erections, I imagine." Peter's very name, of course, is a slang term for "penis," which may be why he can risk asserting that he is "impotent" in order to escape Miss Lomax; alternatively, Peter's "confession" may also reflect some residual male ambivalence about the "softening" effects of a newly emotional and sensitive masculinity. In addition, it allows Peter to "save himself" for marriage, in keeping with the conclusion to *Little Lady*, which also celebrates the redemption of the unwed mother of *Three Men and a Baby*. By virtue of marrying the father with whom, unlike Jack and Edward, she has *not* had sexual intercourse, Sylvia's "lost" virginity is metaphorically restored to her.

Three Men and a Little Lady confirms the importance, the complexity, and the ambivalence of the multiple ways in which gender and culture can interact in contemporary cinematic narrative. Ardolino's sequel recombines the bicultural concerns of its two filmic antecedents within the context of American society in the 1990s. Perhaps the most significant way in which *Little Lady* identifies itself as the sequel to *Three Men and a Baby* stems from a further realization of the potential inherent in Nimoy's film to alter traditional gender roles. Sylvia's refusal to be only a mother challenges the fundamental division between maternity, on the one hand, and the sexuality and autonomy of the adult woman, on the other. Since Peter has incorporated this denial of one's own needs, traditionally imposed only on mothers, into his own conception of fatherhood, the fact that he is forced (or allowed) to express his emotions and to act upon his feelings continues to undermine conventional expectations for parents as well as to revise stereotypical notions of American manhood.

At the same time, *Little Lady* also lends itself to a far more conservative cultural interpretation, whose realization, if not its justification, at times recalls *Trois Hommes et un couffin*. No doubt very real concerns about sexually transmitted diseases and the effects of divorce on children would be quite sufficient to provoke the return of marriage and of the two-parent family in a narrative remade in 1991. Yet the reemergence of particular themes and patterns first encountered in Serreau's film—such as the potential privilege of biological parenthood and its expression in a plot of exclusion and substitution—is also evident. Since this example might seem to suggest the existence of a link between gender and narrative that transcends cultural difference, let me take up in conclusion a counterexample, the one significant aspect of narrative incoherence in *Little Lady* that I have willfully ignored until now.

The action sequence designed to let Peter "make a fool of himself" takes the particular form of the stereotypical plot, already encountered in *I Want to Go Home*, of the unhappy American tourist who endures, in rapid succession and in a highly exaggerated form, the greatest possible number of a foreign culture's most characteristic pitfalls. That Ardolino should film his version of what I earlier suggested is an almost universal story is neither surprising nor inconsistent with the current political climate of the United States. What initially seems somewhat more difficult to explain, however, is the choice of British culture as the focus of *American* dislike. Peter (and Ardolino) would have us believe, for example, that the British manufacture tiny, mechanically unreliable cars, which they then drive on the wrong side of the road; live in a country in which the harshness of the weather is rivaled only by that of the toilet paper; put their children in boarding schools whose barbaric conditions date back to Dickens; and are sexually repressed, class-obsessed snobs who deliberately mispronounce the English language for the sole purpose of provoking Americans.

I want to propose that this particular narrative of cultural clichés serves as a diegetic marker that reminds us that *Three Men and a Little Lady* is a Franco-American co-production. Coincidentally, at about the same time that Ardolino's film was released, Jean Dondelinger, European Community Commissioner for Audiovisual and Cultural Affairs, asserted that "film is not, is no longer, a national product. Film today is by definition a transnational product" (87). Although co-productions have been a largely European phenomenon to date and one specifically designed, moreover, to counter Hollywood's ability to dominate the international film market, American remakes of French originals offer another illustration of the growing internationalization of cinema. Although the increasing fluidity of national and cultural boundaries may well

produce such interesting new hybrids as *Little Lady*, clearly we can also expect changes of such historical and societal significance to be accompanied
by considerable anxiety.[11] Hence, the displacements at work here. The cross-
cultural animosity that American travelers traditionally reserve for the French
is deflected onto the British, the historic focus of French cultural disdain.
(Such national confusion might help explain the idiosyncratic presence of the
vicar, whose obsession with food seems more characteristically Gallic than
Anglo-Saxon.) At the same time, this revolt against our own cultural ancestors, particularly within a context en-gendered by the "return of the mother,"
may well also serve as an apt metaphor for the traumatic interrelationship of a
Franco-American sequel to a Hollywood remake of a French original.[12]

At the Franco-American Crossroads of Gender and Culture

Where Feminism and Sexism Intersect

Perhaps it is only appropriate to introduce a foreign text improperly. At least such a hypothesis might help to explain my insistence on retaining, throughout a series of drafts, a title for this chapter that reveals virtually nothing about its subject matter. If, in retrospect, the title now appears conveniently self-reflexive, given the central location of this chapter within a text that is itself modeled on a crossroads, a place where different cultures meet and where different discourses of gender intersect, I am well aware that this essay could nonetheless be more accurately perceived as a massive roadblock. To the extent that it focuses on a video about the adventures of an American in Paris, filmed in French for an American audience, it would seem at least as much at home in these pages as Euro Disney or Alain Resnais's *I Want to Go Home*. But since the visual text in question, *French in Action*, is, in fact, a text*book*, this essay also finds itself situated at a particularly busy intersection, a place where a number of roads (cultural, ideological, cinematic, linguistic, literary, theoretical, and pedagogical—among others), all of which often lead in different directions, will for once attempt to arrange a meeting—or, at the very least, a temporary crossing of paths.

The recent publication within a matter of months of two new versions of "the American in Paris"—Alice Kaplan's *French Lessons: A Memoir* (1993) and Richard Watson's *The Philosopher's Demise: Learning French* (1995)—reaffirms the status of France as what Tom Bishop has called "the country that fascinates Americans the most, even when it irritates them, or at times scandalizes them" (22). "Listening now to my childhood as the French professor I've become," notes Kaplan, "what I hear first are scenes of language" (5); and indeed, her memoir is structured around a series of encounters in which the language of France, and particularly the spoken language, plays a far more significant role than the country, its culture, or its citizens. Or rather, the former literally embodies all of the latter. Thus, a year in a Swiss boarding school at the age of fourteen transforms both the body and the speech of the American adolescent: "I grew thinner and thinner. I ate French" (53). Years after her failed love affair with a Frenchman during her junior year abroad, Kaplan realizes that what she really desired was her lover's language: "It was the rhythm and the pulse of his French I wanted, the body of it" (94). In contrast, for Watson, a philosophy professor and a Cartesian scholar, French exists only as a written language until an invitation to deliver a paper in France suddenly motivates him to want to speak French twenty-five years after he first learned to read it. What Kaplan, however, experiences as an exhilarating "chance for growth, for freedom, [and for] liberation" (211) becomes in Watson's case a terrifying and frustrating tale of sheer "torture" (9). Moreover, after six months of private tutoring in the United States and a four-month course in intensive French at the Alliance Française in Paris, Watson discovers not only that all he has learned is "how to speak French out loud" (16) but that he particularly dislikes what Kaplan most loves, that is, the sound of the spoken language.

Indeed, Kaplan's and Watson's parallel accounts of learning French, which resemble each other in almost every other conceivable way (same genre, same length, same subject matter), differ only in the attitude that Kaplan and Watson take toward the common experience that both relate. On the one hand, Kaplan recounts "passing in French" (182) as a narrative of (relative) success; not content simply to speak French fluently, she desperately desires, needs, and repeatedly attempts, like Elsie in *I Want to Go Home*, literally "to be" French (92). Watson, on the other hand, repeats Elsie's story from the other side as a tale of endless humiliations and ultimate failure. What Kaplan and Watson both portray as an "obsession" with French therefore logically results, in her case, in a doctorate in French literature and a career as a professor of French, and, in his, in a growing critical resistance both to the French language and to the national mentality that appears to inform it. Watson's growing catalogue of complaints about Paris, ranging from the presence of dogs in restaurants and of their excrement in the streets to a lack of public toilets and a surplus of bureaucratic rigidity, finally makes him as reminiscent of Elsie's father as he is of Elsie. Watson explicitly transforms his inability to imitate Kaplan's conscious choice "to live in not-quite-my-own language, in exile from myself" (210) into a patriotic defense of his own native language and culture: "I'll bet I was having so much trouble learning to speak French because I did not want to pledge allegiance to a foreign language" (79). In short, Kaplan chooses to perpetuate France's "civilizing mission" within the United States, while Watson takes refuge in a discourse increasingly reminiscent of that of "American cultural imperialism" abroad.

Just as France's own *mission civilisatrice* has always served a largely pedagogical function, as the experiences of both Kaplan and Watson make clear, American fascination with France, whether negative or positive, essentially depends upon the teaching of French (language, literature, and culture) in the United States. Indeed, French cinema courses are often located in the modern language departments of American universities with the primary aim of teaching French culture (see Hayward and Vincendeau 1). As Lawrence D. Kritzman points out in a special issue of *SubStance* (1995) devoted to "France's Identity Crises," the particular idea or model of France that is taught in the United States has, of course, evolved over time. To the extent, however, that the study of French has been increasingly dominated since the 1970s by a comparative approach, which focuses on how French and Americans differ (Kritzman, "Identity Crises" 10), teaching French no doubt now involves an increased risk of either indirectly reinforcing the ethnocentricity of American students (à la Watson) or of leading to an uncritical infatuation with the foreign (à la Kaplan) but without producing in either case an accurate understanding of and appreciation for authentic cultural difference. *French in Action*, founded on "the basic assumption" that "French culture must be allowed the right to represent itself, free from the projection of competing cultures and ideologies" (Capretz and Lydgate 11), offers an important, if, as we will see, inevitably controversial, new departure. In this context, it is interesting to recall that Peter Weir's *Dead Poet's Society*, a film that directly informed discussions of possible reforms in the French educational system, was the top box-office hit in France in 1990 (attracting more spectators, notably, than even Jean-Paul Rappeneau's—and Gérard Depardieu's—*Cyrano*, released in the same year). Moreover, the critique of educational institutions and pedagogical strategies has historically played a significant role within French cinema, from Jean Vigo's *Zéro de conduite* (1933), for example, to Louis Malle's *Au Revoir, les enfants* (1987).

"FRENCH COURSE, TERMED SEXIST, WILL BE REVISED." So reads the headline of an article in the April 15, 1990, *New York Times* that announces the release by the Yale French department of the report of an ad hoc committee (Newmark et al.) whose members investigated allegations of sexism in the university's introductory French course. Their findings concurred with formal complaints lodged earlier in the year by four students enrolled in the course.[1] The most important consequence of this media event, which precipitated in the public domain an ongoing debate over the alleged sexism of *French in Action* (1987), was finally to provoke within the profession a long-overdue awareness of the wide-ranging ideological and pedagogical implications of the "action" of "French." The subsequent publication of the second edition of *French in Action* (1994), whose extensive revisions do not, in fact, include any changes in the narrative or visual content, speaks further to the interest and, indeed, the necessity of pursuing this discussion.

Double Takes

The charges ostensibly directed against a particular course at a single institution do and should concern everyone who cares about higher education. The internal report endorsed by the Yale French department bases its conclusions almost exclusively on a review of textual materials. That classroom observation, the only other evidence taken into account, was limited to video presentations further identifies *French in Action* itself as the focus of discussion. More important, the specific context in which this controversy surfaced clearly embraces a broad range of issues—extending well beyond the teaching of French to include larger questions of sexual harassment, First Amendment rights, and institutional practices of discrimination—that currently define the climate and concerns of the academy as a whole. To the extent that many colleges and universities have catalogued these concerns under the umbrella heading of "diversity," a discipline, like French, founded on knowledge of and respect for linguistic and cultural difference(s) seems to afford a uniquely appropriate framework for their recontextualization.

Yet, like mathematics and the majority of the natural sciences, foreign languages remain persistently absent from contemporary feminist projects for curricular transformation. Witness, for example, their exclusion from *Women's Place in the Academy* (Schuster & Van Dyne), a collection of essays that constitutes the most comprehensive proposal to date for "transforming the liberal arts curriculum." The "foreign" is introduced only in relation to "literature," even though the course description of "French Women Writers Today," given as one specific example of curricular revision, includes references to the concept of *écriture féminine*, whose explicit association of gender and language might be expected to affect, at the very least, the study of French. Moreover, those whose professional concerns depend most directly on the teaching of language do not talk about either teaching or language study even in the publications that announce a renewed interest in the newly respectable field of pedagogy. For example, despite the insistent pluralism of the title, the limited range and focus of the essays included in *Reorientations: Critical Theories and Pedagogies* (Henricksen & Morgan) characteristically imply that only scholarly activities as literary critics or theorists bear any relationship to classroom practices.

Alice Kaplan reminds us that this "split between language and literature teaching, the disdain for the language instructors who make their own teaching possible" not only reflects but continues to perpetuate the system of assigned sex roles and gender inequities out of which the division historically arose some twenty years ago, when, according to Kaplan, "French departments divided up into 'literature' sections—husbands—and less prestigious 'language' sections—wives" (179). As I noted earlier, Pierre Capretz and Barry Lydgate, the primary authors of *French in Action*, make a similar analogy between language, culture, and gender. In a discussion headed "American

Cultural Imperialism," Capretz and Lydgate note that "the ways in which Americans view other cultures are analogous to the ways in which men have traditionally viewed women" ("A Statement" 10). Whatever the explanation, Richard Watson represents his chauvinistic resistance to learning French, and particularly to learning the spoken language, whose mastery Kaplan values most, in the specifically gendered terms of a rejection of the feminine: "I have a distinct dislike for the sound of spoken French. Many Americans do. Why? Because it's weak. For American men, at least, French sounds syrupy and effeminate" (52). Watson goes on to attribute this impression that French "cannot be pronounced without simpering" to a notion of Frenchmen that derives directly from French movies: "Certainly no American boy of my generation ever wanted to grow up to be Charles Boyer" (53). One is reminded of Dennis Baron's discussion of the ethnocentrism and "antifeminism" of English etymologists and lexicographers for whom it "is a mark of praise to call a language like English a masculine tongue, while French and Italian are condemned—by English commentators—as feminine, even effeminate" (6).

Coincidentally, in 1982, a special issue of *Yale French Studies*, the journal founded and supported by the Yale French department, proposed a particularly ingenious strategy for conciliating the emergent "pedagogical imperative" and the traditional priorities of the profession. Unhindered by the acknowledgment that "discussions of pedagogy generally deal with classroom procedures for the teaching of texts," the editor, in her preface, immediately reverses the terms and introduces a collection of essays devoted to studying "the way in which the texts themselves dramatize the problematics of teaching" (B. Johnson, iii). I would argue that no "text" seems better designed to satisfy this definition than the foreign-language text*book*—despite its absence from this particular collection, which is explicitly devoted to "works [that is, literary, indeed canonical, works] that represent the pedagogical situation" (iii), as well as from other recent volumes, whose critical framework, like that of *Reorientations*, derives almost exclusively from postmodernist theoretical concerns.

The traditional foreign-language textbook, which can be described as a narrative that fuses content and form and privileges the story of its own construction in and through language, itself provides an exemplary model of the postmodernist text, self-generative and self-reflexive, while simultaneously grounded in sociohistorical "reality." *French in Action* foregrounds the conventions inherent in the genre by adding a coherent fictional narrative to the customary "story" of language. As the writers note in the introductory lesson, "French in Action is more than a traditional textbook providing grammar, exercises, and explanations. It is also a story, a mystery story in fact" (3). Moreover, as every student of the Capretz Method knows—having already learned two facts and two phrases ("nous allons inventer une histoire" [we're going to invent a story] and "ça va être utile pour apprendre le français" [that will be useful for learning French])[2] by the second day of class—this dual narrative structure results in an insistent self-representation of "the pedagogical situation" that also allows the *French in Action* videos to meet the specific criterion for interest outlined in *Yale French Studies*. *French in Action* can be considered to be a paradigmatic postmodernist text that radically challenges traditional boundaries, including the one between literary scholarship and language pedagogy on which modern languages' own professional "order" appears to depend. It is perhaps for this reason that the Yale report begins with and relies on an unusual and untenable effort to distinguish between the "text" and the "book." The review committee officially recognizes *French in Action*'s "status as an artwork in its own right" only to assert that, in this particular case, the literary merit of the text is not only separable from, but irrelevant to, "the pedagogical uses it may have" (B. Johnson, 3).[3]

Thus, even if the current sociohistorical context provides a partial explanation for the charges of sexism that have been directed against *French in Action*, one can fairly assume that something about the text itself also clarifies how it came to be identified as a likely target. In fact, there are three features that most obviously distinguish *French in Action* from similar texts: the emphasis it places on the visual over the verbal, the narrative over the episodic, and the postmodernist over the traditional. As I shall argue, these three features function together in this particular case to produce a still more significant fourth distinction: *French in Action* is also *feminist* rather than *sexist*. Indeed, feminist thought provides a uniquely appropriate theoretical and ideological framework for discussion of the *French in Action* controversy. Contemporary feminist theory and criticism have been largely defined by the work of French and Anglo-American feminist scholars whose most significant contributions of late lie in the areas of film, narrative, postmodernism, and pedagogy. More pragmatically, many students draw increasingly on their knowledge of Women's Studies to take every opportunity, including that of foreign language instruction, to challenge their professors to rethink both what and how they teach.

Yet, the very fact that a same or similar set of assumptions, commonly identified as "feminist," has paradoxically led students and professors alike to diametrically opposed interpretations of a single text can be seen as both a result and an admirable illustration of the extraordinary difficulty we all experience in seeing beyond our own cultural context—even when professional expertise presupposes an ability to do so and even with a methodology specifically designed to facilitate such a process. Not only does feminism name a plurality of ideological positions, more accurately identified as "feminisms," but the general discourse of gender that underlies them all inevitably shares in the cultural specificity through which any sign system takes on meaning. The belief that feminism creates a commonality of thought, impervious to cultural differences, is a frequent misperception. In fact, the "Franco-American *dis*connection" (my emphasis), first addressed in the editorial preface to another special issue of *Yale French Studies* (Gaudin et al. 5; see also Stanton), has remained one highly privileged focus of feminist scholarship for the past decade.[4]

Every lesson in *French in Action* is divided into two parts. The first section of each video focuses on the story of Mireille Bellau, a Parisian university student, and Robert Taylor, an American who has dropped out of college for a year to travel in his mother's native country. Students of *French in Action* follow the adventures of Mireille, Robert, and of their families and friends as they move about Paris, visit other cities in France, and travel in the French countryside. Students also meet a number of colorful and eccentric secondary characters who interact with the heroes in a variety of playfully treated conventional literary and cinematic situations. As accurately described in the preface to the textbook, the plot resembles "a kind of send-up of soap opera" (3). In the second part of each video lesson, the fictional professor narrates explanations of grammar, vocabulary, and culture, which are illustrated by a great diversity of authentic materials (such as cartoons, film clips, commercials, paintings, and interviews). The lexical and structural aspects of the program are closely intertwined with the story line. For example, students learn descriptive adjectives and rules of agreement when the cast of characters is first introduced; they study possessive adjectives when they meet the members of Mireille's extended family; and so on.

In the introductory lessons (Genèse I–III) of *French in Action*, which serve primarily to generate the pedagogical situation within the text itself, we are immediately confronted with the potential for intercultural conflict. The French professor, otherwise engaged in actively encouraging his Anglophone students to participate in the construction and constant *"réinvention"* of the narrative, objects only when the representative student rebel reveals a perspective informed by specifically American expectations and assumptions. The central female character, a French woman, cannot be named "Ethel," for the simple reason that "ce n'est pas un prénom français" (it isn't a French name). To the extent that conflict arises, among men, over the naming of the woman, gender already informs this initial and initiatory experience of cross-cultural disagreement. Certainly, the "préjugés de notre nation" (our national prejudices), the "vérité" (truth) that is alternatively "américaine" or "française" (Lesson 21), which *French in Action* insistently calls to our attention, inevitably include our culturally specific understanding of sexuality and gender.

In keeping with the inseparability of theory and practice posited by most modern critical discourses and particularly important within feminist theory (see, for example, Bowles & Klein), the discussion that follows will use a

97

specific textual example as a recurrent point of reference. I will concentrate on Lessons 11 through 13 because of their centrality within several important contexts. These lessons include an—perhaps *the*—essential episode within the narrative structure of *French in Action* itself: the long-anticipated meeting between Mireille and Robert. Indeed, the promise of the *rencontre*'s imminence at the beginning of Lesson 11 and its realization at the end of Lesson 13 provide a dramatic unity and continuity that organize this portion of the text into a discrete sequence. Consequently, this passage also addresses a key pedagogical concern by providing an interpretive context of a length consistent with student memory at the beginning level of language instruction.

Finally, and most important, Lessons 11 through 13, which involve the two episodes in which the "dragueur" Jean-Pierre Bourdin figures most extensively, are the recurrent focus of the charges of sexism documented in the Yale report and repeated in the national media. For example, all letters of student complaint cite Lesson 11 as, alternately, "a particularly painful example of the propagation of gender stereotypes," "a particularly offensive video," "especially upsetting," and "particularly disturbing." The official response of the Yale French department confirms both the central role of this passage and the reading that the students confer on it: "The single most extreme example of the way the vehicle of the male gaze can work to objectify and exclude women in 'French in Action' is also the one example most often singled out for attention in discussions concerning the course's use of gender stereotyping" (6). In this interpretation, Jean-Pierre's attempt to pick up Mireille is viewed as an exemplary act of aggressive and potentially dangerous male behavior. Similarly, her silence and eventual departure figures as an equally exemplary and potentially equally harmful reaction of feminine passivity.

This critical concentration on "gender stereotypes" or "stereotyping" typifies a particular kind of textual criticism—the evaluation of negative or positive "images of women"—that not only characterized the early stages of contemporary feminist analysis in the United States but continues to be strongly identified with American feminism over its own increasingly frequent objections, particularly when it is structured in contrast to (or *to* contrast *with*) "French feminism." In this context and in terms that appear to draw on general *cultural* stereotypes and stereotyping, American feminists are chided for a naïve realism that (con)fuses textual constructions with "real" women, in apparent denial of the mediating function of language so central to the sophisticated linguistic theory and experimental practice of *écriture féminine* (see Moi).

Clearly, the multiple critical strategies and complex theoretical positions that characterize feminist scholarship in both the United States and France cannot be reduced in either culture to any single or simple position. Yet, most feminist criticism in the United States does in fact take place within the (inter)disciplinary framework of Women's Studies, which in turn has always described itself as the "academic branch" of—and thus subordinate to—the women's movement as a whole (Boxer). Within this explicitly pedagogical context, theories and strategies of textual analysis can be identified as feminist to the extent that they include among their larger goals a political commitment to encouraging change in (real) women's lives. Appropriately, the Women's Studies curriculum has privileged autobiography, biography, and realistic forms of fiction. Thus, the tendency of all the Yale women to use personal experience to justify their complaints and to assume that the text of *French in Action* can be read as directly applicable to their own lives—indeed, in several cases, to substitute autobiographical accounts for textual description—is fully consistent with fundamental principles of American academic feminism. These students appear to be engaged in a restructuring of the learning process that recalls exactly Barbara C. Ewell's description of what happened when the consciousness raising of the women's movement became the pedagogy of the feminist classroom. "Personal involvement in one's own education" and the discovery of "the authority of one's own experience" created "a charged atmosphere," in which "the relationship between literary texts and experience readily collapsed" as "the real object of study" became "students' lives and their perceptions of their lives" (53–54; see also Mills).[5]

The use of a predominantly visual text further complicates this situation, for film speaks a highly specific language of its own, which students must also learn if it is to serve simultaneously as a means for acquiring yet another language and culture. Rick Altman's observations that "the [foreign-language] instructor without a clear notion of how to make use of video's special qualities may inadvertently recreate many problems typical of feature film use" (24) unintentionally identifies the source of the difficulty. The appropriate analogy, however, is less that between two texts within a single context—video and feature film in the foreign-language classroom, as posited by Altman—than between two contexts—the French course and the film course. In both of the latter cases, the professor confronts students for whom linguistic and cultural transparency constitutes a deeply ingrained assumption that leads them to equate, on the one hand, English and French, and, on the other, representation and reality. Countless hours spent in front of television and Hollywood movie screens have produced American students in whom culture-specific habits of viewing and interpretation are firmly established. Mainstream media encourages a form of reception, the passive consumption of apparently referential images, that runs counter to the active critical awareness sought by every instructor of film—and of *French in Action* (see Ellis and Santoni, "Visual Images"). Moreover, current pedagogical assumptions about the use and usefulness of visual materials in foreign-language instruction also contribute

Double Takes

to the confusion. What Altman, for example, characteristically cites as video's unique capacity for "contextualization," for conveying the "authenticity" of the foreign language and culture, inevitably reinforces realistic expectations and responses (10).

The Yale report as a whole reflects the realistic approach typical of both mainstream American media and traditional American feminism. Analysis centers on sexism as conveyed through characteristic gender stereotypes; it includes an equally conventional evaluation of the latter as negative (such as female silence and passivity) or positive (such as active male voice and gaze); and it further assumes that these stereotypes inflict immediate and unmediated harm on Yale students. The faculty review committee validates the students' penchant for realism and relevance by focusing on the reception of the text rather than on the text itself. Indeed, the report stresses that "in itself," the projection of stereotypical attitudes "would not constitute a problem," were it not for the possibility of their "non-critical assimilation" by students who "may identify" with the persons represented (Newmark et al. 4). Since this "problem" is carefully distinguished from "the manner in which literary or cultural artifacts are treated in other courses" (4), it appears to be informed far more by general cultural assumptions about the passivity of film spectatorship than by any specific aspect of *French in Action*. Certainly the Yale evaluators are clearly troubled to see "playful 'exaggerations' not meant to be taken seriously" appear within a text that, at least in their minds, had "assured and repeatedly reminded" them of the "accuracy" of its representation of French culture (Newmark et al. 4).

I want first, then, to reconsider what results from a traditional "realistic" reading of Lessons 11 through 13 of *French in Action* in order to argue that this interpretation, though limited and limiting in many ways, supports the conclusion that the passage in question is feminist, not sexist. Whatever the particular traits associated with Jean-Pierre, his portrayal is explicitly and consistently coded as negative within the textual diegesis. In his central performance as "*dragueur*," he experiences multiple rejections and *only* rejection ("Il essaie, il essaie . . . mais ça ne marche jamais" [he tries, he tries . . . but he never succeeds]); his complementary roles as an aging academic dilettante and a "*resquilleur*" (a person who cuts in line) are respectively greeted with ridicule and hostility; and those who mock him include male characters as well as female. The professor, the textual representative of both linguistic and cultural authority, uses Jean-Pierre to illustrate patterns of direct object pronouns in which parallel grammatical structures highlight a series of ideological contrasts. Initially en-gendered to valorize the female "negation" of the male ("Il la trouve jolie / Elle ne le trouve pas intéressant / Elle ne le trouve pas amusant" [He finds her pretty / She doesn't find him interesting / She doesn't find him amusing]); as the sequence continues, her *opinion* ("Elle le trouve ennuyeux" [She finds him boring]) becomes, first, the *fact* of his behavior ("Il l'ennuie" [He bores her]) and, finally, his very *essence* ("Il est ennuyeux" [He is boring]).

Although one Yale student complains that she "was not even offered the French words to tell Jean-Pierre to go away" and presents her assertion that he is, in fact, "offensive" as a total contradiction of his portrayal in the text, both of the women whom Jean-Pierre approaches in Lesson 13 respond with highly articulate verbal put-downs. Annick not only offers a wide variety of insults (such as "Il est puant, ce mec"; "Quel horrible dragueur," "Quelle tête d'idiot") but when a male friend attempts to defend Jean-Pierre as "inoffensif," she proceeds to an explicitly feminist attack on systemic sexism: "C'est ça, défends-le! Ah, vous êtes bien tous les mêmes, vous, les hommes! Tous aussi sexistes! Quand je vois des types comme toi, j'ai bien envie de m'inscrire [au movement de la libération des femmes]" (That's it, defend him! Oh, you men are all the same! All just as sexist! When I see guys like you, I feel like joining [the women's movement].) Moreover, Annick's antipathy toward Jean-Pierre forces *him* to flee—he claims to have a rendezvous with "une fille superbe" (a gorgeous chick)—in what at the very least offers fitting retribution for those who object to Mireille's departure at the end of Lesson 11. I would also assert that Mireille's determined silence and eventual departure, far from exemplifying "the passively mute role the woman is made to play" (Newmark et al. 6), appropriately accord the most effective—perhaps the only truly effective—strategy to the central female character.[6]

The devaluation of a behavior that the text clearly valorizes exposes an unspoken assumption that frequently underlies and undermines the critical practice of realism. The objections of the Yale students proceed from the belief that a cultural experience clearly foreign to that of the United States can nonetheless be read as American; indeed, that "reality" itself is American, by definition.[7] Thus, they appear to equate the imposition of the French *dragueur* with the "threat of violence women in *our* society live with every day" (my emphasis). This revealing "our" denies the cultural (and linguistic) specificity both of the situation (indeed, the English language has no exact equivalent for the term *dragueur*) and of the response. The difficulty of perceiving cultural difference as "real" may well be reinforced in this case by a methodological contradiction inherent in traditional American feminist theory. The search for gender stereotyping that informs realistic textual criticism clearly involves a risk of imposing predetermined and transcendent categories on specific textual and contextual "realities." Moreover, the standard feminist interpretation of gender stereotypes may pertain similarly, so that female silence, for example, will automatically be read as negative and male speech as positive, regardless of where they occur and how they function.

Double Takes

If, on the other hand, we acknowledge the reality of culture itself, then a "profound difference in the interpretation of conversation" in France and the United States, to which Raymonde Carroll attributes the frequency with which interpersonal relationships lead to cultural misunderstanding (*Cultural* 23), clarifies both the French text and its American reception. Carroll states that "the French person will recreate distance with silence, the American with conversation" (33). In that event, Jean-Pierre's incessant chatter need not illustrate masculine prerogative. Indeed, in the context of gender, it appears to mark a reversal of gender roles. His behavior conforms fully to the "cultural presupposition" that conversation serves to identify those "with whom I have, affirm, confirm, or *want to create* ties" (Carroll 32, my emphasis). Similarly, Mireille is not necessarily silenced as a woman; her refusal to speak effects the culturally approved strategy for denying that any relationship between herself and Jean-Pierre does, can, or will exist. This does not mean, however, that gender is entirely irrelevant. That the French characterize as "promiscuity" the willingness of Americans to converse with strangers (Carroll 32) surely has more than a linguistic bearing on their simultaneous perception that Americans often invite a "pickup," an impression that Carroll describes as "a continual source of problems for unsuspecting American women" (27). Mireille herself illustrates this very danger within the diegesis. Her own words—and not those of Jean-Pierre—precipitate her departure. Clearly the mere fact of speaking far outweighs the content of female speech, for when Mireille finally responds, Jean-Pierre finds her unambiguous putdown sufficiently encouraging to justify proceeding to a new stage of familiarity: he promptly introduces himself.[8]

Let us return for a moment to academic feminism's initial and, in this case, ongoing choice to define itself as "Women's Studies," an identity recently reaffirmed at many institutions in explicit opposition to potential alternative conceptualizations as "Gender Studies" or "Feminist Studies." This particular perception of "self," taken literally, not only imposes unnecessary restrictions on most feminist projects for curricular transformation and virtually excludes some disciplines—notably foreign-language instruction—from consideration, but it also limits seriously the field of "Women's Studies" itself. Certainly the desire to conflate women's interests with those of nonwhite cultural groups surfaces with increasing frequency in recent feminist theory—for example, the insistence of Marilyn R. Schuster and Susan R. Van Dyne that "the most transformative strategy employs *gender, race, and class as categories of analysis*," which closes the introductory chapter of *Women's Place in the Academy* (11). Yet, critics—many of them women of color—continue to charge that not only does American feminist analysis fail to incorporate adequately these categories of race, class, and gender but also that its retention of a primary focus on white, middle class, American women marks its own discourse as racist, classist, imperialist, and, yes, sexist (see, for example, Caraway). Unfortunately, the one-dimensional orientation of the objections to sexism in *French in Action* reconfirms that in some cases such accusations remain accurate and valid.

An explicitly ideological critique that fails to address the potential racism of *French in Action*, which features only a single (and to some extent culturally stereotypical) black character in an underdeveloped secondary role, may be the most astonishing omission. But the invisibility of race functions most significantly as a symptom of the inherent limitations imposed on any analysis constructed in terms of "sexism" alone. The belief that the portrayal of women can ever, even temporarily, be profitably discussed in isolation from other factors of oppression and discrimination and outside a systemic framework reveals the theoretical inadequacy of the entire conceptual construct, regardless of whatever specific results it may yield. Moreover, even if one were to accept race as irrelevant to this particular analysis of *French in Action*, on the grounds that the lone black character, Ousmane, does not exhibit "sexist" behavior and that no female characters of color are present, the comparable absence of attention to class and gender leads to a profound misunderstanding of the text as a whole, including the diegetic treatment of women.

I would suggest that what the Yale report characterizes as "the persistence throughout the course materials of a white, middle-class, male point of view to the exclusion and even detriment of other perspectives" figures far less prominently in the object of interpretation, where the evaluators position it, than it does in their own interpretive framework (Newmark et al. 5–6). Feminism, like any other culturally specific product, inevitably retains and perpetuates some of the precepts of the "dominant" culture it sets out to oppose, and American feminism is decidedly *not* postmodernist in its traditional commitment to the fact of such "cultural dominance" (see Collins and Hutcheon). In selecting and defining "patriarchy" as its paradigmatic enemy, American feminism in essence validates a hierarchical system of male power, which is founded primarily on the privilege of wealth and class. The assumptions and expectations that proceed from such a world view—notably, that men are favorably portrayed as powerful and consistently associated with "truth" and that materialism and class status identify equally positive cultural values—will logically pertain even in the face of conflicting evidence. If anything, such beliefs may be more necessary to those who construct a monolithic identity of their own in opposition to a system perceived as dominant—one which they have also (re)constructed, of course, in terms designed to meet their specific oppositional needs—than they are to those who support that system. The Yale analysis of Lesson 11 neither challenges the "realism" of Jean-Pierre's behavior nor insists on its cultural specificity (within patriarchy, "les hommes [sont] tous les mêmes, tous aussi sexistes" [Lesson 13]). Similarly, Jean-

Double Takes

Pierre's actions and words, though ineffectual and subject to ridicule, are nonetheless presumed to earn him power and authority (by definition, within patriarchy, all men have power).

In contrast to most conventional foreign-language textbooks, *French in Action* complements the distinctiveness of its visual, discursive, and postmodernist textuality not only with the inclusion of a feminist perspective but also with the difference of the feminism it includes. Because *French in Action* primarily reflects a feminism that is conceived in terms of representation rather than reality and of gender rather than women, it constructs its challenge to the traditional sex/gender system as the deconstruction of the discourse of masculinity, notably through the subversion of the heterosexual romance narrative, exposed within the text as a specifically male fantasy. In addition, the critique of masculinity is closely and consistently intertwined with that of class. Let us reconsider Lessons 11 through 13 from this theoretical viewpoint.

If "the woman" is "made to play" a "passively mute role" (Newmark et al. 6) in Lesson 11, she does so only in Jean-Pierre's imagination ("Vous n'êtes pas bavarde, j'aime beaucoup ça. Je n'aime pas les filles qui parlent trop, moi" [You're not a chatterbox, I like that. I don't like girls who talk too much]). In contrast, Mireille's absolute refusal to collaborate with Jean-Pierre (that is, to participate in any way in the narrative he would construct) establishes a very different feminist reality, which functions both to identify the *dragueur*'s fantasy as specifically male and to deny the complicity with traditional female roles that even many feminists (French and American) often attribute to women (see, for example, Moi). In fact, however, the text of *French in Action* already engenders the "love story" as male from the moment of its initial generation in Lesson 4 ("Genèse III"). Because this gender marking coincides with Mireille and Robert's first joint appearance on screen, it also serves to inscribe the sexual dynamics of their *own* narrative within the general terms of the same formal pattern. Moreover, the active oral repetition in which students are required to engage at this point establishes the students' identification from the beginning with Mireille's decidedly assertive dismissal of Robert's hopeful inquiry into her fictional preferences: "Ah *non* [students repeat, with Mireille], je *déteste* les romans d'amour" (Oh *no*, I *hate* love stories).

Lessons 11 through 13 reveal clearly the far more radical feminist critique of masculinity that lies behind women's dislike of the male romance narrative. Mireille's two encounters with men, even as they establish the framework that guarantees the autonomy and coherence of the entire episode, also transform an appearance of dramatic progression into the reality of ideological repetition. Although the meeting with Jean-Pierre seems initially destined to serve as an exercise in contrast, designed to heighten both the students' anticipation of the second *rencontre* with Robert and their pleasure when it finally occurs, the two episodes are in fact reflections of one another. They are

inverted mirror images of the same old story. That the narrative of love and romance turns out to be simply a disguise for a highly conventional sexual fantasy not only identifies the former as specifically male and posits the latter as
virtually coextensive with maleness itself, but, in the process, it reveals more
fully the dimensions of the broad ideological sphere controlled by traditional
masculinity. (In this context, see also my discussion of McBride's remake of
Godard's *A Bout de souffle* in chapter three.)

An analysis of the puppet show that concludes the narrative sequence at
the end of Lesson 13 can help to eliminate any doubts that *French in Action*
deliberately equates the discourses of seduction and romance. This textual
strategy offers a generalized and identifiably feminist critique of the codes
governing masculine attitudes and behavior. In this particular *réinvention* of
textual events, Robert has replaced Jean-Pierre in the role of the *dragueur*,
and his pursuit of Mireille is definitively halted by the puppet's literal re-en-
act-ment—"Les types comme ça, je les tue!" (I kill guys like that)—of what
Annick originally presented as a feminist metaphor ("Ça me tue, des types
comme ça" [Guys like that will be the death of me]). In Lesson 12, however,
the students have already been invited to look through Robert's façade of ceremonious courtesy to what lies behind it: Jean-Pierre's familiar fantasy of the
female as a sexually desirable object, similarly coded through the reduction of
the woman to her clothing and similarly critiqued through the dissociation of
visual imagery and verbal text. Just as Jean-Pierre perceives "une jupe rouge"
(a red skirt) in place of Mireille, Robert's somewhat more graphic imagination
figures "une jupe plutôt courte" (a rather short skirt) and "un pull plutôt col-
lant" (a rather tight sweater), which conflict radically with Mireille's actual
appearance, dressed in what can only be described as a rather long skirt and a
rather loose sweater.[9]

The reappearance of the same strategy in the following lesson uses on-
screen imagery of Jean-Pierre's repeated failures as a *dragueur* to mock his
elaborate verbal scenarios of easy conquests at the very moment he constructs
them. Because the visual evidence involves the reprojection of scenes that students have seen before, it illustrates particularly well the fundamental premise
on which *French in Action* is founded. In a predominantly visual medium, in a
context in which the visual image clearly represents the content most readily
accessible to beginning language students, any discrepancy between what we
see and what we hear can only be resolved, both logically and pedagogically, in
favor of the visual. But because *French in Action* depends at the same time on
postmodernist textual strategies, as the use here of autocitation also clearly reminds us, it defines visual reliability in direct opposition to the passive reception of presumably referential images on which classical realism draws.

To challenge viewing habits based on the passive consumption of trans-
parently referential images, *French in Action*, as we have seen, repeatedly

foregrounds its own construction as a postmodernist text. The first three lessons (Genèse I–III) focus on the collaborative generation of multiple and openly contradictory potential narratives, selected from among forms and patterns explicitly identified as already pre-textualized. Moreover, the methodologically crucial strategy of "réinvention," which reopens each episode just as it is about to close, destabilizes and multiplies meaning(s) throughout the text. The intertexuality of *French in Action*, its juxtaposition of diverse forms of previously established discourses drawn interchangeably from popular culture and "high" art, thus offers an excellent example of what Jim Collins calls postmodernist "bricolage," which functions to "overtur[n] the supposed passivity of mass culture and its subjects" (*Uncommon* 18). *French in Action*'s dependence on such intellectually demanding visual and editing strategies as the jump cut and the montage sequence and such emotionally distancing techniques as parody and irony further undermine the assertion by the Yale review committee that *French in Action* promotes a "non-critical, passive attitude of relaxation" (Newmark et al. 4); the very opposite is true.[10]

Moreover, experimental film techniques identify *French in Action*, both thematically and formally, with an explicitly feminist cinema. As Claire Johnston insisted in "Women's Cinema as Counter-Cinema," one of the most historically influential essays of feminist film theory, "it is not enough to discuss the oppression of women within the text of the film: the language of the cinema/depiction of reality must also be interrogated, so that a break between ideology and text is effected" (28). Perhaps the most important of *French in Action*'s interrogations of "the language of the cinema/depiction of reality" centers once again on the heterosexual romance narrative. Lesson 11 opens with the repetition of the montage sequence (originally screened in Lesson 7) that reintroduces the potential *rencontre* between Robert and Mireille as a rapid succession of multiple and contradictory possibilities. This visual parody of the essential "boy meets girl" plot of Hollywood cinema simultaneously exposes and explodes realistic codes of stylistic and narrative unity, thus transforming what traditionally functions as a guarantee of the "realism" of the romance narrative into the sign of the textual "reality" of a cinematic convention.[11]

Moreover, even as the passage offers important supporting evidence for the explicitly fictional nature of masculine fantasies, its open structure also potentially frees the figure of the woman from her usual narrative (en)closure within the romantic plot and the heterosexual couple of conventional film (see L. Fischer, *Shot/Countershot* 263, and my discussions above of *A Bout de souffle* and *Trois Hommes et un couffin*). Lesson 12 then illustrates with particular clarity the failure of the conventional romance narrative to "contain" Mireille. Positioned between the two encounters in which Jean-Pierre and Robert attempt to enclose both Mireille and the narrative in the formation of the heterosexual couple, Lesson 12 privileges female-female interaction. It focuses almost exclusively on Mireille's friendship with Ghislaine and her close relationships with both her mother and her younger sister.

Interestingly, the content of Lessons 11 through 13 that is designed to further the explicitly pedagogical goal of *French in Action*—to teach the French language—incorporates the same ideological issues that inform the narrative structure and content of the episode. Linguistic concerns focus on grammatical and lexical forms that address the opposition between fantasy and reality or between the verbal and the visual or both in ways that reiterate the feminist critique of masculinity. For example, the choice of Jean-Pierre to illustrate the idiomatic expression *faire semblant* (to pretend) verbally furthers his identification as a poseur. On a larger scale, his presentation in Lesson 11 as a self-absorbed narcissist, lost in a perpetual male fantasy, could hardly coincide with the introduction of a more suitable grammatical structure than that of reflexive verbs! Robert's similar association with the linguistic role-playing of the expression *se prendre pour* appropriately requires that he first "(mis)take himself" for Don Juan (that is, the ideal composite of the lover and the seducer). Moreover, the subsequent "poses" that Robert strikes as Napoléon and Louis XIV appear to acknowledge that within cultural codes of masculinity, fantasies of sexual potency and of political power—of limitless sexual conquest and of endless imperialist expansion—have comparable and parallel importance.[12]

In introducing the "touchy subject" that class constitutes for Americans, Paul Fussell notes that "you can outrage people today simply by mentioning social class, very much the way, sipping tea among the aspidistras a century ago, you could silence a party by adverting too openly to sex" (1). The historical analogy that Fussell establishes between the discourses of class and gender resurfaces in *French in Action*, where the discourses of masculinity and of classism are explicitly associated and textual authority is once again aligned with female opposition to both. Mireille (Lesson 11) and "la fille qui porte la robe verte" (the girl in the green dress) (Lesson 13) reject in turn the assumed value of wealth and class privilege that underlies Jean-Pierre's notion of what constitutes a "compliment." Mireille's democratic assertion that her skirt (*his* fetish) comes from Prisunic not only interrupts his elitist fantasies of *haute couture* but, more important, exposes *as* fantasy his own pretense that he can tell the difference.[13] The woman student's expression of horror at Jean-Pierre's pretentious jet-set allusions to luxury resorts clearly extends to him as well. Moreover, her singling out of "les fils à papa" (daddy's boys) as particularly repellent equates Jean-Pierre with Robert once again and prepares Mireille's subsequent mockery of the latter, who claims to have rejected his father's wealth in favor of independence even as he draws on the fruits of his grandparents' fortune to finance a year's vacation in France (Lesson 15).

Double Takes

The subject of class illustrates vividly how our own cultural beliefs can intersect to erect multiple barriers between us and the perception of textual and contextual difference. Despite the cultural uniqueness of the French *dragueur*, most American students will, of course, tend to identify with Jean-Pierre's preoccupation with symbols of wealth and status; and many fully share Robert's self-serving definition of "independence." They are especially likely to overlook or dismiss a critique of class whose particular focus—money and what it can buy—directly implicates a value system presented within the text as characteristically, indeed stereotypically, American. The fact that the social power and authority that accompany wealth in the United States remain predominantly male privileges no doubt further encourages students to misdirect their sympathy toward the men who represent the American/masculine/materialism under attack rather than toward the French/feminist women who do the attacking.

The Yale report itself confirms this confusion of class and gender, which is particularly evident in the following characteristic student complaint about two recurrent secondary characters:

> Tante Georgette and Tonton Guillaume are used to teach descriptive opposites. While she is poor, annoying, and disdainful of children, he is rich, amiable, and lovingly generous. Georgette, a spinster, embodies the pejorative stereotype of the unmarried woman while Guillaume presents an image of the benevolent godfather. Learning to describe these two characters sets up a pattern of associating negative traits with the feminine gender and positive traits with the masculine gender, a pattern which continues throughout the text. (Newmark et al., Appendix 3)

This particular "pattern," however, clearly reflects the interference of American class values, for the text of *French in Action* openly seeks to undermine any automatic assumption that it is "bad" to be "poor" and "good" to be "rich" by constantly subjecting the consequences of wealth to critical analysis. To categorize, as above, Georgette's and Guillaume's characters and behaviors under gender rather than class—"Georgette, a spinster, embodies the pejorative stereotype of the unmarried woman"—directly contradicts the text. Mireille explicitly grounds all other differences between her aunt and uncle in the disparity of their economic situation ("Il a de la fortune" [He's fabulously rich]/"elle n'a pas beaucoup d'argent, je crois" [I don't think she has very much money]), as does Georgette herself in the explanation—indeed, the *definition*—she immediately provides of Guillaume's generosity: "C'est facile, quand on de l'argent" (It's easy, when you have money). Furthermore, the range of qualities the complaint attributes to Guillaume—"rich, amiable, and lovingly generous"—appears to derive from the conclusion of a culture-specific exercise in "logic": that is, if it is good to be rich, then the rich are good, and giving becomes an "amiable" act of "love" rather than an advantage (or a responsibility) of economic privilege.[14]

In positing the priority of the visual over the verbal as fundamental to the methodology of *French in Action*, I argued that the text further associates the "reality" of the visual with "femininity" as a textual and ideological construct and the "fantasy" of the verbal with a similar understanding of "masculinity." But the implications of this premise for determining whether *French in Action* inscribes its discourse of gender as sexist or feminist are still broader and more significant. Indeed, by delaying discussion of the "male gaze" until now, it may have begun to seem as if I were deliberately avoiding what is arguably not only the central concern of any feminist analysis of the visual image but at least one of the central concerns of the Yale French department. For example, the committee report notes that, in general, "the video portion of the program makes use of a dominant and unquestioned male gaze as a vehicle through which to constitute structures of identity and desire in French" and cites, in particular, the Jean-Pierre episode as "the single most extreme example of the way the vehicle of the male gaze can work to objectify and exclude women" (6).

In "Visual Pleasure and Narrative Cinema," Laura Mulvey argues that "in a world ordered by sexual imbalance, pleasure in looking has been split between active/male and passive/female." The "male gaze," directed at a "female image," results in a "'masculinisation' of the spectator position." That is, mainstream cinematic address constitutes the viewer as male, regardless of the actual sex of any particular moviegoer. Women spectators must therefore choose between the alienating effects of identifying with the "masculine" point of view or the masochistic consequences of identifying with their own visual objectification as "to-be-looked-at-ness" (Mulvey 62). Since Mulvey's germinal essay appeared in 1975, the "male gaze" has remained a, if not the, central preoccupation of feminist film theory, as evidenced by its influence on a number of recent essay collections (such as Constance Penley's *Feminism and Film Theory*; and Mary Ann Doane, Patricia Mellencamp, and Linda Williams's *Re-Vision: Essays in Feminist Film Criticism*) and special issues of reviews (such as Bergstrom and Doane's *Camera Obscura* 20–21: *The Spectatrix*) as well as by Mulvey's own "Afterthoughts" on her original formulation. As Judith Mayne concludes in a review essay in *Signs*: "It is only a slight exaggeration to say that most feminist film theory . . . of the last decade has been a response, implicit or explicit, to the issues raised in Laura Mulvey's article" (83).

Interestingly, these subsequent attempts to revise and expand our feminist understanding(s) of the theoretical possibilities and practical consequences of cinematic address—to reclaim, that is, the gaze for women—appear far

Double Takes

Mireille ignores Jean-Pierre, the *dragueur*, in Lesson 11 of *French in Action*: "Elle le voit, elle le voit, mais elle fait semblant de ne pas le voir" (She sees him, she sees him, but she pretends not to see him). Photo from *French in Action* by Pierre J. Capretz, copyright © 1987 by Yale University and WGBH Education Foundation, Boston, reprinted by permission. All rights reserved.

more applicable to Lesson 11 of *French in Action* than does Mulvey's initial conceptualization of its dynamics. For Lesson 11 does not focus on the "male gaze" that Jean-Pierre directs at Mireille (in part, out of pure necessity, because he rarely looks at her at all), but rather on the active denial of her own "female gaze" that Mireille inflicts upon Jean-Pierre. As the professor insists, "elle le voit, elle le voit, mais elle fait semblant de ne pas le voir" (she sees him, she sees him, but she pretends not to see him). Far from enjoying the "voyeuristic" pleasure inherent in the masculine spectator position, a pleasure that derives from the fact that the female image does not (indeed, *cannot*) look back, here, on the contrary, it is precisely the female *gaze* that functions as the object of male desire. Moreover, our own privileged position as spectators provides us with a "visual pleasure" that derives not only from the fact that this pleasure is refused to Jean-Pierre but also from the fact that such a refusal constitutes a radically subversive challenge to the traditional dominance of the male point of view. An extreme close-up of Mireille's eyes, directed straight at us, foregrounds the active female gaze in a self-reflexive reversal ("Regardez le regard de Mireille" [Look at Mireille's look]) of the usual terms of cinematic address, similar to that which was evident in the final shots of *A Bout de souffle* (see also Penley 42). In addition, this close-up also functions as an establishing shot so that female subjectivity controls not only our subsequent view of the sky but that of Jean-Pierre as well. Thus the female point of view both dominates and subverts the male gaze, forcing it to look not at the woman as object, but at the object of her look.

In Mireille's parallel encounter with Robert, before she bestows the visual reciprocity sought in vain by Jean-Pierre ("elle lui rend son sourire" [she smiles back at him]), the female gaze reaffirms its authority. Mireille sees Robert first, and her point of view dominates the shot/countershot sequence that follows; the camera grants her a greater number of establishing shots (three for Mireille to two for Robert) and holds longer on her. Moreover, since the reality of *her* visual image contradicts what *his* words claim he sees, the camera simultaneously exposes the masculine point of view as effectively blind. Thus the woman retains subjective visual control even when she becomes the apparent "object" of the "male gaze," now revealed to be an empty self-reflexion—a mirror image—of its own visual fantasies.

The intertexuality and self-referentiality that in general identify *French in Action* as a postmodernist text also serve in particular to foreground its cinematic specificity. The en-gendering of this context broadens discussion of intradiegetic concerns of visual authority and address to encompass the creation of film as a whole. Although the Yale report includes Mireille's childhood desire to be an actress (but not Robert's parallel wish to be a fireman) among the examples of sexist stereotyping it cites, both this role and its connotations of visual objectification and the passive repetition of another's text have in fact been reassigned to the male protagonist in the textual present. Robert explicitly defines himself in relation to the actor Robert Taylor, whose poster dominates shots of Robert prior to and in preparation for his self-introduction. Mireille, on the other hand, not only presents her own self in relation to the poet Rémy Bellau, but she is also preparing for a career as an art historian; metaphorically, she claims both verbal and visual authority, and she does so within the cultural context of "high" art.

The filmic allusions that envelop Jean-Pierre as well as Robert reinforce their allegiance to the realm of fantasy. Indeed, by including in his repertory of the "trucs" of the *dragueur* the proposal that he might have met an unknown woman "l'année dernière à Marienbad" (Lesson 13), Jean-Pierre names the very paradigmatic text (Alain Resnais's 1961 film) that he himself seeks to *répète* (both repeat and rehearse)—without, however, ever managing to duplicate Resnais's hero's apparently successful imposition of *his* fantasy as *her* reality. Moreover, as he directs his "male gaze" toward his own imaginary vision of a "Greta Garbo" look-alike in the courtyard below, Jean-Pierre in fact sees "un type en noir" (a guy dressed in black) whom he instantly recognizes as his double. The initial identification of the character who ultimately turns out to be the "cinéaste" as a stereotypical *dragueur* now reverses the terms that have peopled male fantasies with cinematic images of women to equate film itself with the construction of a male fantasy world.[15] *French in Action* thus realizes the very goal that feminist film critics and filmmakers strive to achieve.

But perhaps I have misinterpreted what those responsible for the Yale report understand by "the vehicle of the male gaze." Although this terminology never appears in the written complaints that initiated and often influenced the formal departmental inquiry, students nonetheless appear to be aware of a problem that they conceptualize somewhat differently. With some consistency, the students explicitly focus on the *consequences* of the voyeurism inherent in traditional cinematic address, the fragmentation and objectification of the female body. In a representative example, one student comments: "Mireille is a well-endowed, flirtatious, sexy woman whose legs and braless breasts are often the focus of the camera. This cannot help but make a class uncomfortable" (Newmark et al., Appendix 3).

Without for a moment questioning the sincerity of such responses, I do want to suggest that they once again reflect the culturally specific context of American feminism.[16] In every case, commentary initially identifies some aspect of the "cinematic apparatus" (such as point of view, type of shot, camera movement) as the ostensible object of its interest, only to shift its focus in mid-discourse from the *representation* of women to the *reality* of the women who are represented. Student discomfort (what "cannot help but make a class uncomfortable") originates far less in how Mireille is filmed than in her actual physical appearance ("well-endowed"); its perceived effects on her behavior ("flirtatious, sexy"); and what she does—or, more importantly, does not ("braless")—wear. The tendency evident here—to equate *sexism* with the portrayal of *sexuality*, at best, and, at worst, with any and all depiction of the female body—reflects one of the most consistent and characteristic of the ideological positions in American feminism (see, for example, Rich). Given that such a view also enjoys wider cultural support—a deeply ingrained association of the body with privacy, often identified by the French, in particular, as American "puritanism"—certain students will undoubtedly continue to deplore the evidence of such "sexism" in *French in Action*. However ethnocentric this reading of the text, it certainly denies access to some dimensions of Francophone culture. This seems to be nonetheless a case in which the Women's Studies classroom constitutes the most appropriate context in which to (continue to) address what is fundamentally a question far less of textual interpretation or of language pedagogy than of feminist ideology—at its most complex and potentially divisive.

What may seem like an abrupt dismissal of the very density of context into which I sought initially to introduce this discussion of *French in Action* brings to mind the surprising conclusion reached by the editors of the second and most recent incursion of *Yale French Studies* into the field of pedagogy. This time an explicitly feminist search for "a new form of practical criticism that can actually have an impact on what we as critics do in our other lives as teachers" results in the startling—and unsettling—revelation that pedagogy itself may be a specifically American concern (Dejean & Miller 3). The volume includes excerpts from fourteen interviews with French feminist scholars whose only unifying principle appears to be the shared desire to teach the contributors to *Yale French Studies* that they are asking "American questions, translations of an American academic desire" (Jardine & Menke 230). The French women single out two issues in particular. They challenge, on the one hand, the concentration on the "hopelessly passé" notion of a national canon and, on the other, the concern with "the metaphysical category of 'women'" rather than "the construction of sexual difference through notions of the feminine and the masculine" (Jardine & Menke 231).

In other words, these fourteen women object precisely to the textual hierarchy of the American university system as a whole and to the specific ideological orientation of American feminism within the academy—the two factors that, paradoxically, together either eliminate foreign-language textbooks and teaching from general theoretical discussions of pedagogy or eliminate their difference, their very foreignness, from particular ideological considerations of curricular transformation. *French in Action* suggests the validity and the value of a very different approach. The introduction of the foreign-language textbook, a resource whose content by definition foregrounds teaching methodologies and cultural differences, into future considerations of the pedagogies and the ideologies of the classroom, might result in the very diversity that professors claim they want to introduce into their teaching and their scholarship. In this light, the inclusion in the most recent edition of the Modern Language Association's *Introduction to Scholarship in Modern Languages and Literatures* (Gibaldi) of Claire Kramsch's essay on foreign-language acquisition and learning is indeed, as the author herself comments, "a noteworthy event" ("Language" 53).

Jean-Charles Tacchella's and Joel Schumacher's Kissing Cousins

In/Fidelity in Family and Film

The practice of remaking French films in Hollywood bears a direct, if fortuitous, relationship to the pedagogical issues raised in the preceding discussion of *French in Action*. Indeed, recent essays in such leading professional journals as *French Review* and *French Cultural Studies* suggest that the remake phenomenon as a whole offers a unique potential for expanding the traditional goals of the foreign language and culture classroom. Georges Santoni, for example, maintains that "one needs only to compare a few clips of an original French film with its American remake to be convinced [that] French people do not necessarily organize their visual production and perception the same way as Americans do" ("Visual Images" 68). Michael J. Raby concurs that "such doublings serve as ideal vehicles for understanding both cultures" (838; see also Carroll, "Film"). Although I obviously agree both with the methodology promoted by Raby and Santoni and with the results it promises, I am somewhat less optimistic than they appear to be, at least in the statements quoted above, that the cross-cultural differences revealed by comparative analysis will be immediately visible to all film viewers—and not simply, I hope, because such transparency would render irrelevant my own work along with theirs. As Santoni himself points out, not only the appreciation of otherness but even its very perception depend upon the acquisition of "visual literacy," a skill normally achieved by overcoming a number of obstacles, including the ethnocentric bias and the cultural preconceptions that lead one to see the stereotypical rather than the actual (72). The experience of moviegoers, even at times that of professional reviewers, can be expected to reflect at least some of the difficulties that initially confront students of foreign cultures.

Certainly most reviewers of *Cousins* (1989), Joel Schumacher's remake of

Jean-Charles Tacchella's *Cousin, Cousine* (1975), insist on the American film's remarkable similarity to the French original. Indeed, if one were to believe *Vogue's* Jeffrey Sherman, whose words echo the worst fears of the French film industry, the remake distinguishes itself primarily by its use of the English language: "If you liked *Cousin, Cousine* but can't speak French, don't like subtitles, and hate dubbing, you'll love *Cousins*. The films are strikingly similar." Other views, if more moderate, are nevertheless fully consistent with Sherman's. David Ansen of *Newsweek*, for example, characteristically asserts that both the direction and the screenplay of the remake "follow the original with nearly scene-by-scene fidelity" ("Love" 65). Yet mainstream critics also tend to concur both with Ansen's affirmation that "what's fascinating, however, is what's been changed, to suit a different decade and a different culture" and with his identification of attitudes toward adultery as the single most significant locus of change: "A true American love story in the '80's—especially an adulterous one—must be star-crossed and guilt-ridden, exactly what the French version wasn't." Moreover, although Ansen holds Schumacher's *Cousins* in unusually high regard, a judgment he himself characterizes as a "surprise," he explicitly introduces this judgment as an exception to a general principle that is, once again, widely shared: "Any American remake of a French comedy, as bitter experience has taught us, is guilty until proven innocent."

I have singled out Ansen's review as a privileged point of reference and quoted his exact words with such frequency, because the language in which he expresses his (commonly shared) opinions is of particular interest. Note, for example, Ansen's choice of the word *fidelity*, which clearly names the common subject matter of *Cousin, Cousine* and *Cousins*, to describe the relationship between the two films as well. Similarly, he uses the same vocabulary of guilt and innocence to identify a particular difference between one specific Hollywood remake and its French original and to articulate the general dynamics of French-to-American remakes as a whole. Ansen's review thus functions both to call the relationship between marital and cinematic in/fidelity to our attention and to remind us that the latter is as much a moral issue as the former. (Indeed, *adultery* and *adulteration*—the process of making or, in this case, remaking "inferior by adding foreign substances"—share a common etymology.) Finally, Ansen's own double discourse can be seen as suggestively reflective of the very texts on which it comments, for both Tacchella and Schumacher use theme and structure as self-reflexive metaphors. Or, to put it somewhat more provocatively, not only is *Cousins* no more faithful to *Cousin, Cousine* than the cousins within the two films are to their respective spouses, but the American remake is every bit as preoccupied aesthetically as it is dramatically with the question of "relative" infidelity.

Although Hollywood waited fourteen years before producing an American version of *Cousin, Cousine*, the tendency of journalists to recall the French original explicitly is no doubt consistent with the memories of many of their readers as well. Even if Tacchella's popular hit can hardly lay claim to the critical stature of a work such as Godard's *A Bout de souffle*, it won the Oscar for best foreign film in 1976 and subsequently became one of the first foreign films to be distributed well beyond the East Coast art house circuit to theaters throughout the United States. Indeed, *Cousin, Cousine* is certainly one of the reasons why French films came to represent fully half of the (admittedly always and now increasingly limited) market for foreign films in this country in the last two decades. Those viewers who saw *Cousin, Cousine* even twenty years ago can therefore be expected to perceive a certain superficial family resemblance between the French original and the American remake. In both versions, two distant cousins meet at the wedding of her mother to his uncle as a result of the temporary disappearance of their respective spouses, who have gone off together to have sex. To punish their unfaithful mates, the cousins, now friends and allies, at first merely create the impression that they have begun an affair of their own, but eventually pretense turns into reality. Meanwhile, everyone is continually thrown together at a steady stream of familial and social gatherings that identify the recent British hit, Mike Newell's *Four Weddings and a Funeral* (1994), as a worthy namesake of Tacchella's and especially Schumacher's similarly structured stories.

All that is missing from this description, despite both its general accuracy and its superficial conformity to distant visual memory, is, quite simply, everything that matters, to wit: character, cultural mores, and cinematic style. By chance, Santoni singles out the relationship among precisely these three aspects of filmmaking to illustrate his belief in the specificity of national cinemas: "Today, we know that there is a native understanding of objects, persons, or situations experienced visually and that *stylistic constraints are definitely tied to cultural and psychological context*" ("Visual Images" 68, my emphasis). He goes on, as we have seen, to assert that the comparison of "a few clips" or even "the first fifty shots" of any original French film with its American remake provides ample proof of "this fact." Regardless of the general validity of Santoni's thesis, this experiment certainly leads to convincing results in the case of *Cousin, Cousine* and *Cousins*, in part, no doubt, because both films call attention to their patterns of organization and foreground their visual strategies.

The opening credits of the French film are already playfully self-reflexive and suggest a desire to challenge the conventional boundaries between "reality" and its cinematic equivalent. Tacchella introduces us to the adult characters of *Cousin, Cousine* by the projection of childhood photographs of the actors who play the roles. The initial dramatic episode that follows further focuses our attention on the general dynamics of the relationship between children and adults. Just as the individual photos of the stars are replaced, at the precise moment that the film's title appears on screen, by an anonymous wedding portrait of a large extended family; subsequently, our first direct encounter is with two clearly secondary characters, the heroine's sister and her husband, who are driving with their son and daughter to her mother's wedding. This generic French family is engaged in its single most important cultural task: the instruction of the children in the codes and values of the bourgeoisie. Both mother and father take turns informing their children of the proper way to behave at their grandmother's wedding, since, as the paternal exhortation concludes, "marriage is a serious matter." But, of course, it *isn't* in Tacchella's film, nor do adults themselves necessarily respect the rules of civilized behavior, as the jump cut to the drunken bride downing a huge beer makes immediately evident. Moreover, it is children who perceive social hypocrisy—the discrepancy between appearance and reality, the disjunction between what adults say and what they do—with particular clarity. Beginning with this first wedding and continuing throughout the film, Tacchella repeatedly privileges the clear-eyed gaze of children, who figure, individually and in groups, in a series of establishing shots that set up their perspective as ours as well.

Thus, in the third sequence of the film, when Marthe (Marie-Christine Barrault) and Ludovic (Victor Lanoux) are left alone at the end of the wedding to await the return of their missing spouses, the audience of *Cousin, Cousine* watches them from the position of Marthe's young son Eric. The first shot of the couple, initially seated next to each other with an empty chair on either side and framed against the closed French window behind them, projects at once a sense of imprisonment and a kind of mutual wallflower image that suggests a connection with the bored and abandoned child. In fact, however, what turns out to be only a fleeting first impression serves rather to further clarify the nature of the interaction between children and adults in this film and to set up a visual contrast between the situation in which Marthe and Ludovic apparently find themselves and the reality—or perhaps the fantasy, or both—into which it will be quickly transformed. The waiter brings champagne, the orchestra plays a waltz, he invites her to dance, she smiles radiantly and murmurs, "Music, champagne, what a life," as the lights are dimmed to complete this perfect *mise-en-scène* of the conventional romantic encounter. The child's complaint ("You're having a good time, but it's not any fun for me"), which his mother ignores, establishes a pattern and a message that will structure *Cousin, Cousine* as a whole. The role of children in the French film is a slightly revised version of the famous proverb that still largely dictates their behavior in French society. If children are clearly still not to be heard, they are there *to see* rather than simply to be seen, a task that highlights the importance that children also enjoy in France. Their gaze, as we will see, metaphorically validates the right of the adults they observe to reclaim a certain kind of freedom, fantasy, and fun associated with the young—"You're having a good time," acknowledges even the sulky and envious Eric.

At the same time, of course, this is also a vision of infidelity, our first view of an adulterous affair in the making that has been approved, in some sense, before it has even begun. Even though its romantic perfection contrasts with the disarray and confusion exhibited by Marthe's and Ludovic's guilty spouses, who now return from having sex in a nearby forest, the ironic similarities do not appear to escape even them. When Pascal's (Guy Marchant) guilty conscience subsequently drives him to confess to this "adventure" with Karine (Marie-France Pisier), his final affirmation that "I no longer have anything to reproach myself for" is suddenly followed by an unexpected observation—"I saw you dancing the waltz"—that clearly implies that Marthe, unlike him, still may.

In this context, one would have to conclude that the American remake of *Cousin, Cousine* ends where the French original only begins, even though Maria (Isabella Rossellini) and Larry (Ted Danson) meet at approximately the same moment and for essentially the same reasons. In Schumacher's *Cousins*, however, the champagne is gone, the band is on its way out the door, and when Tom (William Petersen) and Tish (Sean Young) return from their illicit tryst, they find their respective spouses standing chastely on opposite sides of the room. Indeed, Maria and Larry do not dance together until the final wedding reception that concludes the American remake. Yet Larry, who, like his French counterpart, is a dance instructor, does dance in this scene; he waltzes not with Maria but with Chloë, her young daughter, to the child's obvious delight and to her mother's explicit approbation—"You're very good with children," a compliment that Larry immediately justifies by the fact that his job leaves him a lot of time to spend with his son. Thus, whereas the French film validates the desires of adults over those of children (who must wait their turn) and even at times accords adults the freedom to behave like children, that is, to be relatively irresponsible and self-indulgent, the American remake grants absolute priority to the needs of children and thus requires adults to conduct themselves at all times as responsible parents. Like Ludovic and Marthe, Larry and Maria are immediately drawn to each other, but in the American remake, this initial attraction is based entirely on their mutual recognition of each other as good parents. Schumacher offers us an image of the ideal nuclear family, a mother and father amusing their daughter, and not that of the romantic couple, a man and a woman amusing each other, which we encounter early in Tacchella's film. This change in perspective is evident in the respective titles of the two films: the emphasis on gender and sexual difference encoded in the French *Cousin, Cousine* becomes the non-specific familial plural of the English-language *Cousins*.

The way in which Schumacher prepares and contextualizes the first encounter of his cousins further clarifies the distinctiveness of the American remake in comparison to the French original. Before we arrive at the wedding reception, which concludes with the fleeting impression of family harmony described above, we are first introduced to the two dysfunctional families whose problems will simultaneously necessitate and justify their eventual breakdown and reconstitution in the course of the film. *Cousins* opens with a close-up of the glowering face of a very unhappy little girl whose father tries to prevent her from dragging her wet blanket across the leather seats of his new BMW, until the mother intervenes on her daughter's behalf: "It's just a car." Thus, from the moment we first meet Tom, he stands accused of what in the American film will prove to be a far more serious crime than infidelity: he is a bad father. The (mis)adventures of Tom and Chloë—on the way to the wedding he has to retrieve her blanket from the middle of the highway—are intercut with a parallel narrative sequence that features another father and child. In direct contrast to Tom, however, Larry is immediately established as a good father, prior to and in preparation for his encounter with Maria and her daughter. Larry clearly has a close and affectionate relationship with his adolescent son Mitch (Keith Coogan), who confirms, "As dads go, you're okay." The outsider in this family is Tish, Larry's second wife, less because she is a bad mother than simply because she is not a mother at all, as Mitch will explicitly remind her when she attempts to act like one in a subsequent episode. Like Tom, however, Tish has questionable values, which similarly delay her family's arrival at the wedding; she too places too much importance on appearance(s), in this case her own: "Just think of her as a work in progress," Larry tells the impatient Mitch.

In keeping with the opening wedding sequences in *Cousin, Cousine* and *Cousins*, which leave us with differently composed but similarly "picture perfect" visions of happiness, whether romantic or familial, both French and American families next gather for the express purpose of reviewing the wedding in pictures. Nelsa (Catherine Verlor), Ludovic's teenage daughter and the wedding photographer of *Cousin, Cousine*, shows slides of her new great-aunt Biju's (Ginette Garcin) marriage on the occasion of another family ritual: Biju entertains her grandchildren once a month. As a result, Nelsa's audience is composed primarily of children; indeed, the bride and groom and Marthe and her sister are the only adults whose presence is visually called to our attention. This relationship between children and adults corresponds exactly to that established at the wedding reception itself, where Tacchella singles out Nelsa's camera as representative of a privileged childlike gaze by tracking between shots of (these same) children watching and of Nelsa taking pictures. Although the use of the technique of *mise en abyme*, usually associated with more experimental narrative structures, might seen somewhat surprising in a romantic comedy (even a French one) aimed at a popular audience, Tacchella's internal duplication has the mainstream merit of being both explicit and transparent. Nelsa's slide show reproduces at once the filming, the editing, and the screening of *Cousin, Cousine.*

Moreover, we inevitably view wedding photos within the additional context of a much larger and in this case unquestionably familiar visual tradition, one that Nelsa's photo montage is precisely designed to call into question. By convention, the generic family photo album reproduces the daily reality of family history as the limited record of its "happy moments." From this perspective, wedding photos function as the ideal representative of the genre as a whole, not simply because weddings actually *do* tend, at least more dependably than vacations or holidays, to be unusually happy occasions, but because most weddings are already staged with a degree of fantasy and artifice that helps assure that their reproduction will almost necessarily remain reasonably faithful to the desired "reality." Perhaps it is because most photo albums are (re)constructed *around* the lives of children but *by* their parents that the adults in *Cousin, Cousine* react with shock and horror to what their offspring clearly consider entertaining. Presumably the children find Nelsa's slide presentation realistic as well, since she shows us much that we have already seen and reveals nothing that we do not already know.

Nelsa's slides are arranged in chronological order, but their structure also respects, both thematically and figuratively, an evolution from "fidelity" to "infidelity." If the early shots are somewhat unconventional—we see, for example, clearly bored faces at the wedding reception and the groom mooning his guests—they nonetheless remain acceptably faithful to what everyone is willing to remember. Nelsa's great-aunt objects only after she has seen three consecutive photos of Uncle Eugène peering down the blouse of the woman beside him, a drunken Uncle Gaston pissing into his hat, and Aunt Hélène throwing up in the garden; and she does not interrupt the projection until Nelsa shows two additional slides that first reveal Pascal and Karine leaving the reception together and then another clearly amorous couple taking off their clothes in the cloakroom. The brief verbal exchange that ensues between Nelsa and her great-aunt makes it perfectly clear that their disagreement concerns not factual reality but only its visual representation:

> **Biju**: That's horrible, my little Nelsa, people don't show things like that.
> **Nelsa**: Why? They exist. I didn't make them up.
> **Biju**: At your age one takes an interest in the pleasant aspects of life.

In fact, Nelsa's version of *cinéma vérité* appears to be much more harmful to adults than to children, even though the latter are immediately chased from the room ("This isn't suitable for children") when the lights come back on to reveal that Nelsa's slide projection has unexpectedly transformed their grand-mother from a bride to a widow. Certainly Tacchella provides no other expla-nation for the sudden death of a man seen to be in perfect health moments earlier. Truth, or the transgression of social convention, or both—that is, the visual revelation of impropriety apparently has, at least metaphorically, the power to kill.

In Schumacher's *Cousins*, Edie's (Norma Aleandro) new husband also has a fatal heart attack at a similar family gathering, but it occurs several hours after the showing of the wedding photos, and there is no suggestion, coinci-dental or otherwise, that the two events are in any way related. In general, "A Wedding, a film by Mitch," who defines himself as "a multimedia artist with an emphasis on video," receives better local reviews than Nelsa's slide projec-tion does. Although the video includes the same examples of individual im-propriety, Mitch's project is much more ambitious; the revelation of family se-crets interests him less for its own sake than as raw material from which to construct a broader social critique. To the music of "Happy Days," Mitch creates an ironic montage of visual images: shots of the wedding guests gorg-ing themselves are juxtaposed with those of the starving bodies of famine vic-tims; the cutting of the wedding cake is followed by a shot of a knife slicing through a breast; and a clip of Tom and Tish heading off into a field comes to a "climax" with a shot of nuclear rockets exploding into the air. Although Tom interrupts the screening at this point and Mitch's elderly Aunt Sofia calls Mitch "a very sick young man," Larry proclaims it "interesting work." More-over, whereas Nelsa abandons photography after her initial experience ("It serves no purpose. No one understands."), Mitch is encouraged by the nega-tive reactions his video has provoked ("Alienation—great!"); and we will see him filming at all subsequent weddings.

Mitch's enthusiasm for "alienation" suggests the particular significance of the *mise en abyme* within a film that is itself "based on" an earlier film, as the opening credits of *Cousins* clearly announce. Just as *alienation* denotes the estrangement from family and friends that partially identifies the thematic interests shared by *Cousin, Cousine* and Schumacher's remake, the derivation of the word simultaneously marks the distance between the French original and its American cousin: *alien*, foreign, characteristic of another and very dif-ferent place or society. The increased importance that Schumacher grants to the duplication of the film within the film, an idea he clearly inherits from Tacchella, suggests a desire to foreground not only the reflexivity of all re-makes, faithful or adulterated, but the internal repetitiveness of film itself. The title of Mitch's video repeats that of Rick Altman's similarly satirical study of a wedding (1978) and the knife slicing through the breast cannot fail to recall the razor and the eye, in itself a self-referential cinematic image, of Luis Buñuel's *Un Chien andalou* (1929).

Double Takes

One of the most obvious differences between *Cousin, Cousine* and *Cousins* is that of the sex of the teenager who serves as the diegetic representative of the filmmaker within both Tacchella's and Schumacher's movies. I have sought in vain to find a meaningful explanation for a change that nonetheless seems to cry out for an interpretation, which, once found, would surely illuminate the relationship between the two films in fascinating new ways. Yet, despite the fact that the substitution of Mitch for Nelsa seems ideally suited to focus our attention on the significance of gender, I am forced to conclude that this is simply not the case, however much it might suit my own purposes if it were. (No doubt it is useful for a feminist critic to be reminded that not only is gender not the only issue, sometimes it's not an issue at all.) The substitution of sons for daughters—and vice versa (Chloë also replaces Eric)— plausibly follows directly from the divergent narrative interests of the American remake. *Cousins* requires Larry to be a good parent, and visual affection and closeness between a father and a teenager are unquestionably easier to convey when the latter is male as well (that is, when gender is not an issue).

Still, I remain convinced that Tacchella and Schumacher mean to call *something* to our attention, given the particular prominence that each accords to Nelsa and Mitch. If it isn't the difference, that is, the gender of adolescence, that counts, then it must be the similarity, that is, adolescence itself. *Adolescent* and *adult* refer to two separate stages in the life cycle, but both derive from different forms of the same Latin word meaning, respectively, "growing up" and "grown up." As the transitional stage that mediates between childhood and maturity, adolescence serves as an ideal metaphor for films that both focus, albeit very differently, on the relationship between children and adults, a dynamics whose initial presentation we have already seen and which I now want to explore in greater detail.

According to Raymonde Carroll, the majority of French people recall adolescence as "a burst of freedom" (*Cultural* 53), a description that applies equally well to *Cousin, Cousine*. A longer version of the same recollection, which characterizes the period between childhood and adulthood by "the freedom to do what [one] want[s], that is, to stay out late, to 'have a good time,' maybe to get drunk, to have sexual experiences, to travel, and so on" (51), identifies not only the principal episodes of Tacchella's film but even its narrative progression. "I respect the freedom of others. I can't help it," Ludovic tells Marthe the second time they meet. The most overt announcement of theme in *Cousin, Cousine* is appropriately attributed to the character who best represents the particular understanding of freedom portrayed in Tacchella's film, indeed, whose very name contains within it an explicit reference to the "ludic." Ludovic explains his current—and temporary—choice of profession by a combination of capriciousness and the desire to have fun; he became a dance instructor "by chance, to have a good time." (His actual childhood dream was to be a "clochard" [bum], but unfortunately his parents objected. In direct contrast to adolescence, according to Carroll, "childhood is full of restrictions" [53].) In keeping with Ludovic's carefree philosophy that "You must always go in search of adventure—even if only for an hour from time to time," he and Marthe spend their first afternoon together "playing hooky" from their jobs at a Laurel and Hardy film.

In this context, *Cousin, Cousine* reveals itself to be less about adultery than about sexual freedom; moreover, sexual freedom is itself significant primarily as an illustration of a more general concept of freedom that Tacchella's film seeks to explore. Marthe's mother provides perhaps the clearest evidence for this interpretation. On the same day that her daughter first runs off with her future lover, that is, on the same day that Biju buries her late husband, she meets Thomas (Hubert Gignoux), Ludovic's widowed father, a serious, stable, settled man of approximately her age who is openly presented as a promising—and eager—candidate for a remarriage. But when Biju subsequently returns from a visit to Thomas not only without him but with Serge, the very young lover (indeed, barely beyond *adolescence*) whom she has acquired somewhere along the way, she happily explains to Marthe and Ludovic that "freedom is a wonderful thing." Similarly, just as our first impression of Marthe and Ludovic themselves is one of imprisonment, the final shot of the film configures their liberation: we last see the lovers outside the same French windows that now contain the rest of the family. (As if to underline the freedom that Marthe and Ludovic have chosen, the situation of Marthe's mother is, at that moment, one of entrapment. As the lovers leave, we hear her screaming to be released from the box in which Serge, who turns out to be a "charmer" by profession as well, has enclosed her in preparation for performing a magic trick.)

Still, if *sexual* is just one possible adjective to modify *freedom*, there is never any real doubt in Tacchella's film that Marthe and Ludovic will have an affair—nothing less and, in all probability, nothing more. After their romantically encoded first encounter, which establishes them as a couple, they next meet in a pastry shop. In France, eating, let alone gourmandism, qualifies in and of itself as a sensual activity; and the appetite with which Marthe and Ludovic gorge themselves on *gâteaux* functions suggestively as sexual metaphor. (Hence Marthe uncharacteristically declines to eat on the day they first make love: "No, nothing before.") Similarly, when the cousins subsequently spend their lunch hour swimming, Tacchella's camera openly eroticizes the scene. The composition of the initial image, in which Marthe is positioned behind Ludovic so that his torso dominates the foreground of the shot and we see only her head and shoulders, makes the couple appear to be nude; a two-shot of the couple facing us in close-up subsequently creates the identical effect. In addition, their bodies are bathed in the same reddish-golden light, suggestive of passion, that will later color the room in which they first make love.

This event takes place in a clearly disreputable hotel (it openly substitutes for one where a friend of Ludovic's "used to take his girlfriends") whose rules, personnel, and decor are all designed to invite us to equate it with the stereo-typical brothels of our movie memories. In context, however, there is nothing remotely degrading about this allusion; rather, its theatrical playfulness con-veys the sheer hedonistic excess with which Tacchella's lovers conduct their affair. A similar effect is achieved by the curious fact that virtually everything in *Cousin, Cousine* seems to come in pairs. Marthe and Ludovic dance to-gether twice, devour pastries and go swimming on two different occasions, at-tend two weddings, spend two afternoons making love, and so on. Such an internally repetitive structure might seem peculiarly predestined to provoke external repetition in the form of a remake, and indeed we have seen this pat-tern before, notably in the case of *Trois Hommes et un couffin* and *Three Men and a Baby*. Although every event that Tacchella repeats either disappears from Schumacher's *Cousins* or is reduced to a single occurrence, doubling it-self, as we will see shortly, continues to play a very important role in the American remake.

Just as sex first occurs simply because it is the logical next step in Ludovic and Marthe's eroticized march toward freedom, sex itself is only one stage in a rebellion that continues to escalate. In particular, the profession of self-indulgence ("Let's think about us"), which determines the decision to con-summate their affair, comes increasingly to characterize the lovers' behavior. Ludovic and Marthe now begin to flaunt their relationship. At the next family gathering, their second dance together is willfully sexy and ends in a very pub-lic embrace. In the final sequence of the film, they spend Christmas eve locked in a bedroom making love, while the other members of the family try to distract themselves with more traditional activities, including a televised midnight mass. The lovers emerge only to say goodbye to their children and leave. Clearly, out of context, such behavior would appear to be not only ego-centric but excessively irresponsible. In context, however—and the emphasis that Tacchella's camera places on the framing of these two scenes makes it clear how important context is to interpretation in this instance—the com-portment of the film's heroes is, well, in some sense at least, heroic.

I mean this metaphorically as well as literally. No doubt it takes a certain courage to ignore conventions of social propriety, let alone to exhibit one's dis-regard for such codes, even in a country in which, in the words of Robert Darnton, "it is good to be bad" (65); but the final third of *Cousin, Cousine* also takes place in a setting increasingly resistant to film's own traditional codes, in this case, those of cinematic realism. The first time that Ludovic and

Marthe publicly appear as lovers, at an annual family party, they enter a world that looks—and is—familiar, except that it represents a kind of mirror image, an inverted reflection, of conventional "reality." (Rear projection might constitute a more apt metaphor—or perhaps the relationship between most remakes and the original films on which they are based.) The very terms in which the film describes this event further destabilize the usual relationship between reality and fantasy: "The children invite the grown-ups once a year; it gives them a sense of reality." At the end of the party, consistent with the controlling inversion of roles, the adult guests stand watching the children dance with each other, until Marthe and Ludovic join the dancers, at which point the children also temporarily stop to watch. In a final realization of the pattern set up from the beginning of the film, the (mis)behavior of the adults is thus implicitly equated with the harmless (indeed, the useful) fantasy of a childhood game, while it is publicly sanctioned by the curious, but nonjudgmental, gaze of the children. The importance of fantasy and its association with the freedom and the tolerance of youth becomes even clearer in the closing sequence of *Cousin, Cousine*. When Ludovic and Marthe finally emerge from the bedroom, which the spectator has entered periodically through the gaze of children peeking through the keyhole, they return to an enchanted world in which a magic show is underway and the children are dressed in costume. Their masked faces watch the lovers' departure from behind the French windows, and the final shot of the film is a long hold on a little girl who is smiling.[1]

The conclusion to *Cousin, Cousine* retrospectively clarifies the ambiguities of Jacques's "murder" by slide show.[2] The inclusion of elements of fantasy confirms that it is neither sexual indiscretion nor social impropriety nor even their revelation per se that metaphorically kills, but rather the fidelity of the representation. In other words, aesthetic choices, not moral ones, are at issue. Even if Nelsa herself attempts to blame society (that is, real*ity*) directly at the end of her photographic career ("It's too real; it lacks fantasy"), her aunt appropriately reproaches her for excessive real*ism* ("People don't show things like that . . . one takes an interest in the pleasant aspects of life"). In an essay on "French Film Remakes" (other than *Cousins*), informed by the standard critical assumption of the necessary inferiority of such films, Marc Mancini nonetheless makes the perceptive suggestion that charges of the "moral incompatibility" of French and American films may, in fact, be part of "an even broader, more subtle cultural trait" that reflects different cross-cultural traditions of realism (40). In this context, he cites the screenwriter Larry Gross, assigned to adapt *Les Ripoux* for Hollywood before the project was abandoned, who attributes the impossibility of remaking certain films to precisely this factor: "The French have a playful, comfortable role with reality that is hard for Americans to understand" (qtd. in Mancini 40).[3]

Still, the absence of guilt, indeed, the general approbation that accompa-

nies the departure of the adulterous (adolescent) lovers is neither exactly unrealistic nor entirely morally irresponsible. Although the conclusion is appropriately open-ended, in keeping with Tacchella's thematics of freedom, the
film encourages its audience to assume that Marthe and Ludovic will return
shortly. "*A Bientôt*" ("See you soon"), Marthe's final words to her son, mean
precisely that in French. The only future plans the couple has ever discussed
project nothing more than a vacation ("You know what would be terrific? To
take a trip together"). Marthe and Ludovic never profess to be "in love" and
never mention the possibility of divorce; they make love, not commitments.
In short, the lovers' affair is coded as an escapade, an exercise in independence and personal freedom. As such, this behavior certainly includes elements of daring and defiance and no doubt represents the desire to shock
("épater les bourgeois," as the French say), but ultimately it also constitutes
only an act of revolt and not the beginning of a revolution. Notably, although
the lovers themselves temporarily abandon their families and societal conventions, they also leave the structure of the family, traditional guardian of social
order, very much intact.

Georges Santoni may well be right that *Cousin, Cousine* owed its original
popularity with American audiences to the fact that it "responded to a certain
idea that America has of the French" ("Stéréotypes" 84, n. 1). Certainly the
reputation that France enjoys in the United States as a country where sex,
pleasure, romance, and infidelity thrive owes a great deal in return to the
French film industry, at least as represented by its American distribution.
Ironically, however, in this case, *Cousin, Cousine* derives its cultural authority
and authenticity less from the stereotypical image of the French that is circu-
lated abroad than from the reality of cultural specificity at home. Liah Greenfeld, in his recent study of the historical development of a unique sense of
French national identity, recalls that the very name of the country encodes
the fundamental importance of freedom (*France*, from *franche*, freedom)
(94). If the original sense of the term, which extolled the historical fact of
France's freedom from foreign domination and influences, dates from the late
Middle Ages (97), remnants of this foundational pride continue to resurface
periodically, as in France's current opposition to "American cultural imperialism" and, in particular, to the international domination of Hollywood. More
generally, Greenfeld describes the French understanding of freedom in terms
that make Tacchella's *Cousin, Cousine* an excellent illustration:

> "[L]iberty" in France retained an intensely individualistic, in fact egocentric,
> connotation, as unqualified in its rejection of all authority and all limitations
> (including those imposed by the rights of other individuals), . . . Such libertar-
> ianism, a spirit of revolt for the sake of revolt, inconsiderate of others and un-
> mindful of its own implications, was characteristic . . . (523, n. 199)

Luigi Barzini, in his classic study of Europe, speaks similarly of French *liberté* as the egocentric desire to free not only the nation but ultimately the individual self as well from all constraints. But since the "rigorous discipline" of constraints is every bit as necessary as the drive toward "anarchy" that characterizes freedom, France and the French live in an endless cycle of "order" and "liberty" (142–43). Significantly, the works of Greenfeld and Barzini are strongly comparative in nature and both see the parallel study of France and the United States as essential to the full understanding of the cultural distinctiveness of each nation; indeed, Barzini includes France and the United States on equal terms in a book accurately entitled *The Europeans.*

On occasion, one has the good fortune to encounter particularly compelling images of Franco-American cultural difference. The Michelin guide to Euro Disney, for example, constitutes one such telling metaphor. Recent history provides another. In France, an entire nation, unexpectedly united in mourning at the death of a former president, was most deeply affected by a photograph of Danielle Mitterrand and her sons standing next to François Mitterrand's longtime mistress, Anne Pingeot, and their daughter, Mazarine. Newspapers raved about Danielle's "generosity" and Anne's "discretion"; everyone exulted over Mitterrand's "final victory." As an American, I was perhaps inevitably struck less by this final gesture of reconciliation than by the former president's ability to have concealed the existence of his "second family" from the nation and, to some extent apparently, even from his first, for some thirty years. In the United States, during the same week of January 1996, when France was preoccupied with Mitterrand's death and funeral, which Bill Clinton did not attend, the Supreme Court decided that Paula Jones had the right to sue a sitting president for sexual harassment; suddenly Clinton's reelection campaign promised to be a repeat performance with Jones in the role that Gennifer Flowers had played four years earlier.

On one side of the ocean, marital infidelity is first politely ignored and then formally eulogized; on the other, it is considered to concern everyone and it costs elections. Yet in a larger context, both men want(ed) the same thing and define(d) themselves in much the same way. François Mitterrand will be remembered as "le grand séducteur" for his ability to charm even his enemies and to turn every situation to his own advantage. Bill Clinton too has an endless need to *séduire*, both to please and to be loved in return. I have left the word in French for good reason, since in this context Clinton's only misfortune may be to have been born in the wrong country. In France, *séduction* not only has no negative connotations, it has a great many positive ones, including the assumption of strong personal attractiveness and almost irresistible charm. In the United States, in contrast, the act of seduction continues to bear the full moral weight of its linguistic origins (from the Latin *seducere*, to *lead astray*), making its practice singularly problematic for the leader of the nation.[4]

Double Takes

In this context, Schumacher's *Cousins* initially seems to be as much a confirmation of certain conventional beliefs about the French, which are popular among Americans, and of similar images of Americans, which circulate widely in France, as it is a direct response to Tacchella's *Cousin, Cousine*. In part, that is, Schumacher remakes a film widely perceived as a playful French comedy about sexual infidelity within the far more serious framework of Americans' reputed puritanism. In the director's own words, "The original French version took adultery very much for granted. It's not as popular a concept in America, so we had to deal with it from a different point of view—not so live-and-let-live" (qtd. in Sherman 268).[5] Within *Cousins* itself, Schumacher explicitly announces this change of moral perspective early in the remake by first reproducing and then rewriting a speech that is essential to the French original for its important revelations about theme and character. When Maria asks Larry whether he thinks their spouses have had sex, he first casually professes the same commitment to freedom that characterizes Ludovic: "Sex is not that big a deal. I believe in people's freedom of choice. Tish needs to grow up to be her own person. What people do is their own business." A moment later, however, Larry follows this statement, whose repetitiousness already suggests its insincerity, with an atypical outburst of anger and a reversal of position: "I'm so full of shit. I'd like to kill them both."

Subsequently, Maria and Larry's own relationship develops at a pace and with a restraint that contrast sharply with the hedonistic indulgence of their French counterparts. In *Cousins*, as I have already suggested, less is more; Schumacher counts out the pleasures he borrows from Tacchella with considerable parsimony. Just as Maria and Larry do not dance at the opening wedding, they do not eat when they next meet, even though the American cousins, unlike Ludovic and Marthe, actually go out to lunch. On the day of the funeral, a visit to Larry's boat and a serious conversation substitute for an afternoon spent laughing at a comic movie. Maria and Larry go swimming only once, and there is never the slightest doubt that they are wearing properly conservative bathing suits. They also make love on only one occasion—a possibility that Ludovic and Marthe also propose, and then immediately reject. Moreover, not only is this initial adventure never repeated, but it lasts only a few hours in the American remake, unlike in the original French version, in which a Saturday afternoon rendezvous lasts until late Sunday night.

Still, the quantitative and qualitative changes that Schumacher makes in the episodes he inherits from Tacchella do not result simply from Anglo-Saxon moralism in the face of adultery (even if the denial of pleasure or its enjoyment in limited quantities does recall yet another example of American presidential problems: Clinton's now famous explanation about his experience with marijuana). The same or similar events serve a very different purpose in *Cousins* than in *Cousin, Cousine*, since, as the comparison above makes clear, nothing that could properly be described as an affair ever takes place between Maria and Larry, who first become friends and then fall in love. In strictly parallel scenes in the French and American films, the two couples discuss the possible evolution of their relationships in revealingly different language. For example, while Marthe and Ludovic use the verb *coucher* (to have sex) to characterize their dilemma ("Either we have sex or we don't"), Maria and Larry talk about "making love." The former propose to remain "an unusual *couple*," whereas the latter plan much more specifically— and innocently—to become "very special *friends*" (my emphasis). At the second wedding in the American remake, a stranger mistakes Larry and Maria for husband and wife, and they talk openly about the kind of married couple they might make, even as each also confirms that the other has indeed become his or her "best friend."

At the comparable point in *Cousin, Cousine*, Marthe and Ludovic escape from the wedding reception in an episode that confirms their personal commitment to freedom, fun, and self-indulgence. Notably, they try to visit the shop of a friend of Ludovic who turns out, to their admiration, to have taken the day off "for no reason at all"; and Marthe reveals, on the one hand, that she explicitly blames "her job, her husband, her child" for a recent bout with depression, and, on the other, that she found a previous affair with a colleague "a lot of fun." Moreover, the departure of the French lovers is specifically motivated by the desire to make Pascal and Karine jealous. In contrast, Maria and Larry can't even sustain the illusion of an affair, let alone actually have one, for fear of hurting their own unfaithful spouses. Indeed, at one point, Maria actually apologizes to Tish for "playing a little game to get back at you and Tom." Consequently, the growing anxiety of Tom and Tish serves throughout the film as a constant reminder of the real stakes of this very serious "little game." Quite early in *Cousins*, when Tish assures a terrified Tom that "Larry would never have sex with a woman like your wife" (no doubt an accurate statement, though not for the reason Tish thinks; Maria is clearly the kind of woman with whom men like Larry fall in love), Tom replies, "I'm not worried about them having sex but a relationship." Precisely because their "relationship" is not about sex, even when Maria and Larry finally do make love, their adventure is visually encoded as romantic rather than erotic. In contrast to the charmingly bordello-like hotel where Marthe and Ludovic first meet, the idyllic tryst of the American lovers takes place at a moonlit cabin on a lake.

In the American version of *Cousins*, falling in love apparently constitutes such a serious crime in and of itself that Schumacher invents a variety of strategies for exonerating his lovers. (One could argue, for that matter, that even the love story serves primarily as a fictional device for clearing the American cousins of the charge of adultery.) Indeed, Schumacher so thoroughly structures the remake of *Cousin, Cousine* around this effort that the film at times curiously recalls French classical tragedy, although I am well aware of how strange such a comparison must seem. Rather like Racine in the case of Phèdre, for example, Schumacher suggests that his lovers are initially more the victims of fate than of their own free will and that they subsequently act heroically to overcome their guilty desires. Thus, in the American remake, even a single sexual encounter, which will never be repeated, occurs by chance rather than prior arrangement, so that it appears to be beyond Maria and Larry's control rather than consciously chosen ("Let's think about us") as in the French film. Moreover, in direct opposition to the smile of approval that sanctions Marthe and Ludovic's affair at the end of *Cousin, Cousine*, Maria and Larry's liaison is marked from the beginning by remorse, which appears in the contrasting form of a little girl's stare, seen in close-up, as the lovers first embrace on a crowded subway platform. This child clearly stands in for Maria's daughter, whose scowl opens the film, and to whom Maria will be forced to lie, to her horror, during the few hours that she and Larry spend together.

In continued contrast to *Cousin, Cousine*, where the recurrence of events demonstrates the intensity of the lovers' affair, internal repetition in *Cousins* furthers their vindication (in both senses of the term—what excuses them often functions simultaneously as an act of revenge). Tacchella favors the jump cut and the use of contrasting images, also evident in Nelsa's slide presentation, as an appropriate metaphor for the passion that characterizes Marthe and Ludovic's adventure; Schumacher, like Mitch, prefers crosscutting between analogous scenes in order to establish revealing connections. Ironically, given the fundamental differences in the nature of the two relationships, Maria and Larry's love finds a first reflection in the infidelity of their own spouses.

Both the French original and the American remake include a montage of successive scenes in which we see Pascal and Tom, respectively, breaking up with their current lovers on the morning after the opening wedding scenes. Initially, the only difference seems to be one of quantity. Consistent with the French film's greater acceptance of and enthusiasm for sex in general, Pascal sacrifices six women to Tom's three. Only comparison with the American remake retrospectively reveals the omission of Karine's name from Pascal's checklist, for within the specific context of the French film, he obviously has no reason to end a relationship that doesn't exist, that consists of a single sexual encounter so brief it hardly even qualifies as a one-night stand. For the duration of the film, not only does Pascal barely speak to Karine, even in public, but he does an impressive job of honoring his promise of marital fidelity, particularly for a man whose professed goal in life is "to beat Casanova's record" and who, by his own admission, still has "thirty to go." Pascal's only subsequent transgression occurs the day after Marthe has spent the weekend with Ludovic, and the comic scene clearly fails to bolster his wounded male pride. Although his partner politely attempts to reassure him ("It was good . . . not bad . . . *oh là là*, it was *very* good"), she also firmly rejects his offer to "start over."

In the American remake, Tom includes Tish among the lovers he forswears, but his farewell visit in fact perpetuates their liaison, which will run parallel to that of their spouses throughout the film. Although this dramatic transformation of Tacchella's original might seem inconsistent with the American film's greater commitment to marital fidelity, in two very important ways it actually sustains and supports the stricter ethical code of *Cousins*. In the first place, the explicitly sexual attraction that links Tom and Tish simultaneously contrasts with and justifies the authentic affection that Larry and Maria feel for each other. Whereas spousal infidelity in *Cousin, Cousine* functions at most as the initial impetus for a relationship that quickly takes off on its own merits, Schumacher assures that sympathy remains with Larry and Maria by keeping their far guiltier spouses quite literally within constant sight of the audience. Whenever Larry and Maria are together, beginning with their chaste afternoon walk on the day of the funeral, Schumacher intercuts scenes of Tom and Tish preparing to have sex, having sex, or talking about having had sex. These scenes, moreover, increasingly frequent as the film progresses, indirectly offer yet another justification for Maria and Larry, since even Tom and Tish blame only themselves ("They're in love—and it's our fault," says Tish; "Maria's too good for me," confirms Tom).

In the second place, however, Tom and Tish's ongoing affair ironically ends up exonerating them too to a certain extent. Like their spouses, to paraphrase Tom, he and Tish end up having not just sex but "a relationship"; Tish, moreover, clearly entertains the possibility that the liaison might evolve into something permanent. If this change confirms Schumacher's commitment to what the French would no doubt characterize as an excessively puritanical—and American—refusal to countenance casual sex on any account, it also reaffirms the importance, evident throughout *Cousins*, of friendship, love, and marriage. To emphasize this double message, Schumacher alters yet another relationship inherited from the original French film. Just as Marthe's mother implicitly condones her daughter's liberation by her own unconventional behavior, Maria's mother and now, significantly, Larry's father as well, offer their children an analogous and therefore very different model.

In contrast to the open-ended ambivalence that characterizes the final shots of *Cousin, Cousine*, *Cousins* comes full circle to achieve perfect closure. Indeed, in a curious conjunction of what Daniel Serceau describes as two alternative possibilities—"Films can be either remade or rerun" (8)—Schumacher's film concludes by repeating its own opening sequence. Not only does Edie remarry (yet again), but she does so in essentially identical circumstances and to virtually the same man, or, at least, his brother. Moreover, by unexpectedly crosscutting the single episode in which Larry and Maria make love with the story of Vincent (Lloyd Bridges) and Edie, rather than with that of Tom and Tish, Schumacher reinforces his distinction between sex and love and recontextualizes adultery as a prelude to marriage. Vincent prepares for his "big date" with Edie by passing his pornographic magazines on to Mitch. His explanation—"I'm going for the real thing"—not only announces his rejection of meaningless sex but constitutes a declaration of love as well. Subsequently, Larry and Maria's lakeside idyll is intercut with the equally romantic—and, as I will argue shortly, similarly metaphoric— scene of Edie and Vincent dancing on a cruise ship.

The final strategy that Schumacher uses to exonerate the lovers in the American remake requires greater infidelity to the French original than any I have yet noted. The alteration, even the inversion, of elements borrowed from *Cousin, Cousine* no longer suffices, and *Cousins* becomes, in the final third of the film, a very different movie from its predecessor. The American lovers are required to pay for their affair in ways that certainly seem to reinforce a cultural reputation for fidelity to moral codes inherited from our Puritan ancestors. Retribution is first exacted in an almost biblical sense of "the sins of the father being visited upon the sons"—or, in this case, those of the mother upon her daughter. Maria returns from the final afternoon she spends with Larry not only to face an angry husband but, more important, to learn that Chloë has been misbehaving at school. Although Maria accurately attributes her daughter's lying and aggressivity to her relationship with her father ("She's acting out her anger toward Tom"), she nonetheless blames herself: "I'm not doing a good enough job. My husband and my daughter need me." In keeping with *Cousins'* emphasis on responsible parenting, Maria immediately sacrifices the man she loves, with his approval, to parental guilt and to her perception of maternal duty. Moreover, she and Larry owe their eventual reunion to a decision made once again, at least overtly, for the good of the child. Maria finally justifies leaving Tom for Larry on the grounds that "Maybe Chloë deserves more than a bargain." The closing coda to *Cousins* appropriately recreates in reality this time the virtual family—Maria and her daughter, Larry and his son—evoked in the opening prelude to the film. Significantly, Mitch films his new family in the realistic black and white of the home movie.

The long montage sequence, which unfolds while the lovers are apart, exists, like the separation itself, only in the American remake. This passage consists of fifteen successive images, linked by dissolves, that chronicle the two- to three-month period from Halloween (children in costume open the series) to the New Year (the closing shot shows Maria putting away Christmas decorations). The sequence variously features all four principal characters (Tish, Tom, Maria, Larry). They are sometimes filmed with a child but never with a spouse or a lover; and each of the four is seen in turn in an identical setting: in bed, late at night, awake, and alone. What unifies this composition is the picture that emerges of loneliness and unhappiness.[6] The addition of this original montage confirms the sense in which *Cousins* most clearly reveals itself to be not just a remake of a French film but a specifically American movie as well. Everything else—responsible parenting, mature adult behavior, moralistic attitudes toward adultery, the importance of marriage and family—is ultimately subordinate to and in the service of a cultural thematics of happiness that is as American as Tacchella's notion of freedom is French.

To clarify my argument, I want to return to the parallel scenes in which Marthe and Ludovic and Maria and Larry originally meet. I quote first from *Cousin, Cousine*, then from *Cousins*:

Ludovic: I change jobs every three years.
Marthe: As soon as you're successful, you make a change.
Ludovic: No, I'm not looking for success.

Larry: I change jobs every two to three years. If it looks like I might be successful, I move on.
Maria: You don't want to be successful?
Larry: I want to be happy.

Despite the obvious similarities, this juxtaposition also points to interesting differences, consistent with those revealed between the two films within a broader comparative context. Ludovic is completely indifferent to success, a notion that Marthe introduces into the conversation, as well as to anything else that might tie him to a particular profession; he changes jobs systematically and on principle, in keeping with the permanent commitment to freedom that characterizes him and informs Tacchella's film as a whole. In the revised version of this exchange, Larry replaces freedom with happiness, a value he sets in explicit opposition to that of success. He thus identifies a dialectics of personal happiness and professional success that is fundamental not only to Schumacher's remake but also to an understanding of American culture in general.

References to happiness as well as the word itself punctuate the dialogue of *Cousins*. Larry, for example, banters encouragingly with the senior citizens whom he is teaching to dance the cha-cha: "Happy, happy, happy—it's okay to smile." On the day they go swimming, the contentment of Larry ("I would die a happy man just now") and Maria ("It's a long time since I've been this happy") spreads to the world around them ("Fish must be so happy"). In conversation with her mother, Maria appeals to happiness to justify her attraction to Larry:

Double Takes

Maria: I haven't been happy with Tom in a long time.
Edie: Who says you're supposed to be happy?
Maria: Excuse me. I dare to want to be happy.

Later, however, when she says goodbye to Larry, Maria worries that "maybe people aren't supposed to be happy."

Among these, and many other, examples, the first two are particularly revealing, for Larry consistently defines happiness through the metaphors of dance and of movement through or on the water. Schumacher, of course, does the same thing visually, notably when he crosscuts between Larry and Maria making love and Vince and Edie dancing on a ship. Similarly, toward the end of *Cousins*, just before Larry finally asks Maria to dance, Schumacher represents Larry's point of view through a series of alternating shots of Maria's face and of a sailboat on the lake. Larry articulates his philosophy of happiness to Maria on the first afternoon they spend together, when he takes her to see his sailboat: "Isn't that what everyone wants? A smooth-sailing life. It can be achieved for a minute out on the dance floor—or the water." His dream to "sail off into the sunset," which Maria initially dismisses as a sign of Larry's "rich fantasy life," nonetheless finds literal realization in the final shot of the film, an image whose already quite evident romanticism is further reinforced by its juxtaposition with the immediately preceding family portrait framed in black and white through the lens of Mitch's video camera. Throughout *Cousins*, however, Schumacher's aesthetic preferences, which often distinguish the American movie from its original French model, for a slower rhythm, a more fully developed narrative, parallel editing, transition by dissolves, and analogous structures combine to produce a consistently "smooth-sailing" film.

Not surprisingly, given the frequency of Franco-American comparisons in cross-cultural studies, French intellectuals have traditionally figured among the most astute cultural commentators of the United States. Indeed, as I noted earlier, virtually all attempts to understand the distinctiveness of American culture pay homage to Alexis de Tocqueville, who published the first such analysis, now a seminal work, in 1835. By chance, a much more recent contribution to the genre, which as a whole has produced remarkably consistent results over the years, renews previous interpretations in at least one way that is curiously reminiscent of how Schumacher remakes Tacchella's film. Hervé Varenne, whose book *Americans Together* (1977) is based on his experience of "everyday life" in a small town in the United States, is particularly struck by "the constant talk of happiness" that he hears around him (180). Admittedly, one need not be a cultural anthropologist to realize that "the pursuit of happiness" is not one of the officially declared rights of the citizens of France (or that *liberté* is, and in first place, as illustrated by that country's motto). Most French observers, however, simply tend either to take for granted Americans' puzzling belief in happiness or to dismiss it with a Gallic shrug as an unfortunate, but incomprehensible, obstacle to true cross-cultural understanding. Varenne, in contrast, looks more closely and discovers that happiness is an inherently relational concept that, on the one hand, never applies to individuals alone and, on the other, most often applies to marriage. (Hence the montage of isolation and unhappiness that intervenes in Schumacher's film between the original formation of the couple and its final confirmation.) In short, Varenne defines (American) happiness as "the realization of love in interpersonal relations" and argues provocatively that love represents the fundamental precept that underlies the organization of social interaction in the United States (202).

At the same time, Varenne himself points out on several occasions that he is quite aware of "how astonishing it is" not simply to use the category of love in a sociological analysis but, more important, to ignore America as a "capitalist society" in the process (207). Materialism or an equivalent concept (such as commercialism, obsession with money, cult of success, competitiveness, and so on) probably shows up in comparative studies of American culture more often than any other national trait. Indeed, unlike Varenne, Schumacher complements the discourse of happiness, which dominates his version of *Cousins*, with an important secondary plot that both recalls and critiques the importance of "success" in American society. As the contrasting dialogue quoted earlier suggests, perhaps no American, including Larry, can remain as indifferent to success as Ludovic appears to be in *Cousin, Cousine*. Although Vincent describes his son as "a failure at everything but life," some of Larry's previous professional incarnations (securities analyst, real estate broker) suggest that even he may have flirted with middle-class respectability if not outright prosperity. (Ludovic's jobs, in contrast, appear consistently whimsical—he has studied mushrooms, played the trumpet in a jazz band, and drilled for oil with a buddy in Normandy.)

More generally, in keeping with American cultural myths and values, periodic allusions to success figure in the narrative structure of *Cousins*. Vincent, for example, characterizes his life as an American success story, and his relationship with Edie begins as a joint business adventure. The generally positive context in which financial stability and career achievement are presented within Schumacher's film serves two important functions. On the one hand, it devalues the two characters—Tom and, at least initially, Tish—who are obsessed with money, professional ambition, competition, and collegial rivalry to the exclusion of all else, including their spouses and families. On the other hand, it simultaneously validates the heroes of *Cousins*. In the American film, the nonconformity of the lovers takes the form of indifference to money and to professional success rather than indifference to social conventions and adult responsibilities as in *Cousin, Cousine*. At the same time, in keeping with the American cultural idiom, Maria and Larry also endure a period of separation and suffering so that they can "pay for" their infidelity and "earn" the right to happiness.

I made two statements earlier in this essay that now appear to me to require further consideration. In arguing that the translation of *Cousin, Cousine* as *Cousins*, although perfectly accurate, also points to the substitution of the family unit for the heterosexual couple at the center of the narrative, I may have seemed to suggest that gender concerns as a whole disappear from the American film. Similarly, in attributing the many differences between the French original and the American remake primarily to cultural rather than temporal change, I clearly overlooked the significance that historical context may have *within* a given culture as well as *between* distinctive cultures. The fact that *Cousins* has four central characters and *Cousin, Cousine* only two results in the importance in the American remake of an internally comparative structure that is almost entirely absent from the French original. In *Cousin, Cousine*, virtually no contact occurs between the two women, between the two men, or between Karine and Pascal. The latter represent static fictional types without even minimal psychological complexity: Sleeping Beauty (Karine is only happy during her repeated "sleeping cures") and Casanova. Although these are certainly gendered stereotypes, they are also consistent with the playful fantasy world that surrounds Tacchella's lovers and should not, I think, be interpreted outside of that context. In *Cousins*, however, Schumacher sets up a virtual *chassé-croisé* of similar and contrasting pairs that highlights gender issues within the framework of contemporary American feminism.

Curiously, Schumacher's *Cousins*, filmed fourteen years after Tacchella's *Cousin, Cousine*, nonetheless has a slightly retro air about it in comparison to the original French film. Perhaps remakes inevitably evoke a certain nostalgia, although in this case Schumacher's 1970s referents include not the climate of sexual freedom reflected in Tacchella's film but rather the happy world of the family sitcom, recalled through musical allusions to *Happy Days* and *The Brady Bunch*, and perhaps the countercultural rejection of material success, evoked in Larry's deliberate cult of failure. More than anything, however, the vaguely old-fashioned impression left by *Cousins* comes from the character of Maria as played by Isabella Rossellini.

A "foreigner" both literally and metaphorically, Maria is not only "too good" for Tom but almost too good to be true, at least in the late 1980s. A "Catholic school girl" and a virgin on her wedding day, she remains too modest (or too sexually repressed) to say out loud what it is that she wants Larry to tell her if their spouses are doing. Always dressed in skirts that reach to her ankles, Maria has a soft, almost matronly, prettiness. She is shy, self-effacing and self-sacrificing, and so exceptionally "nice" that even Tish is won over. When Larry asks Maria what she does, she responds with her husband's profession even though she also has a full-time job. Maria defines herself as wife and especially as mother. Her conventional femininity is further reinforced by her frequent juxtaposition to Tish, who contrasts with Maria in almost every way possible. Tish is openly sexy, and her striking beauty is clearly artificially enhanced. She wears short, tight, brightly colored dresses that make her the constant center of (male) attention. She is sexually aggressive and professionally ambitious. She has no children, and she is unfaithful to her husband.

Reviewers tend to adore Isabella Rossellini and to rave, in particular, about her "Madonna-like" quality as Maria. In contrast, they make consistently negative comments about Sean Young's character. Even those critics who find Tish rather charming nonetheless use such terms as "ditsy" to describe her; others prefer "frantic" and "obnoxious" (see, for example, Kael; and Ansen, "Love"). Such a division of opinion seems to reflect the belief that *Cousins* encourages a preference for the traditional wife and mother over the modern career woman. But in that case the critics seem to be watching the wrong movie. At the very least, they badly misinterpret the character of Tish and thus misread Schumacher's film as a whole, which in fact escapes the simplistic dichotomization of what might be called "the *Fatal Attraction* syndrome."

Despite the differences between the central female characters in *Cousins*, both are positively portrayed. Early in the film, Larry describes his wife in the following terms: "Tish is a really good person. She just wants to be appreciated for more than her looks; she's afraid people think she's dumb"; in the course of the film, Tish will prove him right as she increasingly demonstrates competence, intelligence, and sensitivity. In effect, Tish grows up in *Cousins*, and she does so, moreover, in culturally sanctioned ways. She reads self-improvement manuals and learns to "approve of [her] self" so that she no longer needs to seek the approval of men attracted only by her beauty. Tish succeeds in her professional as well as her personal life; by the end of the film, she has been promoted three times and has advanced from trying to sell makeup to fellow wedding guests to heading her own department. Much more confident and mature, Tish leaves Larry by her own choice and with her self-esteem intact. Indeed, her departure, which she welcomes as an overdue opportunity to "face up" to her mother, clearly functions as a declaration of independence. Thus, despite the many differences between Tish and Maria, the one area in which they reach total agreement reaffirms the intelligence and good judgment that the two women share. Tish, in fact, sets an example that justifies Maria's eventual decision to leave Tom by her own prior rejection of a man whom she too dismisses as insensitive and irresponsible.

Schumacher accomplishes something quite remarkable for the director of a mainstream Hollywood movie. On the one hand, *Cousins*, like a great many other films, creates two contrasting female characters, who not only select radically different roles from among the choices available to women, but who also exist within a narrative that explicitly positions them as rivals. On the other hand, the choices of both women prove equally valid and valuable, each views the other more as ally than as enemy, and the audience ends up liking and respecting both. I certainly have no reason to believe that Joel Schumacher sought to make an explicitly feminist film nor would I characterize *Cousins* in such terms; its women characters no doubt owe more to reality than to ideology. Yet *Cousins* does show us a picture of contemporary women that accurately reflects the evolution and cultural influence of the feminist movement in the United States. As many others have pointed out, American feminism no longer fits, if it ever did, either of two perfectly contradictory media images: it is not a monolithic movement nor can it be constructed as a "catfight," either among feminists or between feminists and non-feminists (see, for example, Douglas and Faludi). Modern America has long offered women a number of different acceptable roles, and the pluralistic discourse of contemporary feminist voices may be nothing more than a confirmation, like Schumacher's own film, of this new freedom. Many feminist writers, for example, have recently reclaimed the right to such traditionally feminine concerns as beauty and clothes for career women like Tish (such as Naomi Wolf); others have turned back after years of political activism to the essential importance of self-esteem (a problem for Maria as well as Tish) in order to escape from a history of negative relationships with men (such as Gloria Steinem). Few feminists have been hostile to women, like Maria, who choose to define themselves as wives and mothers, but, in any event, Betty Friedan, whose *Feminine Mystique* may have been responsible for the belief that they were, has since written *The Second Stage*, which emphasizes the importance that the family retains for most women and encourages the active participation of men in feminism as a prerequisite for the transformation of gender roles and the achievement of gender equity.[7]

In terms of changing male roles, Larry, appropriately enough, recalls the heroes of *Three Men and a Baby* (1988) and *Three Men and a Little Lady* (1990). (Indeed, by choosing family and fidelity over career and seduction, this time Ted Danson finally ends up with the wife and the daughter that his character loses in *Three Men*.) In particular, Larry offers us an image of the "New Man" similar to that which emerges from Nimoy's and Ardolino's films of the same period. The multiple internal comparisons within *Cousins*, however, now introduce further complexity into old—and new—questions of gender difference. Larry is gentle, sensitive, kind, family-oriented, and a good parent; he is nonaggressive, refuses to fight, and does not measure his self-worth by his success as a breadwinner. By embracing traditionally female values and rejecting traditionally male ones, Larry becomes a radically different (and better) kind of man.[8] Yet Maria, who resembles him like a twin sister for her similar fidelity to traditional femininity and traditional female roles, nonetheless seems a bit old-fashioned, as I have noted earlier. Two characters who share the identical traits are differently valued because of their sex. This might seem to be a new version of a very old story, were it not that Schumacher simultaneously remakes it, in reverse.

By rejecting traditional female traits and roles (such as dependence upon men and sexual passivity) and embracing traditionally male ones (such as ambition, career, sexual freedom, and independence), Tish presents within the context of the film a positive image of a nonconventional woman. At the same time, *her* twin, who exhibits all the standard traits and values of conventional manhood (such as sexual prowess, aggression, competitiveness, and workaholism), appears to be left over from another era. More important, Tom is devalued not simply as the representative of an outmoded form of masculinity but explicitly because of the attitudes he holds towards women as a result. Tom himself equates his skill as a car salesman with his success with women ("That's the thing in sales; you have to concentrate on the women"), and the attempted sale is his favorite alibi for marital infidelity. Thus, by his own admission, Tom's entire life is given over to the constant need to prove himself sexually. Throughout the film, at every family gathering, both the script and the camera repeatedly associate Tom with two other men, clearly comic characters, whose sole preoccupation is evaluating women's bodies and speculating on the possibility of having sex with them. In the version of the magic show that concludes the final wedding in Schumacher's *Cousins*, one of these men is about to be sawed in half at a point that quite clearly corresponds to his genitals. It is difficult not to interpret this scene as a metaphoric and much needed emasculation—or rather de-masculinization—of Tom and of any other men who still resemble him.

I have thought a good deal about how this chapter differs from those that precede it, just as I considered a number of alternative ways to approach and to structure this comparison. In the final analysis, however, I do not think it is simply self-serving to conclude that the length of this discussion, as well as the amount of space that I have devoted to each film in isolation from the other, is a direct consequence of the films themselves and particularly of the relationship between them. Distant relatives at best, despite their unquestionable family resemblance, and constantly unfaithful to each other, Schumacher's *Cousins* comes as close to a total reconceptualization of Tacchella's *Cousin, Cousine* as any pair of films I have yet explored. Such an enactment of infidelity, however, confirms the general value of comparing American remakes with the original French films on which they are based in order to perceive and to analyze cross-cultural differences. (Indeed, in this case, the tendency of some reviewers to describe *Cousins* as an "Americaniza-tion" rather than a "remake" seems entirely appropriate, although one cannot but wish that the critics in question had at least *seen* the French original [see O'Brien].) At the same time, the comparison of *Cousin, Cousine* and *Cousins* also reveals that different Franco-American pairings will produce different in-sights, including in the area of gender and culture. If the study of *Trois Hommes et un couffin*, *Three Men and a Baby*, and *Three Men and a Little Lady* led me to conclude that cultural context directly affects how an essen-tially similar discourse of gender will be differently inscribed, the comparison of *Cousin, Cousine* and *Cousins* appears to reverse this process. The discus-sion of gender here plays a subordinate and supportive role that primarily identifies and defines important differences between French and American culture. I am reminded once again of the excellent advice offered in *CinémAction*'s special issue on Franco-American remakes to avoid "con-structing a theory of the remake too hastily" (M. Serceau 9).

Other Ways of Looking

Re-Visions of Feminism and Film Theory in François Truffaut's and Blake Edwards's *The Man Who Loved Women*

As the visual practice of the verbal theory advocated by *Cahiers du cinéma*, New Wave French cinema literally read and wrote itself into existence. Indeed, according to Jacques Aumont, *Cahiers'* conception of filmmaking as an extension of its own initial function meant that "each individual film would therefore be a re-reading, a re-writing, of the entire history of cinema" (222), an ambition clearly evident in Jean-Luc Godard's *A Bout de souffle*. If François Truffaut's dual role as the *Cahiers* critic who theorized the auteur ("Une Certaine Tendance") and the director who made such films as *Les Quatre Cents Coups* (1959) and *Jules et Jim* (1961) assures his reputation within the context of the *nouvelle vague*, his subsequent career seems to many to have been a virtual revision of its own beginnings. By the mid-1970s Truffaut is generally perceived not only to have abandoned the New Wave innovations of his earlier films but to have begun to author precisely the kind of mainstream cinema he had previously critiqued. Moreover, a filmmaker once highly praised for his originality, he is increasingly accused of repeating himself, in part, no doubt, as a result of his periodic return to the Antoine Doinel cycle begun in *Les Quatre Cents Coups* (see, for example, Forbes 105–11). Still, this is far from the only evidence one could cite of what seems clearly to have been on Truffaut's part both an entirely consistent and a fully conscious commitment to exploring multiple patterns of recurrence. The curious question is why critics not only end up lamenting what they originally find fascinating but why they fail even to recognize the same and the similar upon their return.

L'Homme qui aimait les femmes (1977), for example, is nothing if not internally repetitive within Truffaut's career, a fact readily pointed out by the director himself, who also appears within the film, in both the aptly named *Truffaut par Truffaut* (154–57) and *Le Cinéma selon François Truffaut* (353–

67). Truffaut explicitly conceived *L'Homme* as a vehicle for Charles Denner who reprised in Bertrand Morane an extended version of the same character he had played ten years before in *La Mariée était en noir* (1967). Moreover, the death of the hero, whose hearse Truffaut salutes during the opening credit sequence of *L'Homme*, results from the visualization of an anecdote first recounted in the even earlier *Tirez sur le pianiste* (1959), itself an homage to American film noir that no doubt further justifies Truffaut's brief cameo à la Hitchcock. Truffaut's Morane may not be directly inspired by either Don Juan or Casanova, as the character insists within the film and the director without, but Truffaut simultaneously acknowledges that he "was working on something mythical"; and the description of Morane, again both intradiegetic and extradiegetic, as "simply *a man*" no doubt grants him an even broader field of potential reference than would the imitation of any particular masculine model, however multivalent and recurrent.

The autocitational practices out of which *L'Homme qui aimait les femmes* was originally generated make its subsequent reproduction as an American remake, in the form of Blake Edwards's *The Man Who Loved Women* (1983), seem not merely inevitable but almost necessary. *CinémAction* proposes that Edwards's interest actually resulted from the recognition that *L'Homme qui aimait les femmes* resembled his own *10* (1979) (Protopopoff, "Sur Quelques Films" 110), a theory that would be fully consistent with Truffaut's desire to depict a certain kind of generic male character. If Edwards initially saw *The Man Who Loved Women* as a sort of sequel to an earlier film of his own, however, his transformation of the Morane character from a writer into a sculptor also curiously recalls Truffaut's own precursory film, *La Mariée était en noir*, in which Charles Denner originally played a painter.

The cinematic allusions favored by New Wave directors and the recurrent phenomenon of the remake are, of course, far from the only examples of a fondness for repetition and revision that appears to be virtually coextensive with the history of cinema and perhaps even integral to its constitution as an art form. Lucy Fischer recently categorized feminist films in general as "'remakes' of the canon" (*Shot/Countershot* 16); and the work that she singles out as the best example, a film that expands this practice to the point that it "swallows the dominant cinema whole" (302), happens to be a film by Yvonne Rainer entitled *The Man Who Envied Women* (1985). Despite the suggestiveness of the title, of which the director says only that it "came very early" to her (44), Rainer's film is not a direct remake of Truffaut's (or Edwards's) *L'Homme qui aimait les femmes* but rather an extraordinarily complex (re)reading of classical narrative cinema as a whole and of contemporary film theory as well. Moreover, *The Man Who Envied Women* simultaneously exposes the Franco-American text for which it is named as a virtual textbook illustration of both. In the ensuing discussion of Truffaut's *L'Homme qui aimait les femmes* and

Edwards's *The Man Who Loved Women*, I intend to include Rainer's text in the mediating role that it already plays for the films themselves. That this explicit use of "bifocality," the inclusion of "at least a third case" that Michael M. J. Fischer considers essential to "successful cross-cultural comparison" (199), first occurred in the analysis above of another New Wave film and its remake, Godard's *A Bout de souffle* and McBride's *Breathless*, reaffirms the importance of "repetition with a difference" (Ellis 34) within not only the *nouvelle vague* but also modern cinema as a whole.

The structure of Truffaut's *L'Homme qui aimait les femmes*, as *its* title suggests, respects the repetitive pattern of the central character's obsession. Indeed, in keeping with the use of the past tense, the story of Bertrand Morane's undying passion for women would have no reason ever to end were the hero not already dead when the film begins.[1] Thus the narrative of Bertrand's successive encounters with women, most of which he recalls in order to record them in the novel he has decided to write, unfolds within the framework of his funeral as witnessed by Geneviève Bigey (Brigitte Fossey), the editor of his book, in the opening and closing shots of Truffaut's film. Edwards retains the general narrative structure of the French original in his American remake, although the funeral of David Fowler (Burt Reynolds) is attended by his analyst Marianna (Julie Andrews), to whom David relates his amorous adventures in the course of Edwards's version of *The Man Who Loved Women*. An initial comparison would therefore seem to suggest one of two patterns: either differences of quantity rather than quality—Bertrand remembers far more women than does David—or the direct substitution of similar kinds of things—the sculptor for the novelist, the analyst for the editor—that seem essentially superficial and even arbitrary. Indeed, despite Georges Santoni's usual attentiveness to the significance of cultural differences and the general validity of the methodology he uses for this purpose, which I tested in an earlier comparison of *Cousin, Cousine* and *Cousins*, one would have to include the actual examples he cites in just such a category:

> French people do not necessarily organize their visual production and perception in the same way as Americans do. One needs only to compare a few clips of an original French film with its American remake to be convinced of this fact and to convince students. As one good example, compare the first fifty shots of François Truffaut's *The Man Who Loved Women* with Blake Edwards' American remake: from Montpellier to eternal California, from Jaubert to Mancini, from writer to sculptor, from editor to psychologist, from mini-coopers to limousines, there is a world of difference. ("Visual Images" 68)

I have nonetheless reproduced Santoni's words in their entirety in order to return to them later. In fact, he is right that a "world of difference" separates the two films and even that a comparison of their opening sequences makes this visible, although he does not provide—nor do we yet have—enough information to undertake this analysis effectively.

Edwards retains Truffaut's title, *L'Homme qui aimait les femmes*, for his own version of *The Man Who Loved Women*. Such concordance between an original French film and its American remake does not occur as often as one might expect, if only because a rigorously literal translation that respects syntax as well as meaning—what translation theory calls a *calque*—is often linguistically impossible (as in *A Bout de souffle/Breathless* and *Cousin, Cousine/ Cousins*). Frequently, however, change is introduced even when it is totally unnecessary, as if to mark the very fact that repetition inevitably results in difference (as in *Trois Hommes et* **un couffin**/*Three Men and* **a Baby**; *Les Fugitifs*/*The* **Three** *Fugitives*; and *Le* **Grand Blond** *avec une chaussure* **noire**/*The* **Man** *with* **One Red** *Shoe*). In the case of Truffaut and Edwards, the title shared by the French original and the American remake encodes and repeats the importance of gender and, at least potentially, that of the past as well. Within this framework, confirmed by the reprisal at the beginning and the end of each film of the hero's funeral, at which only women are present, some scenes are retained (though often altered and differently contextualized, issues to which I will return) while others are either omitted or added. The first group, I will argue, presents gender stereotypes perceived as universal and therefore transcultural; these tend to show how men—and film—traditionally view women. The second group, in contrast, which includes scenes that focus more exclusively on men, reveals masculinity to be a culturally specific social and historical construction.

Of the more than twenty women whose names Truffaut's hero can still recall (the fear of forgetting theirs too partially motivates Bertrand to write), Edwards retains only six, two of whom play far more episodic roles in the French original than several of those who disappear entirely from the American remake. Both versions of the film begin with a similarly paradigmatic passage in which a passing glimpse of the legs of an unknown—indeed, an *unseen*— woman drives the hero to unusual lengths, first, metaphorically, to discover her identity, and then, literally, to track her down in a city some distance away. In both cases, Bertrand and David succeed in meeting the woman in question—Martine (Nathalie Baye) or Agnes (Marilu Henner)—only to learn that the legs they saw really belong to her cousin, who has since returned to Canada. In some sense, then, Truffaut and Edwards inaugurate the amorous adventures of their heroes under the sign of failure; indeed, this is inevitable, since the search for an elusive ideal, for the perfect incarnation of female beauty, is precisely what keeps Bertrand and David on the prowl. "Failure," however, remains a relative concept, since it takes place in the realm of the hypothetical, rather than in that of the real or of the sexual. At any given moment, beginning with this first example, the two men always discover a willing and "perfectly," if only temporarily, acceptable version of the ideal they seek. Since only death can end the quest, Edwards also retains the final woman in Truffaut's film, who is at once the double and the necessary counterpart of the first. Bertrand and David are hit by cars as they rush into busy holiday traffic in pursuit of yet another vision of female legs; and both subsequently die reaching toward a literal realization of their Platonic ideal, the transitory reflection of a nurse's legs outlined against her uniform in the doorway of their hospital rooms.[2]

To the extent that Truffaut introduces—and Edwards retains—a "real" exemplar of the hero's feminine ideal, she appropriately figures in both films in episodes that stand out for their structural centrality and their extended narrative development. Beyond superficial differences of name and national identity, Delphine (Nelly Borgeaud) and Lulu (Kim Basinger) are fundamentally alike: capricious, contradictory, and consistent only in their unpredictability. They are also eager, passionate, and exciting lovers who prefer to have sex in unusual and semi-public situations (such as cars, department stores, and stadium boxes) where the risk of discovery, including by their husbands, is always acute. Both will eventually shoot their husbands after deliberately arousing their jealousy and suspicions. In short, Delphine and Lulu are a comic version of the femme fatale. They incarnate traditional Western associations of sexual passion with danger and violence; and their initiation of sex in any place and at any time makes them the perfect realization of the popular media's portrayal of a standard male fantasy. Thus the adventures of the "man who loved women" with this *particular* woman stand as a microcosmic version, a *mise en abyme*, of the film as a whole that serves, in particular, to explore the single reality behind the constant (con)fusion that Truffaut and Edwards create between women as individuals and Woman as eternal essence. The emptiness that inevitably follows the arrests of Delphine and Lulu plunges both Bertrand and David into an extended period of depression and chastity, whose origins the Frenchman perceptively articulates: "I finally had to admit to myself what really mattered: with Delphine I had never been bored! Because she was all women rolled into one, Delphine could not be replaced by any single woman."

With the fourth type of woman whom Edwards directly borrows from Truffaut, he once again retains what comparison increasingly reveals to be the original film's system of parallel patterning. Both *L'Homme qui aimait les femmes* and *The Man Who Loved Women* include a single example, but one present throughout the film, of a woman with whom Bertrand and David could have had an affair but didn't; rather each rescued her from difficult circumstances and gave her a permanent job as his assistant. This "exception that proves the rule" clearly functions as the counterpart of the sexually obsessed character of Delphine and Lulu and demonstrates that the hero, far from reducing all women to the status of sexual objects or even that of past, present, and future lovers, is, in fact, also a chivalrous savior and protector of vulnerable women.

The final two episodes incorporated directly into Edwards's remake from Truffaut's film confirm the use of what appears to be doubling or repetition in order ultimately to conflate the multiple into the single, the different into the same. In this case the two passages follow each other immediately; indeed, their sequentiality provides the visual evidence that confirms the analogies simultaneously announced in voice-over by the hero. The sequence unfolds in three stages; my description is based on *L'Homme qui aimait les femmes*, which the American remake essentially reproduces somewhat more concisely. The color film changes to black-and-white footage as Bertrand recalls his initiation into sex by a prostitute, an experience he claims as characteristically male: "Like nine out of ten men of my generation, my first erotic memory is a memory of a bordello." Although the fourteen-year-old Bertrand originally goes upstairs with an older woman, she proposes her own replacement by a younger and prettier prostitute whom she judges better suited to the boy's youth and inexperience. To this "generous initiative" Bertrand attributes not only a pleasant memory of his first sexual encounter but also, and more important, "a lifelong fondness [*un goût qui ne s'est jamais démenti*] for the women one meets in the street."

The deliberate ambivalence of this designation—"women *one meets* in the street" (and not, as in the American remake, the unambiguous but consequently less effective "women *of* the streets")—serves as a subtle transition to the second stage of the sequence. Truffaut's hero challenges the theory that "virtuous women" can be distinguished from prostitutes by the speed at which they walk. The narrator first recalls a prostitute whose rapid pace served as an erotic stimulus to potential clients, who could briefly fantasize that they were about to seduce "une bourgeoise," and then he immediately goes on to note that "my mother also walked very quickly." The visualization of the scenes described, which we see unfold simultaneously on screen, unquestionably confirms the implication of the words we hear, for the two women who successively walk rapidly down the street, pursued by the stares of male bystanders, are played by the same actress. This relatively matter-of-fact revelation that his mother was a prostitute is followed by the hero's similarly straightforward and still implicit, although now predictable, indictment of her as a mother: "Everything in the way she behaved toward me as a little boy seemed to say: 'I would have done better to break my leg the day I gave birth to this little idiot.'" Indeed, although Truffaut certainly encourages the spectator to interpret his hero's subsequent actions and character development as the direct consequence of Christine Morane's (M. J. Montfajon) profession and comportment, Bertrand not only never complains but indirectly portrays himself more as a jealous and unsuccessful rival for his mother's affections than as her unloved and rejected son.[3]

The third segment of this sequence shifts from the past back to the present and from the personal to the general. Bertrand rhapsodizes over the beautiful spectacle of women in motion, irrespective of their particular rhythms or their actual physical attractiveness. He once again proceeds to divide all women into two categories but this time accurately, that is, not by the presence or absence of "virtue" but by body type: "les grandes tiges" (tall saplings) and "les petites pommes" (little knobs). His seasonal analysis—after four months of female "hibernation" that marks the desolation of winter, women suddenly reappear "by the dozens" at the first sign of March sunshine and "then life begins again"—confers an almost mythical status and function on women. At the same time, however, Truffaut's "man who loved women" reminds us that they are all fundamentally indistinguishable, reducible to a never-ending parade of available prey whose "bodies are there for the taking" since "they want the same thing I do, they want love." Constant shots of female bodies and particularly female legs walking through the streets, which accompany Bertrand's ode to female sexual availability, underscore what now clearly appears as the message of the sequence as a whole. Women spend their time walking through the streets offering their bodies, literally as well as metaphorically, to the men who watch them—or, to state it more directly, all women are prostitutes.

Feminist film theory, whose rapid and increasingly important development also began in the mid-1970s, has remained a predominantly Anglo-American phenomenon, both in terms of the national origins of its principal practitioners and of the Hollywood model of classical narrative cinema that has been the most frequent target of feminist critique. Hence the "surprising omission" of France from the special issue that *Camera Obscura* devoted in 1989 to Laura Mulvey's work: "There is a distinct absence of film theory written in France that is concerned with feminist theory" (Bergstrom & Doane 22). Nonetheless, as Yvonne Rainer clearly realized, the sexual dynamics of looking in *L'Homme qui aimait les femmes* makes Truffaut's French film a literally "picture-perfect" illustration of feminist concerns about the cinema and especially those of Mulvey. Since "Visual Pleasure and Narrative Cinema," Mulvey's highly influential essay, appeared in 1975, feminist film criticism has been dominated by discussion of the sexual divisions within cinematic address, as I noted in an earlier discussion of *French in Action*. Indeed, Judith Mayne concluded in a 1985 review essay in *Signs* that "it is only a slight exaggeration to say that most feminist film theory . . . of the last decade has been a response, implicit or explicit, to the issues raised in Laura Mulvey's article: the centrality of the look, cinema as spectacle and narrative, psychoanalysis as a critical tool" (83; see also Bergstrom & Doane). Mulvey originally argued that "in a world ordered by sexual imbalance, pleasure in looking has been split between active/male and passive/female" (62). This tendency to position men as the subject of the cinematic gaze and women as its object turns mainstream film into a "voyeuristic enterprise," essentially devoted to the fetishistic display of the female body or what Mulvey calls the visual objectification of women as "to-be-looked-at-ness" (62).

That *L'Homme qui aimait les femmes* is crucially concerned with "the centrality of the look" (Mayne 83) should already be quite evident. Truffaut's film includes innumerable scenes in which Bertrand's gaze tracks women through the streets, stores, and restaurants of Montpellier. His voyeuristic tendencies are underscored by his persistent attraction to unknown women and by his ready habit of following them home. Truffaut's camera privileges shot/countershot sequences that first establish the hero's point of view as dominant and then linger on the female bodies that are the focus of his gaze. His fetishistic attachment to women's legs in particular frequently results in the visual dismemberment of the female body. Notably, the film opens and closes with scenes that show us the legs of the women at Bertrand's funeral from the position of the deceased, who, as Geneviève notes in voice-over, "is well placed to look one last time at what he loved best about us." Moreover, the disembodied legs that frame the film reappear on several occasions within the text in the form of the hero's hallucination. Their materialization out of nowhere and their projection onto or superimposition over the external reality that actually constitutes Bertrand's visual frame of reference at once equate the hero's look with the screening of the cinematic image and identify the content of both as male fantasy. Thus the pair of legs for which he is prepared to die appropriately appear to be backlit against a white screen formed by the nurse's uniform.

In other ways as well Truffaut foregrounds the problematics of the gendered gaze as specifically constitutive of "cinema as spectacle and narrative" (Mayne 83). Bertrand first discovers the pleasure of looking in the curious games of hide-and-seek initiated by a female playmate, a childhood event that his memory repositions within the filmic narrative so that it follows immediately upon his first sexual encounter—a displacement that occurs in part, no doubt, because the prostitute and the young girl just happen to share the same name. The "innocent" version of Bertrand's early experiments with desire involves chasing Ginette through the many corridors and doorways of her parents' apartment until they collapse onto a couch, games that are always "pimentés" (spiced up) by her insistence on first turning off the lights. This dialectics of light and dark, of movement and desire—repeated throughout the film in the numerous "motion pictures" of women walking, their bodies outlined in silhouette—once again metaphorically recalls the "voyeuristic enterprise" that according to Mulvey defines cinema as a whole. Bertrand's narrative voice explicitly confirms this association: "Thus it was while playing with Ginette that I came to understand that the company of women was in-dispensable to me or, if not their company, then *at least the sight of them*. For me, nothing was more beautiful *to watch* than *a woman who was walking*" (my emphasis).

L'Homme qui aimait les femmes also contains an explicit scene of *mise en abyme* that further clarifies the conflation of film with the visual construction of a male fantasy world. During a brief period of solitude, Bertrand's endless quest for the indispensable sight of women ("or, if not their company, then at least the sight of them") takes him into a movie theater "where a documentary was playing—I who have always loved only fiction." What may well be an ironic allusion to the *cinéma vérité* practiced by the first generation of New Wave directors, many of whom began their careers in the audience of the Paris *cinémathèque* where they were as likely to view the ethnographic films of Jean Rouch as Hollywood film noir, serves to recall the identification between the director and his fictional hero that is established in the opening scene of the film, where Truffaut is the only (other) man present at Bertrand's funeral. More important, however, this breakdown of generic boundaries an-nounces the inversion of fact and fiction, the substitution of the theater audi-torium for the movie screen, or, rather, the definitive extension of cinematic fantasy into the gendered world of "reality." "That evening the spectacle was in the audience," Bertrand quickly realizes, as he watches the usher insis-tently use her flashlight to light up her own pretty legs rather than to show lat-ecomers to their seats. Moreover, when Bertrand succeeds in seducing Ni-cole (Roselyne Puyo) on a return visit to the theater, he discovers in her the ideal object of the desiring male gaze. Like her cinematic counterpart, this off-screen vision can neither hear nor speak (back); she is, in short, the pure incarnation of what Mulvey calls the "to-be-looked-at-ness" of women that lies at the origins of cinema.

Similarly, Delphine's exhibitionist tendencies no doubt contribute to the exceptional status she enjoys among the women Bertrand encounters. Al-though she willingly offers her body to the male gaze, a fact she even occa-sionally admits ("When I left the table to go upstairs, it was so that you would look at me"), she most often engages in a pretense of denial and sometimes outright interdiction ("I forbid you to look at my legs") that provides the illicit pleasure characteristic of voyeurism. E. Ann Kaplan argues that the prosti-tute—for Bertrand, the prototype of the women he loves—most perfectly cap-tures this sense of "split subjectivity" in which the woman both becomes the object of the male look and remains a subject, since she is fully aware of her self-presentation for men and consciously uses her body as spectacle (39). Such a foregrounding of the viewing process no doubt has the potential to dis-rupt its usual dynamics, particularly in terms of distinguishing the theoretical positioning of the spectator, the issue that concerns me here, from the actual viewing experience of a given man or woman—a subject to which revisionists of Mulvey, including Mulvey herself, have increasingly turned their attention (see Mulvey, "Afterthoughts"; and Bergstrom & Doane).

Feminist film criticism, beginning with Mulvey, inherited "psychoanalysis as a critical tool" (Mayne 83) from such French theorists as Jean-Louis Baudry, Raymond Bellour, and Christian Metz, who dominated film analysis in the 1970s. In general terms, psychoanalytical studies draw upon the work of Freud and Lacan to establish an analogy between the movie screen and the fantasy world of the unconscious. Metz, in particular, equates pleasure in looking (scopophilia) and the voyeurism of film viewing with a regression to childhood (Hayward, *French* 227). More specifically, in addition to this metaphoric interpretation of the cinematic apparatus as a whole, psychoanalytic critics follow Bellour's example in also reading individual texts within the framework of Freudian theory; particularly common, according to Susan Hayward, has been "talk of male representation/characterization as a reiteration of the Oedipus story" (*French* 228). Although Truffaut's own contributions to film theory clearly predate the dominance of psychoanalytic criticism by over a decade, the movie whose release coincided with the period of their greatest influence nonetheless lends itself remarkably well to Freudian analysis.

One hardly needs to read Truffaut's explanation in the "Avant-Propos" to the *cinéroman* based on *L'Homme qui aimait les femmes* to understand that the hero of his film suffers from an unresolved Oedipal complex: "If one sentence could function as the common denominator for Bertrand's love affairs, it would be that of Bruno Bettelheim in *The Empty Fortress*: 'It appeared that Joey had never known success in relation to his mother.'" Bertrand's mother simultaneously arouses her son's sexual desire and denies his very existence: "My mother was in the habit of walking around half naked, not, of course, in order to arouse me but rather, I imagine, in order to confirm to herself that I didn't exist." Thus Bertrand seeks to satisfy his desire for the rejecting and forbidden mother in every woman he meets. Even his decision to narrate the story of his life by describing all the women he has ever loved is explicitly modeled on his mother's habit of carefully documenting her own sexual adventures; and the publisher of Bertrand's completed manuscript immediately identifies it, on the basis of a single passage, as "the story of a womanizer who has remained a child." Indeed, there is nothing remotely subtle about the structure and the significance of Truffaut's film within the context of Freudian theory. Most of Bertrand's lovers, for example, quite obviously recall his mother in terms of character and behavior: Nicole rejects her own young son to be with Bertrand; Ginette, who similarly ignores the baby brother she is supposed to be babysitting, is the subject of fond memories that stem from the perception that his mother was jealous; Delphine alternately offers and refuses her body; and so on. In addition, in the course of the narrative process itself, the constitutive act of psychoanalysis in the view of such theorists as Roy Schafer and Peter Brooks, Bertrand's repetition in the present of events he has unconsciously repressed leads constantly to the resurgence of the past (see also Gillain, *François Truffaut* 254ff).

Although Freudian ideas in general have traditionally met with far greater scepticism in the United States than in France, not only as part of a therapeutic practice but also—and perhaps even more so—as the theoretical foundation of an intellectual and artistic tradition,[4] the American remake of *L'Homme qui aimait les femmes* nonetheless explicitly reframes Truffaut's entire film within the context of psychoanalysis. David enters classical Freudian therapy for treatment of anxiety and depression, and his appointments with Marianna both establish the visual rhythm of Edwards's film and form its narrative core, thus repeating, but differently, the recurrent scenes of Bertrand writing that serve similar functions in the original French version of *L'Homme*. Since David is also a professional sculptor, whose work therefore specifically centers on visual imagery, and since he literally undergoes in the course of Edwards's film what his analyst classifies as a "regressive experience" in which "David, the child" temporarily reemerges, one might well expect that the dominant interests of feminist film theory—"the centrality of the look, cinema as spectacle and narrative, psychoanalysis as a critical tool" (Mayne 83)—would find Edwards's remake to be an even more promising text for analysis than Truffaut's original. Initially, however, this seems not to be the case because of two significant ways in which the American version of the film differs from its French model.

In the first place, with the exception of those scenes, described above, that Edwards simply incorporates into his own film without revision, the American remake provides little direct evidence that its hero is a "man who loves women," let alone an American equivalent of a "wolf" (*coureur*), a "womanizer" (*cavaleur*), or a "ladies man" (*homme à femmes*), all self-definitions that his French counterpart considers reasonably appropriate to his own situation. Indeed, in the remake, the past tense of the title appears to refer less to the fact that the story as a whole unfolds after its hero's death than to the change that has taken place within him just prior to that period of his life related in the film. For example, the identical scene with which both films open (the hero's obsessive search for a second glimpse of a woman's legs) functions quite differently in each case. Whereas it serves in *L'Homme qui aimait les femmes* to establish a present and typical pattern of behavior that Bertrand will incessantly repeat, David, for whom the event is already in the past, specifically recalls it in order to convince Marianna—and, perhaps more urgently, the audience of the film—that his current state of paralysis is "out of character." Consequently, however, *The Man Who Loved Women* does not actually portray its hero in visual terms as a man whose life revolves around the voyeuristic pleasure of looking at women. There are no scenes of him prowling the streets, an activity on which Bertrand's very life depends, nor does Edwards invite the spectator to view the women in the film from the perspective of David's "male gaze." (Indeed, if anyone is visually objectified as the target of desire, it is far more likely to be David himself, an issue to which I will return.) In fact, apart from the hero's own assertion, Edwards's version of *L'Homme qui aimait les femmes* provides so little evidence of any kind of the knowledge that the audience is nonetheless expected to assume—that David and Bertrand are fundamentally the same type of man—that the American film almost seems to be conceived as much as a sequel to the French original than as a remake.[5]

In the second place, although David suffers from truly disabling psychological problems as an adult and identifies his mother as a prostitute within the specific context of a Freudian analysis, no direct causal connection between the two facts is established in Edwards's film and certainly not one of blame. Rather, David appears to remember a reasonably happy childhood, at least in terms of maternal affection. By his own admission, the bruises he acquired in losing his fights with the kids who taunted him for having "a thousand fathers" were "a small price to pay for his mother's comfort." Moreover, the consequences of his mother's prostitution are very different than they are for Bertrand. Far from resulting in an endless search to replace the maternal love of which he was deprived as a child, his mother's profession explains, as Marianna speculates, "why all women are yearned for, forgiven all, protected." Thus Edwards subsequently treats the transition from the specific case of the hero's love for his mother to his continued interest in "women of the street" literally rather than metaphorically. The next passage in the American remake replaces Bertrand's ecstatic ode to the variety of women who roam the world with the specific example of Nancy (Jennifer Edwards), a young prostitute whom David picks up in order to save her from a life in the streets ("I wanted her, but if I had her, what would her chances be? It earned me time in heaven").

Since Mulvey's inaugural work in feminist film criticism, another theoretical development has privileged a "symptomatic" method of interpretation that seeks to identify moments of textual conflict or incoherence at which mainstream cinema reveals its ideological contradictions (see, for example, Cook, "Approaching"; and Johnston, "Dorothy"). By chance, the scene that opens up such a "gap" or "rupture" within *The Man Who Loved Women* simultaneously confirms the tenets that lie at the foundation of Mulvey's original theory. That elements apparently absent from Edwards's remake reemerge unexpectedly strengthens Mulvey's argument even more forcefully than their constant repetition in Truffaut's original movie. Moreover, the language of criticism turns out to be unusually appropriate to its interpretive functions in the American film, since a textual fissure occurs as the direct result of a real one. An actual earthquake takes place in the middle of one of David's appointments with Marianna, and this geological "release of stress" has similar effects on Edwards's hero.

Prior to this seismic shift, which occurs approximately midway through *The Man Who Loved Women*, David's psychological condition has suddenly worsened as a result of his affair with Lulu, and he has become increasingly dependent on his analyst. From the beginning of the film, David has been frequently shown curled up in fetal position on Marianna's couch, and she now confirms that "he was to be David the child for some time to come." He alternately refuses to cooperate during appointments and phones Marianna in the middle of the night in tears. In Freudian terms, this regression to childhood clearly corresponds to the patient's successful transference onto his doctor as a substitute maternal authority. During the earthquake itself, David panics and wants to leave the building, but Marianna persuades him to lie back down and continue the session. Almost immediately, however, David sits up again, announces that he doesn't "feel like associating anymore," and begins to ask Marianna questions about her personal life. When he lies down a second time, he relates a memory in which he recalls being sexually aroused at the age of eight by the sight of his mother in the bathtub.

Subsequently, David appears to have been miraculously cured; he begins to sculpt again and to behave for the first time in the present of the film like "the man who loved women." Marianna, in contrast, is so uncomfortable with "David on the prowl, David resurrected" that she turns in desperation to Simon Abrams (Joseph Bernard), the doctor with whom she originally underwent psychoanalysis in the course of her own training in Freudian therapy. When Marianna claims that she is particularly troubled by her inability to understand what has caused David's sudden transformation from a "helpless, indecisive, impotent child" into a "lickerish billy goat sniffing the wind for sexual sweat," Simon proposes that she may have caused it herself. More important, however, he warns her not to sleep with David as long as he is her patient, even if, as Marianna readily confirms, she has fallen in love with him. Like Simon's suggestion that Marianna herself is somehow responsible for David's dramatic transformation, her own final speculation is similarly perceptive: "Maybe he's seen some great truth in a mirror that's just not accessible to me—it's liberated him." At the same time, however, both Simon and Marianna are also remarkably obtuse for two psychoanalysts presumably well versed in Freudian and Lacanian theory. Their conversation serves for precisely this reason as an important transition between the earthquake and David's revelation of its significance. In spite of themselves, they provide hints that allow spectators of Edwards's film both to confirm the meaning of

Double Takes

When David (Burt Reynolds) lies back down after the earthquake, he metaphorically discovers that his psychiatrist Marianna (Julie Andrews) is a woman. A mirror has been displaced that now allows him to look up Marianna's dress even though she is still seated in the position of the classical Freudian analyst, behind the patient and out of his sight. *The Man Who Loved Women*. Courtesy of the Stills Archive, Museum of Modern Art, New York. Copyright © 1983, Columbia Pictures, Inc. All rights reserved.

two short sequences that we see along with David and to enjoy our privileged position of understanding.

As a result of the earthquake, David does indeed see a "great truth in a mirror," one that is liberating for him and inaccessible to Marianna, in both cases because of their sex. When David lies back down, he discovers that the shaking of the earth has displaced a mirror so that he is now able to see Marianna, even though she is still seated in the position of the classical Freudian analyst, behind the patient and out of his sight. More particularly, the reflection in the mirror actually reveals Marianna's legs or, rather, her genitals; as David finally confesses, "I could see up your dress." In other words, what he sees for the first time is biological reality: Marianna is (only) a woman. Thus the earthquake, a phenomenon of Nature, restores the natural order of the world. The reempowerment of the male gaze, explicitly voyeuristic and fetishistic, results both in and from the visual objectification and fragmentation of the sexualized female body. The inversion of the dynamics of looking immediately leads to a similar reversal of roles and to a transference of power. David now assumes the right to question Marianna, notably about her marital status, that is, her sexual life, and she will have to seek help from Simon. Metaphorically, control and authority are restored to men (the "father" and the "son," now allied), and the woman (the "mother") is redefined as helpless and submissive. Indeed, Marianna subsequently abandons her professional relationship entirely to become simply a "woman," the latest lover of the man with whom she now announces she is hopelessly in love. David, in turn, recovers from "the tragic state of inertia" that he has always qualified as "impotence" and regains his sexual prowess.

The subsequent memory of sexual arousal at the sight of his mother's naked body also confirms the explicitly Freudian interpretation of the passage. Edwards, deliberately or not, films an astonishingly exact *mise en scène* of Lacan's "mirror stage," the moment at which the male child becomes aware of his own "self" as distinct from the mother, that is, the moment at which he is "gendered" or enters into masculinity. The child's initial fears of castration at the sight of the sexual difference of the mother are countered by scopophilia or the pleasures of voyeurism. In this case, moreover, David repeats the mirror stage as an adult with a "mother" who is not taboo. His love affair with Marianna, who neither rejects him nor withdraws her love when he subsequently leaves her for another woman, finally allows David to achieve a healthy resolution of his Oedipal complex. Even in the specific terms of psychoanalytically informed feminist film theory, *The Man Who Loved Women* proves to be remarkably self-reflexive. Susan Hayward sums up the ideas of Lacanian theorists in a form that seems simultaneously to describe the mirror passage in Edwards's film: "What these authors [Jean-Louis Baudry, Raymond Bellour, Christian Metz] are saying in a nutshell is that at each film viewing there occurs a re-enactment of unconscious processes involved in the acquisition of sexual difference (mirror stage), of language (entry *of* the symbolic) and of autonomous selfhood or subjectivity (entry *into* the symbolic order and rupture with the mother as object of identification) (*French* 227, Hayward's emphasis).

Yvonne Rainer has revealed that the preparation for her fifth film, *The Man Who Envied Women*, included "reading the feminist theories of the last ten years about the way the cinematic gaze 'exploits and controls women's bodies'" (Reynaud qtd. in Rainer 26). I would suspect that this same interest also led her to reflect on the two films to which her title clearly alludes, since Truffaut and Edwards provide such excellent examples of the textual evidence on which that theory is based and which Rainer's own text so radically revises. Even brief consideration of Rainer's film dramatically increases the complexity of this intertextual dialogue, however; I am well aware that the following discussion of her extraordinarily innovative work is incomplete. Indeed, to a

Double Takes

large extent, I will limit my analysis to the opening sequence of *The Man Who Envied Women*, which establishes the framework of the film and introduces the primary narrative and visual strategies that are repeated throughout.

Nonetheless, let me first attempt to provide an overview of a work that no doubt resembles an encyclopedic essay far more than it does even an unconventional film. Rainer herself has noted the impossibility of summary: "I can give a description of the film and make it sound like a Hollywood movie, but the story isn't the main thing. All my films deal with develop[ment] and destruction of the narrative" (qtd. in Fischer, *Shot/Countershot* 305). Trisha, an artist who has recently turned fifty, leaves her husband and, at the same time, literally disappears from sight to become only a disembodied voice. The camera follows her husband Jack as he goes about his normal daily activities. For example, he lectures to his class, seduces a student in his office, eavesdrops on the conversations of others in the street and in restaurants, exercises and reads his mail at home, and contemplates the wall covered with his wife's artwork. Eventually, Jack and a female friend engage in a lengthy discussion of sexual politics in the corridor outside a party. At regular intervals throughout the film, we also hear Trisha's voice as she reflects upon a variety of subjects, including Jack, marriage, female identity, public housing, the role of art in the modern world, and feminism.

Rainer's film begins with a close-up of Jack Deller (William Raymond) whose words—"Doctor, I'll tell you all you want to know about my sex life"— clearly indicate that he is speaking to his psychoanalyst. In the second shot, however, the camera zooms back to reveal that in reality a movie screen figures in the position of the classical Freudian analyst, behind and to the left of Deller. As we watch the opening shots of Buñuel's *Un Chien andalou* projected on this screen, we simultaneously hear the soundtrack of Rainer's film. Trisha (Trisha Brown) complains in voice-over about the difficulties of her personal life in the past week, which began with her separation from Jack and ended with the death of her gynecologist. Just as she pronounces the word *speculum* in the context of the latter event, by far the more tragic of the two, we see Buñuel's famous close-up of a woman's eye being slit by a razor. Rainer then cuts to a coffee shop where the next sequence of the film takes place. After tracking through the shop, the camera returns to rest on Jack Deller (now played by Larry Loonin), who appears to be eavesdropping on a joking conversation critical of men that the two women in the booth behind him are having.

Analogies that remain implicit and metaphoric in Truffaut's *L'Homme qui aimait les femmes* and Edwards's *The Man Who Loved Women* become an integral part of the text in *The Man Who Envied Women*. The opening sequence explicitly links psychoanalysis to film as the realm of dream or of the Freudian subconscious. The analyst disappears, to be replaced literally by the theater audience. Like the intradiegetic *cinéaste* in *French in Action*, the film clips themselves, which function throughout Rainer's film as a projection of Jack Deller's subconscious, equate classical narrative cinema as a whole with male fantasy. Selected primarily from a variety of mainstream American movies, they offer diverse examples of Hollywood's favorite images of women, ranging from the *femme fatale* (King Vidor's *Gilda* [1946]) to the "good girl" infantalized by men (Edmund Goulding's *Dark Victory* [1939]).

As re-presented in Rainer's text, the films she quotes both recall and critique the way in which the dynamics of looking have been traditionally gendered within mainstream cinema. Notably, Buñuel's close-up of an eye being slit at once constitutes an attack on female visual subjectivity and reminds us that women's on-screen appearances have been primarily limited to the fetishistic representation of the female body. At the same time, however, Rainer's own film eliminates any possibility of objectifying the image of women with a voyeuristic male gaze, since her female lead performs only as an invisible verbal presence; Trisha never actually appears on screen. As Rainer suggests, such radical innovations may be necessary at present to challenge the long history of cinematic scopophilia: "There's been a lot of feminist theory about how the female image is manipulated and sexually objectified in film. I took this writing at face value and decided that my character was not going to be there in the flesh at all." Jack, if anyone, now serves as the object of the cinematic gaze, since he is incessantly visible on screen and often addresses the audience directly. Rainer avoids a simplistic reversal of conventional gender relations, however, in which the image of her hero would be unproblematically objectified, by using two different actors interchangeably to play a single character (Rainer 42).

Similarly, the constant visual presence of Jack no more makes him the primary focus of *The Man Who Envied Women* than does the comparable visibility of female characters in classical narrative cinema, including Truffaut's and Edwards's films. In particular, the importance of the female voice ironically subverts the power of a man whose very name, as Trisha explains, derives from the authority he presumes to have over women: "Deller, a euphemism for 'Tell her.'"[6] Although voice-over in visual media has traditionally been male and aligned with authoritative knowledge, Trisha not only acts as controlling narrator and frequent political commentator but also explores the realities of women's daily lives that have been frequently passed over in silence within mainstream cinema. It is important to note that female voice-over plays a significant role as well in both Truffaut's *L'Homme qui aimait les femmes* and Edwards's remake, where Geneviève and Marianna at the very least share responsibility for the cinematic narrative with the male heroes of the films. Not only are Truffaut's and Edwards's female narrators totally preoccupied with telling the men's stories, however, but as editor and analyst they arguably do little more than repeat words that originated with Bertrand and David.

In short, unlike Rainer's overtly woman-centered revision of cinematic relations between the sexes, there is never any doubt that the primary interest of both Truffaut's and Edwards's films lies with "the man" of their titles. The first page of Truffaut's *cinéroman* makes this fact amusingly, if unnecessarily, clear. The film's cast and characters are divided into two categories. The first, "PERSONNAGES," which appears in boldface and large capital letters, has only a single entry, despite the use of the plural: "Bertrand MORANE, played by Charles DENNER." All of the female characters figure in a second listing, positioned below the first and under a new heading that is lower case, in a much smaller typeface, and, most important, modified: "Personnages *féminins*" (my emphasis). The short description that accompanies each name (such as, "Hélène, a shopowner who sells delicate lingerie" or "Martine DESDOITS, a pretty resident of Béziers") is a no doubt necessary stimulus to the spectator's memory, and for that very reason further emphasizes the women's secondary status. Simultaneously, however, even such limited information also individualizes the women somewhat within their generic categories; in contrast, the apparently unqualified status of the hero might seem to equate him with "Everyman" or, at least, "every man," an association clearly reinforced by a psychoanalytical reading of the film. But just as the relationship *between* the two categories of characters, already announced in the title, confirms that "the man who loved women" refers, by definition, to a specifically male human being, so too does the contrast between the French film and its American remake reveal similarly important distinctions in his national identity.

What the title of Truffaut's and Edwards's films also makes clear is the obvious fact that the study of men not only does not exclude that of women but that the one is indeed essential to a full understanding of the other. This same conviction underlies a major change within feminist criticism, beginning as early as 1980 according to some sources (see, for example, Jeffords), that has increasingly replaced exclusive attention to women and their specific concerns with a broader interest in the construction of gender and, in particular, of masculinity. Such a shift in focus has prompted considerable controversy. In one striking example, Tania Modleski recently withdrew her essay on Leonard Nimoy's *Three Men and a Baby* ("Three Men and Baby M") from *Male Trouble*, edited by Constance Penley and Sharon Willis. Modleski's dissatisfaction with a collection of essays designed to examine masculinity from an explicitly feminist theoretical and historical perspective is a bit surprising, since the dominant critical influence on the volume as a whole remains that of psychoanalysis. Modleski's hostility to an approach fully consistent with her own exemplifies the fear of many feminists that the study of masculinity as a gendered discourse in its own right, rather than simply as a context illustrative of "patriarchy" or sexism, will somehow result in diminished attention to women and their interests (see Modeleski, *Feminism Without Women*). Such fears may also stem, correctly no doubt, from the suspicion that this new approach to the study of gender will eventually challenge the dominance of the essentialist model of psychoanalysis. Indeed, one of the most promising consequences of the evolution of feminist criticism lies in emerging evidence of a renewed interest in gender as a culturally specific construct. The introduction to *Male Trouble* states the two key premises of contemporary feminist film theory with particular clarity: "The study of masculinity is never the study of masculinity as such. Rather, focusing on male subjectivity inevitably leads us back to issues of femininity and sexual orientation, as well as to masculinity as it is constituted in relation to race, class, and national identity" (xv).[7]

In *The Cinema in France*, one of the few general studies of French film to be devoted entirely to the period after the New Wave, Jill Forbes singles out "the question of male identity" as a theme that distinguishes French films of the seventies from those of previous decades (183). Curiously, however, she then dismisses Truffaut, who merits mention in her book primarily because of his continued influence on younger filmmakers, as a director who ignored the world of the 1970s (105), citing in particular the "repressed misogyny" of his films, which is also a familiar theme within the relatively limited feminist criticism available on Truffaut and which largely predates more recent attention to masculinity (111; cf. Gillain, "The Script" 196–97). In relation to *L'Homme qui aimait les femmes*, my first reaction is to wonder what, if anything, would remotely qualify as "repressed" about those attitudes held by Bertrand Morane that might indeed be fairly described as misogynistic. My second is to fear that labeling Truffaut in this way risks seriously underestimating the complexity of what this film in any case has to say about "the question of male identity." Bertrand Morane is nothing if not a man of the seventies, which means, in context, that he is both full of contradictions and already a man of the past.

Toward the end of *L'Homme qui aimait les femmes*, at a point when exact correspondence between Truffaut's film and Bertrand's book has been fully achieved, Geneviève explicitly describes the latter text to its author as "a testimonial to what relations between men and women will have been in the twentieth century" and then immediately adds: "You realize, of course, that all of that is now changing?" When Bertrand expresses his fear that new possibilities for friendship between men and women ("the buddy-buddy side") will eliminate the game playing ("cette part du jeu") that he considers essential to heterosexual love, Geneviève quickly reassures him: "But game playing will always be a part of it. It's just that the rules of the game are being changed. And what is going to disappear first is the power struggle. We'll still play but as equal partners." At this point Bertrand abruptly backs down, professing, on the one hand, that he does not have a clear opinion on the subject after all, and, on the other, that he senses that he too is "changing," to which Geneviève responds with both encouragement and caution: "Bravo, bravo, but don't change too much; I don't think you're too bad as you are." This changing dynamics of male-female relationships, which is destined to erase male dominance and to allow women to compete in the game of love on an equal footing with their male partners, finds expression throughout *L'Homme qui aimait les femmes* in a pattern of rejection and reversal whose total disappearance from the American remake simultaneously highlights its importance within the French original and suggests its potential for revealing key areas of cultural difference. Although scenes of rejection tend to center on the hero and scenes of reversal on "the women he loved"—or rather, precisely because of this distinction—both types of episode are equally important and often specifically constructed to reveal their mutual interdependence. Truffaut's film expresses the transformation taking place in gender relations through a kind of process of substitution, in which different but complementary changes take place simultaneously for men and for women.

Despite Bertrand's conviction that all women are potentially seducible, he experiences a series of rejections, notably by women of approximately his own age. Although no doubt also intended to recall his childhood rejection by his mother, the similarity in age between the adult hero and the women who resist him visually identifies them on sight as the female doubles that their behavior subsequently proves them to be. Take, for example, the woman whom Bertrand calls "the beautiful Hélène" (Geneviève Fontanel). In their frequent conversations, it is difficult to tell them apart, given the ease with which she discusses the merits of the sexy lingerie she sells, details the body parts of her clients ("that one has splendid breasts; it was the speciality of the Japanese clinic she went to"), and generalizes about women as a group ("woman will always be woman"). By profession, Hélène devotes herself to displaying the objectified female body for the pleasure of the male gaze, as evidenced by the fact that men, including Bertrand, often pause in the street to watch her dressing the mannequin in her store window. Yet, even though Hélène defines herself, on the model of Bertrand, as "a woman who loves men," a connoisseur of the male sex ("I know men well") who has had a great many lovers, she refuses to have sex with Bertrand because of his age. Her attraction to much younger lovers, in whom the freshness and beauty of youth remain intact, distinguishes her, for once, from Bertrand, but her preferences are fully consistent with those frequently displayed by a great many other men: "I'm forty-one years old; I'm very sentimental, but I'm only attracted to boys younger than I am . . . if they're over thirty, I don't even *look* at them" (my emphasis).

Geneviève responds very differently to Bertrand himself, but her behavior nonetheless confirms the pattern of role-reversal set by Hélène. Immediately after predicting the disappearance of male dominance, Geneviève seduces Bertrand. There is not the slightest doubt that she both initiates the seduction and carries it out in accordance with a conventionally masculine model. Indeed, she explicitly claims that her behavior directly contradicts a passage in Bertrand's book in which he attempts to distinguish women's attitudes toward sex from those of men: "There's one thing I don't agree with, it's when you write that 'women think about love more generally than men do.' I assure you that we also experience curiosity and sudden desire." The example she offers of her own sexual attraction to Bertrand specifically describes him as a visual object of desire. Her interest is aroused when she watches him remove his sweater and is sustained when she subsequently sees him having lunch with a female rival. Moreover, after his death, Geneviève imitates Bertrand to the point of literally replacing him. Casting herself in the role of his "accomplice" at his funeral, she examines the women present and enumerates their various attractions much as Bertrand would have done in any other circumstance; but Geneviève uses her own words and, as the scene progresses, she identifies different qualities from those that actually appealed to her masculine double.

In short, *L'Homme qui aimait les femmes* portrays gender relations in the seventies as the integration of women into an essentially unchanged society in which men may no longer dominate, as Geneviève asserts, but in which the game of heterosexual love is nonetheless still played according to rules originally written by and for them. Women's sexual freedom, along with salary equity and new career opportunities, was originally an important part of the feminist agenda in the United States as well as in Western Europe. Still, given the fundamentally positive connotations of the art of *séduction* in France, which I explored in the last chapter, as well as a generally greater cultural openness to issues of sexuality, the sexual revolution of the 1970s may have had a more immediate and especially a more lasting appeal in French society than in American.[8] Moreover, the reversal of gender roles is a progressive solution fully in keeping with an essentially conservative society, since it can in no way lead to radical social transformation; even if power occasionally changes hands and different individuals occupy new positions, the structure remains fundamentally intact. In the movie at hand, the traditional "battle of the sexes" goes on. Indeed, in keeping with a deep cultural belief in *la différence*, Truffaut seems convinced that women cannot claim certain rights traditionally reserved for men without men's being forced into feminized positions. As Truffaut conceives this scenario, what promises to be a dream come true for women risks turning into a nightmare for men.

Initially, Bertrand claims to welcome change. He professes, after all, not to be a vulgar *dragueur* ("No, I don't try to pick up women. I despise men who do that; I think it's appalling") in the opening sequence of the film; and he far prefers the title of "the man who loved women," which Geneviève bestows on him and his memoirs, to any of the alternatives that he came up with (such as *Le Cavaleur, Le Coureur,* and *L'Homme à femmes*). Just before he confesses that even he may be "in the process of changing," Bertrand offers his willingness to let Geneviève drive as evidence of his relative freedom from "masculine vanity," a conclusion with which she concurs: "You don't try to appear virile at any price." The example is a particularly telling one, since shots of Bertrand in the early part of Truffaut's film frequently show him in the driver's seat of his own car in pursuit of some woman. Ginette Vincendeau claims that French cinema, in contrast to that of the United States and other nations, has a history of projecting a "gentler" version of masculinity, constructed to incorporate rather than to oppose traditional feminine values. In keeping with this image of a "feminized French man," which Vincendeau promotes to the stature of an international film cliché, on the surface Bertrand accepts with relative equanimity the rejections and reversals to which he is increasingly subjected.

On another level, however, the visual imagery of Truffaut's film and his hero's subconscious dreams and fantasies suggest a very different scenario, in which the changing roles of men and women represent a source of profound anxiety and a serious threat to traditional masculine identity. As metaphors for change, for example, Truffaut favors storms and car accidents, which foreshadow his hero's death and which are so frequent as to stress their inevitability. Notably, Bertrand's final conversation with Geneviève is framed by a storm and a car accident. In a particularly crucial scene, although Bertrand appears at the time to accept Hélène's rejection with good humor, it nonetheless provokes an "unpleasant dream." In his nightmare, Hélène is dressing a male mannequin in the window of her lingerie shop. Seen in close-up, her hands descend the length of the male body with unquestionable eroticism in order to adjust the *supports-chaussettes,* visually reminiscent of a garter belt, that hold up his socks. This spectacle has attracted the attention of a group of women who crowd around the window, staring and talking among themselves. As the camera tracks back up the body of the mannequin, Bertrand recognizes with horror that it has his own face.[9] Bertrand no doubt remembers his nightmare so vividly because he is awakened from the dream in the middle of the night by an unexpected phone call from a woman he knows only as "Aurore" who works for the wake-up service to which he subscribes. Aurore, a voice in the dark who rejects all of Bertrand's efforts to meet her and refuses to divulge any information about herself, chooses this particular night to reveal that she is a female voyeur who has been stalking him for days and can describe him and the women in his life in remarkable detail.

Consistently, then, and at least at some level to his own discomfort, Bertrand is cinematically feminized, positioned as the sexualized object of the desiring gaze. What are we to make of this? Truffaut seems to propose at least two contradictory explanations. One possible interpretation focuses on the book that Bertrand writes—and therefore, ultimately, on Truffaut's film as a whole—as an act of revenge directed against the women who threaten traditional masculine identity.[10] Bertrand begins to write as a direct consequence of Hélène's refusal to sleep with him:

> So the pretty bra merchant can only make love with young boys whose skin is fresh and soft. Obviously it's not my first failure but it's the most unexpected. I was certainly aware that it would happen some day, but I thought that it would be with a young girl and suddenly a woman of my own age sends me packing. That's why I'm going to try to write this book.

Subsequently, moreover, Bertrand realizes that the book also responds not only to his mother's original rejection but to his abandonment five years earlier by Vera (Leslie Caron), the one woman whom he may really have loved or whom he has at least subsequently convinced himself that he did ("It's only now that I realize that this book was written because of a specific woman, and that woman isn't even named in the book"). If the book is motivated by Bertrand's romantic failures, then the actual act of writing functions as a form of compensation that allows him to regain control through the narrative process over both his own life story and the women he has known.[11] Thus all of the titles he originally proposes for the manuscript leave women out entirely.

Throughout the film, shots of books and bookshelves are omnipresent, and Bertrand associates his love of reading not only with women but explicitly with sex. Reading is the only activity his mother allows him while she entertains her lovers; the room in the brothel where he first has sex is lined with empty bookshelves; he is sexually attracted to women he sees reading; his lovers read in bed; and so on. Writing, however, although still associated with sexual activity, seems to replace rather than to support it. Even if this is eventually justified as a necessary substitution while Bertrand undergoes treatment for gonorrhea, in fact he stops searching for new women from the first moment he begins to create in writing textual portraits of those he has known in the past. In his own words, Bertrand emerges from the completion of his manuscript "as exhausted as after twenty nights of lovemaking but lighter than air."

More important, however, writing—a metaphor, no doubt, for artistic creativity in general, including filmmaking—excludes women for the simple reason that Truffaut defines it in *L'Homme qui aimait les femmes* as a specifically male activity. The visit to his urologist (Jean Dost) constitutes the single exception, remarkable for that very reason, to what a colleague of Bertrand represents as one of his absolute principles: "You'll never see that guy put up with the company of men after 6 P.M." Bertrand and Dr. Bicard share something much more significant than the doctor's initial admiration for his patient's sexual appetite. Although this context certainly helps to establish a conventionally jocular ambiance of male comradery, what really links the two men is the fact that both write. Bicard has published his history of trout fishing at his own expense, but when he learns that Bertrand has written "a kind of novel," he strongly encourages him to seek a commercial press: "Nothing is more beautiful than seeing a book you wrote appear in print. Nothing is more beautiful with the possible exception of giving birth to a baby you've carried inside of you for nine months, but we're not capable of that, well, at least not for the moment!" This telling analogy suggests that writing has the potential not only to compensate Bertrand for the maternal and female rejection he has experienced in the past but actually to usurp the only power still exclusive to women ("at least for the moment" to paraphrase Bicard) by metaphorically transforming him into a mother.

There is, of course, nothing original either in comparing a woman's ability to reproduce biologically to a man's right to produce artistically, or in justifying the latter as a poor substitute for the former, but this traditional distinction may remain particularly influential in France. Women's reproductive powers also figure as a major source of male creative anxiety in Coline Serreau's *Trois Hommes et un couffin*; and the love of literature and the love of women have always tended to be closely associated among French men (Mitterrand is only the latest example). Thus, when Bertrand's typist, Mme Duteil (Monique Dury), refuses to continue transcribing a manuscript she pronounces repellent ("These stories of interchangeable women make me dizzy; they make me ill"), he is momentarily tempted to abandon his book ("A mere novice as a writer, I had already been blacklisted by my first reader [*ma première lectrice*]") until the decision to consult "the memorialists of the past" in order to learn "how [you] should write when your subject is yourself" quickly restores his confidence. Despite the originality, indeed the virtual textbook version of the New Wave's auteur theory, that he claims to discover—"I realized that there were no rules, that every book is different and expresses its author's personality"—what he necessarily encounters is one of the most distinctively male autobiographical traditions in existence. Moreover, Jean-Jacques Rousseau's *Les Confessions*, the work that inaugurates its modern history, portrays both a "man who loved women" and a voyeuristic male gaze and begins to establish, as Philippe Lejeune has repeatedly shown, that there *are* rules, ones that Bertrand's own text fully respects.

Tracking shots of walls lined with books also typify Yvonne Rainer's *The Man Who Envied Women*, whose title character is a university professor well versed in French literary theory, including, in particular, that of Michel

Foucault. In an interview with Mitchell Rosenbaum, Rainer notes that the complexity of her hero—the fact, for example, that the diverse sources from which she has constructed his speech range from Raymond Chandler's letters to far more "intellectually progressive" texts—often baffles spectators of her films, especially men, who fail to understand the director's sympathy for Jack Deller: "There are women who find him vulnerable and appealing. Men are much harder on him . . . They see him as utterly reprehensible and ludicrous, and they can't take anything he says seriously. But he says a lot of right-on things, including the Foucault stuff" (43). Indeed, Rainer believes that even Deller's obsession with women "has taken a new form. The feminist man. Feminism as it is used by certain kinds of womanizing men" (44). One is inevitably reminded in this context of how differently men and women also respond to Bertrand Morane. If such reactions figure within the diegesis of *L'Homme qui aimait les femmes*, they nonetheless function *en abyme* to recall Truffaut's actual spectators, since they explicitly comment on a book of the same name as the film.

The two male members of the selection committee at Editions Bétany are openly hostile to Bertrand's manuscript and oppose its publication. If the first simply denounces "this character who thinks he's an irresistible seducer" as "uninteresting," the second expresses precisely the kind of frustration and confusion at the complexity of the character that Rainer attributes to spectators of her film: "It doesn't hold together psychologically; it's a tissue of contradictions, so much so that when you reach the end of the book, you really don't know what to think of the character. Is he sick? A sex maniac? A pathological case? A disabused romantic?" At one point Rosenbaum remarks to Rainer that most of the men to whom he has shown her film deny that they identify with the title character and that this denial is particularly vehement in the case of those men for whom such identification would be most appropriate (43). "Women," replies Rainer, "recognize him instantly" (44). Similarly, Geneviève, in contrast to her male colleagues and even though she too is fully aware of the hero's faults and the contradictory nature of his story, readily accepts him for what he is: "He's just *a man*" (her emphasis). Moreover, as we know, she also reads *L'Homme qui aimait les femmes* as a kind of feminist document ("a testimonial to what relations between men and women will have been in the twentieth century"), whose style and form appear consistent with many texts produced in the context of the 1970s women's movement. Bertrand's "novel" is narrated in the first person by a self-effacing narrator, spontaneous and sincere in tone, realistic in its achronological structure and accumulation of detail, true to life precisely because it is both pointless and plotless by conventional standards.[12]

But does this make Bertrand Morane "the feminist man" ("feminism as it is used by certain kinds of womanizing men")? Does this make him "the man who *envied* women"? Despite Geneviève's—and Truffaut's—assertions that he is "just *a man*," there seems to me nothing remotely simple about this particular man's masculinity. In an interview that also dates from the mid-1970s, Truffaut says that he has learned from experience that the public tends to dislike those of his films in which male characters are the center of attention, particularly if they are his own age; he goes on to note his personal preference for working with women: "I identify with female characters more easily than with male characters, which does not mean to say that my films are feminist" (Porter 3). This certainly seems to apply to *L'Homme qui aimait les femmes*, given the advice that Truffaut offers Charles Denner on how to handle the questions about feminism that the director expects to arise in pre-release interviews: "I'm in favor of responding that we didn't try to suck up to the women's liberation movement, but that the female characters, although few in number and episodic, are strong enough to stand up to Bertrand Morane" (*Truffaut* 156).[13]

Like Truffaut, his hero seems to "identify" with women more easily than with men, even to the point of wanting to become one. As we know, Bertrand avoids men, whom he seems to dislike; has no male friends; and neither he nor anyone else ever makes the slightest allusion to his father in the course of the entire film. In the scene that immediately follows the highly gendered critique of his book, Bertrand finds himself in an airport lounge surrounded entirely by men. He experiences such horror at the sight that in the fantasy sequence that ensues his visual hallucination substitutes female legs for the suit pants and briefcases he cannot bear to see. In the absence of any explanation, and Truffaut offers none, visual memory and logic require that the scene be read in conjunction with the opening sequence of the film, in which Bernadette (Sabine Glaser), the first woman with whom Bertrand has sex, shows him a map of an unknown island whose existence clearly fascinates and excites him: "It's an island where women who want to live alone, among themselves, without a single man, came to settle." Although the only reasonable assumption at this early point of the film is that Bertrand's enthusiasm ("Then, there are only women, nothing but women? How many are there?") stems from the irresistible challenge such a place presumably represents for an inveterate—and still ambitious—seducer, the reality turns out to be quite different. After the accident that puts him in the hospital and just prior to his death, Bertrand recasts the publication of the book he has written—and thus, metaphorically, Truffaut's film as well—as the means to a single end: "He will leave everything and take off for this island where women settled to live among themselves. He will try to make them accept him. Yes, they will accept him, he will explain to them."

Since the island described clearly has to be Lesbos, this ultimate example of Truffaut's pattern of rejection and reversal appears to lead to the denial of one's own sexual and gender identity and to suggest that, to at least some extent, Bertrand's transsexual fantasies should be taken literally. In this context, "the death of his character," which concludes Bertrand's novel, in keeping with what both Geneviève and Truffaut characterize as "logic itself" (*Truffaut* 155), seems not merely "logical" but also necessary and even inevitable. On the one hand, despite Bertrand's efforts to change and to attenuate his own virility—with some success, as Geneviève confirms shortly before his accident ("You're not a Casanova, you're not a Don Juan . . . You don't try to appear virile at any price"), he nonetheless remains a man of the past in a new world of gender relations in which women are no longer content simply to be beloved, desired, and pursued. Thus Bertrand must die, and his death is appropriately accompanied by the transformation of the female characters he once created and controlled into the authors of their own text. In the words of the woman who has herself evolved from his editor to his "accomplice" to his double and, finally, his replacement: "I now have the impression that all these women are writing the last page of his novel." On the other hand, Truffaut insists that Bertrand's death should not be conceived as a "punishment" (*Truffaut* 156). His hero cannot fully realize the desire to *be* female in any world except that of fantasy and the imagination. He therefore dies in order to "give birth" metaphorically to the text by and in which he sought most fully to achieve traditionally female powers of creativity.

If the originality of Truffaut's *L'Homme qui aimait les femmes* stems from a pattern of rejection and reversal, then that of Edwards's remake lies in what might be called, *allitération oblige*, the repetition of the relational and the risible. Although only a few years separate the 1977 French film from the 1983 remake, they represent an especially significant period in terms of the influence of contemporary feminism, marked, in particular, by rapid changes in the conception of gender roles. *The Man Who Loved Women* seems already to represent what Betty Friedan in 1981 identified as a "second stage" of feminism, during which increased opportunities for women to integrate a still largely male-dominant society no longer seemed adequate to bring about further change. Subsequently, feminism in the United States increasingly targeted the evolution of men's traditional roles and alternate constructions of masculinity as the key to a more egalitarian future. To some extent, no doubt, this constituted a logical historical development, since it also occurred, for example, with particular ease and rapidity in several of the Scandinavian countries. Within a specifically Franco-American cultural context, however, the transformation of masculinity remains far more characteristic of the United States than of France, as already shown in our comparisons of French films and their Hollywood remakes and now confirmed by that of Truffaut's and Edwards's versions of *The Man Who Loved Women*. Bertrand Morane is already a man of the past, David Fowler the "New Man" of a potential future.

Double Takes

The psychoanalytical structure of Edwards's film immediately establishes the relational model that characterizes the American remake as a whole and distinguishes it most remarkably from the French original. Truffaut's hero thrives on solitude, affirms his freedom at every opportunity ("You're free, I'm free, everyone is free"), and refuses on principle to allow the women he seduces to stay overnight. Certainly Bertrand has no intention of repeating the mistake he made with one of his first "mistresses": "[I]n order to make her conquest, I had given her the impression that I wanted to be a part of her life even though that was out of the question. It's a mistake that I've avoided repeating." David, in contrast, is not only involved in a series of relationships in the course of Edwards's film but his psychological problems stem precisely from his inability to sustain any one of them both permanently and exclusively. At the beginning of the film he describes himself as "semi-living" with Courtney, a pattern that later repeats itself with Swetlana. Although both *L'Homme* and *The Man* share the same opening sequence, Bertrand immediately loses interest in Martine once she tells him about her cousin and heads back to Montpellier to seduce Bernadette. In identical circumstances, David refuses to believe Agnes, continues to pursue her over the next several days, and after she finally has sex with him, promptly proclaims her "the only pair of legs in my life." Although this quickly proves not to be the case, David and Agnes do establish an ongoing relationship, and she finally breaks it off to marry someone else only because she "needs commitment," the one thing that David cannot provide.

In the case of Edwards's hero, therefore, Marianna rightfully asserts at his funeral that "he really and truly loved all these women." Unlike Bertrand, who can pass easily from one lover to the next precisely because each encounter helps to satisfy more fully a passion whose object is essentially woman rather than women, David values not only the femaleness but, especially, the individuality of each of his partners. Hence the confusion and paralysis that characterize his psychological illness and constitute, in the words of his analyst, "a mirror, reflecting an infinity of doubts concerning staying or leaving." Each relationship that David establishes deprives him, at least temporarily, of all other women; yet the end of each liaison also brings him a deep sense of sadness and loss. In contrast to Bertrand, who cynically dismisses marriage as analogous to "believing in Santa Claus" and for whom it would indeed be a senseless disaster, David, who desperately wants to believe in Santa Claus ("I want to settle down and have children in a *Leave It To Beaver* house"), interprets his desire to marry Marianna as a "psychiatric breakthrough" and proof that he is "cured."

Even though it is only a matter of time, as Marianna is well aware, until David suffers a relapse ("We both knew that sooner or later he would be compelled to move on. The pursuit of new women was indispensable to his well-being"), she nonetheless describes the two months of their liaison as "the most loving, original, stimulating" of her life. Moreover, her adoration of David, whom she characterizes, for example, as "the most intelligent man—intuitive, gentle, almost soulful," is shared by every woman in the film. Indeed, in contrast to Bertrand, who regularly—and realistically—encounters failure, rejection, indignation, and anger, David, though equally incapable of fidelity, is portrayed not only as the perfect man but as a virtual saint. No woman ever refuses him, and none of the lovers he abandons (albeit regretfully) ever appears to experience the slightest resentment or the briefest remorse. Ultimately, there is something deeply disturbing about this portrayal of female passion for a man who, however perceptive and sensitive he may be, is also, by definition, emotionally ill and whose symptoms directly undermine his masculinity. Edwards's hero certainly seems to support the theory that the depiction of the "feminized" male characterizes "masculinity-in-crisis" movies (see Cook, "Border"), since David is a caricature of many of the most negative stereotypes traditionally associated with femininity. As we saw earlier, he is passive, weak, indecisive, dependent, and fearful, with, at times, a tendency toward hysteria. Moreover, his sexual impotence turns him into a kind of seducible object who may not be able to initiate sex but who is simultaneously unable to say no to any woman who pursues him, as exemplified by his repeated submission to Lulu's insistence that he perform oral sex regardless of the circumstances. Notable too is his assertion that his sculptures are designed to appeal to touch as much as sight and his singling out in this context of Michelangelo's aptly named "David" as a "very sexy" statue.

Does Edwards really mean to suggest that the women of the eighties require the men they love to be everything that they no longer wish to be? There is no question that the director conceives of his hero as representative, even though the feminist context of the American remake remains less explicit than that of the original French film. As in Nimoy's *Three Men and a Baby*, gender relations are most openly addressed on the film's sound track in the words of the theme song, Henry Mancini's "Little Boys," here sung, significantly, by Helen Reddy. The lyrics clearly recast David's personal problems with commitment and immaturity as those of men in general:

> You ran away the closer you came to love,
> Always the same, the closer you came to love.
> Once, in my arms, you were happy,
> But while I was singing,
> What long ago voice did you hear?
> Women have a way of running

Double Takes

To little boys who run away like you.
It's foolish but then I'd do it again,
For sometimes little boys run away
And grow up to love someday.

As expressed in the theme song, the message of Edwards's film also intersects not only with that of *Three Men and a Baby* but especially with that of Ardolino's sequel, *Three Men and a Little Lady*. In both cases, the feminist "New Man" distinguishes himself above all else by his capacity for permanent commitment to a single woman in a long-term relationship. Despite the obvious condescension toward men that characterizes Mancini's lyrics, especially as interpreted by Reddy, they also convey hope for future change and call into question traditional codes of femininity as well as those of masculinity. "Women" must share responsibility for the irresponsible behavior of the "little boys" they love ("Women have a way of running to little boys who run away"). Moreover, in 1983, it is apparently still enough for a man to *try* to change, even if he ultimately fails, in order to win feminist accolades. Ironically, of course, the perfection of the hero of *The Man Who Loved Women* inevitably includes the fact of his death, which may well provide the best explanation for the miracle of female solidarity that allows Marianna and her "sisters" to join together at his funeral as "lovers in weeds, widows without marriage" beyond all "jealousy, envy, [and] rage."

Still, there is a more disturbing interpretation of Edwards's views on gender relations in the eighties. In another example of the use of the hero's particular character and situation to refer to the construction of masculinity on a broader scale, David periodically portrays himself as "Fokker Febleman" (that is, feeble-man), a self-imposed alias that certainly appears to define male impotence as a fact of gender, particularly since the film offers no diegetic explanation for the pseudonym. In this context it is important to remember that *The Man Who Loved Women* also fails to provide any information about what caused David's sudden psychological breakdown in the first place. All that Edwards reveals is the incident that cures it: the reduction of his psychoanalyst—intelligent, successful, and independent, like every other woman in the film—first to a female body, an available sexual object, and then to a submissive lover. In the absence of any other causal explanation, it seems logical to reason in reverse and to deduce that changes in women's traditional roles are responsible for producing symptoms of illness and impotence in men. According to Susan Faludi and others, the newly conservative social and political climate of the 1980s resulted in a "backlash" against feminism, supported, in particular, by the popular media, including television and film, which delivered the message that women's new confidence and public visibility increasingly led to the "emasculation" of American men.

The selection of Burt Reynolds to play a hero whose masculinity is threatened might seem like an odd choice, particularly given Marc Mancini's conviction that Hollywood's fondness for "glamorizing" its actors sharply distinguishes American from French cinema, including remakes from their original models:

> To cite one example: Blake Edwards cast Burt Reynolds in the lead of his remake of *The Man Who Loved Women*; the lead in Truffaut's original was Charles Denner, who can hardly be called attractive. Indeed, that was a *point* of Truffaut's version, one that French audiences readily accepted. Americans, though, used to a realistic approach to character behavior, would have had great difficulty in accepting, say, Eugene Levy, as a man who easily seduces women. It's the ultimate irony that a fantasy-figure movie star can abet the realistic conventions of American cinema. (41)

Certainly Reynolds's tall, athletic build and his conventionally handsome face contrast with the appearance of Denner, who is a slight, dark, serious man of average height. Still, what the citizens of a particular nation find physically attractive may be almost as culturally specific as what they are willing to laugh at, and in this instance the two things appear to be closely connected. As in the case of *Trois Hommes et un couffin* and *Three Men and a Baby*, where Mancini's argument would presumably apply with equal accuracy and for precisely the same reasons to the casting of Tom Selleck in the role originally played by Roland Giraud, the issue appears to be one of *genre* as much as *gender*, or rather, of both at the same time. Edwards remakes what the French would no doubt classify as *comédie dramatique*, if not *drame* or even *drame psychologique*, as outright *comédie*.[14]

To be honest, I would personally find Bertrand Morane far more appealing if I were able to discern some sign of ironic self-awareness or even open self-mockery in either his character or in Denner's performance. But despite the justification that Bertrand provides for initially choosing *Le Cavaleur* (the womanizer) as the title of his autobiographical novel because it "best summed up the derisory and feverish nature of my pursuits," in general he appears to take himself very seriously. Nor do any of the relatively extensive comments that Truffaut made about either his film or its hero suggest anything different. In one interview, Truffaut even accepts a journalist's characterization of *L'Homme qui aimait les femmes* as a "tragédie dynamique," although he more typically emphasizes the realism of the title character, even to the point of identifying by name men whom he considers Bertrand's real-life counterparts (*Truffaut* 155). What interested Truffaut about Denner's physical appearance was not what Mancini perceives as the actor's relative unattractiveness but rather "his wild appearance and his savagery" (*Truffaut* 155). The

Double Takes

Charles Denner's physical appearance—he is a slight, dark, serious man of average height—contrasts with Burt Reynolds's tall, athletic build and conventionally handsome face in the American remake. The feminization of Denner's character often associates him visually with the women of his obsessions. *L'Homme qui aimait les femmes.* Courtesy of the Stills Archive, Museum of Modern Art, New York.

single description provided within the film stresses similar characteristics. Aurore, the voyeur and stalker who phones Bertrand in the middle of the night, confronts him with the following self-portrait: "You are of average height, thin, very dark, with a rather hollow face and a gloomy air. You move your head like a bird of prey. When you walk down the street, you always seem preoccupied and sometimes you have the look of a killer." As befits a professional seducer, Denner physicalizes a somewhat dark and mildly dangerous sexuality—even if, in the final analysis, Truffaut's hero arguably ends up more "ladykilled" than "ladykiller."

The remaking of French realism as what I called, in reference to *Three Men and a Baby*, "masculine American comedy" is even more pronounced in Edwards's case than in Nimoy's. The former adds a series of episodes of outright farce to his *The Man Who Loved Women*, to the point that it literally supports *CinémAction*'s presumably ironic suggestion, in mock homage to

Marx, that the remake phenomenon is "also perhaps a way of recalling that some stories can only be repeated as farce" (Oms 67). Not only do all four of the major slapstick sequences focus in some way on the hero's interactions with other men but male characters other than David appear only in these scenes. Since this nonetheless grants men in general a more visible presence and a more significant role than in Truffaut's *L'Homme qui aimait les femmes*, where Bertrand directly interacts only with his doctor (and fellow author), it further reinforces the probability that comedy and an American version of masculinity in crisis are somehow closely linked ("some stories can only be repeated as farce"). Indeed, of interest is the precise nature of this connection, for even if Reynolds is primarily a comic actor and Edwards what David Ansen of *Newsweek* calls "one of our finest farceurs" ("Don Juan"), Edwards's use of comedy is too consistent and too particular in *The Man Who Loved Women* to be simply dismissed, as a number of (male) reviewers have tended to do, with praise, to be sure, but without interpretation.[15]

Although David is always the primary comic figure and the focus of laughter in the scenes of farce, in every case he also manages to triumph in some sense over men who officially function as authority figures. Thus, as David chases after the legs he has glimpsed at the beginning of Edwards's film, he is almost hit by a police car and then carried off by a pickup truck filled with plants and fertilizer. Despite the fury of both cop and truck driver, David nonetheless succeeds in getting Agnes's license plate number. A few days later he follows her to her aerobics class, where he manages to get another look at her legs, even though his frantic efforts to do so require him to attempt repeatedly to peer through a very different pair of legs, those of a huge black male guard who eventually throws him out. In the third example, David valiantly battles with Nancy's pimp in a supermarket until she knocks the pimp out with a frozen leg of lamb. In the most elaborate sequence (and the favorite of most reviewers), David escapes discovery by Lulu's husband only after an unfortunate encounter in a closet with Krazy glue that subsequently forces him, first, to convince a black garage attendant to give him the keys to Lulu's Mercedes and, then, to drive it away with one hand in his mouth, a small dog stuck to the other hand, and pieces of carpet glued to both feet.

In general, all of this appears to be consistent with the interpretation of Edwards's *The Man Who Loved Women* as a film about the emasculation of the American male in the 1980s. If Mancini is right that Edwards selected Reynolds to play the lead at least in part because he is sufficiently attractive to be convincing in the role of a man who easily seduces women, the director of the Hollywood remake goes to a great deal of trouble to counterbalance the physical strength and appearance of his "fantasy-figure movie star" (Mancini 41). Not only is Reynolds constantly made to look ridiculous, even if often engagingly so, but, more important, he is repeatedly confronted with and contrasted to men who, by either their legal or moral authority (the policeman and the husband) or their sheer physical size and threatening behavior (the guard and the pimp), further diminish the hero's virility. Juxtaposed with conventionally strong and authoritative men, David's relative "feminization" comes to include an element of sexual ambivalence and/or homoeroticism. Although the most explicit scene, that of David crouched in the triangle formed by the gym guard's legs, is unique, it is also visually striking and therefore particularly memorable. According to Ginette Vincendeau, the comic male persona, which she sees as a mainstay of French cinema from Jean Gabin to Gérard Depardieu, derives its humor from the contrast set up between the definition of the character and the performance of the star. In this case, Vincendeau's argument clearly applies better to Edwards's American remake than to the French film on which it is based. Burt Reynolds's physical appearance and his well-known heterosexuality are played off against David Fowler's feminine sensitivity and sexual impotence so that the "sexual axis" of Reynolds's comic image, like that of Depardieu's, "involves a play on regression and emasculation, in which his body and performance provide the 'evidence' of heterosexual virility . . . against narrative attempts to undermine it" ("Gérard Depardieu" 349).

Roger Vadim cites Truffaut as "a good example" of a filmmaker whose work is particularly resistant to cross-cultural reproduction: "He was the most French of directors. His manner was to take a mediocre story and coat it with layers of French psychology and personal insight. Remake one of these thoroughly attractive films, but lose one of these two elements, and what would you really have left?" (qtd. in Mancini 42). I quote Vadim's statement not because I agree with it—I'm not sure that I even understand it—but because its very lack of precision and clarity suggests the importance of cross-cultural comparison. *L'Homme qui aimait les femmes* may well reflect both elements of Truffaut's own autobiography and a specifically French construction of masculinity. Still, the film *can* be remade and "what you really have left" in that case is no doubt something very like Edwards's *The Man Who Loved Women*. What I would emphasize, then, in analyzing how the opening sequences of the two films already make visible a "world of differences"—to return, as promised, to Santoni's assertion—would not be superficial changes of place, profession, or make of car. Rather, I would point out the metamorphoses of genre (from myth to farce, from fiction to psychoanalysis), of gender (from *their* love for *him* to *his* for *them*, from *his* power to *her* authority), and, finally, of the general (from Freudian thought to individual psychotherapy, from multiple affairs to meaningful relationships) that will continue to structure the interaction of the French film and its American remake from beginning to end.

Conclusion

Contemporary French-to-American Comedy or the Compulsion to Compare

Like the potentially endless quest that structures both versions of *The Man Who Loved Women*, this book could continue indefinitely, especially since Hollywood's passion for remaking French films seems, if anything, to be growing. Indeed, it is somewhat discouraging to realize that the American film industry can apparently produce remakes faster than I, at least, and perhaps any single individual, can hope to analyze them. During the eight months I initially spent working on this project in Paris in 1995–1996, Hollywood released new versions of Henri-Georges Clouzot's *Les Diaboliques* (1955) and Edouard Molinaro's *La Cage aux folles* (1978) and announced plans to remake Jean-Jacques Beineix's *Diva* (1982) and Francis Veber's *Les Compères* (1988). The relative diversity represented in this array of films becomes even more remarkable if one also includes Chris Marker's *La Jetée* (1962), which Terry Gilliam absorbed into *Twelve Monkeys* (1995). Given this rate of productivity, it would be nothing short of astonishing if every American version of a French film were effectively reconceived and revelatory of cross-cultural differences. The nearly unanimous chorus of reviewer's complaints that most Hollywood remakes are little more than pale copies of French originals, produced for the sole purpose of attracting a large American audience uninterested in foreign films, must be accurate in at least some cases, though not in all.

John Badham's *Point of No Return* (1993), the American version of Luc Besson's *La Femme Nikita* (1990), seems to provide a likely example. Despite minor changes in emphasis and interpretation, including some of potential cultural significance, even I will readily admit that the two films are far more alike than different. Both versions of the movie open with an attempt by a group of young drug addicts to break into a pharmacy that goes badly wrong. The only survivor (Nikita in the French film, Magge in the American one) is first sentenced to death for killing a cop and then offered the opportunity to assume a new identity if she agrees to be trained as an undercover hitwoman for a covert government agency. Under the supervision of Bob, an experienced agent, Nikita is gradually—and with considerable difficulty—transformed into a computer expert, a sharpshooter, and, perhaps most important, an attractive, worldly, and well-behaved young woman. Once Nikita has recovered her independence and created a new life in the outside world, however, she soon discovers that the periodic assignments she must complete not only complicate her personal life and her relationship with a new lover but so seriously bother her conscience that she must find a way to escape.

The most interesting change between *La Femme Nikita* and *Point of No Return*, one consistently ignored by reviewers, takes place in the importance of the parent/child subtext that underlies the reeducation of the heroine of both films. In Besson's original, Nikita's retraining explicitly and consistently takes the form of what the French call *éducation*, a word closer in meaning to the English *upbringing* than to its own exact cognate, since it refers to a specifically parental right; and Bob (Tcheky Karyo) and Amanda (Jeanne Moreau) clearly function as educators in the French sense, that is, as substitute parents. In this context, although Bob's real feelings for Nikita (Anne Parillard) are no doubt ambivalent, the love he actually demonstrates for her never exceeds the boundaries of the affectionate and the protective. Invited to dinner as "Uncle Bob," for example, he tells her lover the story of a little girl with long braids who used to imitate frogs. In the American version of the same scene, Bob (Gabriel Bryne) describes an explicitly erotic vision of Magge (Bridget Fonda) riding bareback on "a wild, black horse," which is fully consistent with the openly sexualized relationship between Bob and Magge that characterizes Badham's remake as a whole.

There is, however, nothing particularly perverse about this attachment, since Bob never really functions as a father figure in the American version of the film. After repeating the opening sequence of the robbery in which an armed pharmacist finds himself face-to-face with his drug-addicted son, Badham essentially abandons the parent-child thematics that continue to structure Besson's film. Nikita, for example, "dies" crying for her mother; in general, she is much more savagely childlike than her American counterpart. Her rehabilitation consequently takes much longer and she still retains signs of her original wildness at its conclusion; her departure from the retraining center clearly recalls that of the young adult leaving home; and so on. Badham's Magge, in contrast, is unquestionably a woman, that is, in traditional cinematic terms, a visual object filmed for the pleasure of the "male gaze." Notably, the remake includes repeated scenes of Magge seen from Bob's voyeuristic perspective; she is visually reproduced in huge photographs taken by her lover; and her final assignment requires her to portray the most stereotypical of dumb, sexy, voluptuous blonds in marked opposition to Nikita's impersonation of a male ambassador. Still, the substitution of a Hollywood *femme fatale* for a well-brought-up French daughter, while potentially revelatory in a larger context of Franco-American cultural differences, including specifically cinematic questions of genre, narrative, and realism, remains in this particular comparison very much a question of background. Despite somewhat different frameworks, *La Femme Nikita* and *Point of No Return* are virtually indistinguishable in terms of anything that the two films tell us really matters: plot, action sequences, violence, stylishness.

Nor is there anything at all surprising about this essential similarity, since in this case the remake and the original, which already enjoyed an unusually successful run in the United States for a foreign film, are virtually contemporaneous. Moreover, Todd McCarthy, as did many reviewers, describes *La Femme Nikita* as "one of the most Americanized French films in memory"; alternatively, Joe Chidley describes Badham's "clone" as "a new-wave French film"; and reviewers of both versions generally cite a host of common references, ranging from *Pygmalion* to James Bond to *Charlie's Angels*, which not only further suggest the fundamental resemblance between the original French film and its American remake but also confirm the breakdown of the once rigid boundaries of national cinemas.

In this context, a third reincarnation in the form of an American television series was perhaps inevitable. *La Femme Nikita*, which debuted on the USA Network on January 13, 1997, has the same kind of curious, cross-cultural, hybrid quality as *Three Men and a Little Lady*, that other sequel to a remake of a French film. In this case too, the second American version initially appears to bypass its most immediate ancestor in order to trace its lineage directly back to the French original. Not only is *La Femme Nikita* surely the only show on American television to have a foreign-language title, but the opening episode essentially repeats the transformation of Nikita from street punk to government assassin that originated with the French film. Described by Peta Wilson, the show's star, as a multi-generic hybrid—"It's kind of MTV/soap opera/drama/action" (qtd. in "Editor's Choice")—the television series has the same high-tech visual style as Besson's film, as evidenced, for example, by the quick cuts, the rapid montage of shots filmed from different angles, and the bright colors that are equally characteristic of music video and computer games. In this context, the transformation of the mentor of Besson's film into an attractive young man seems designed more to appeal to a young audience than to avoid its moral discomforture. Michael (Ray Dupuis) still acts as Nikita's protector, but he is now more friendly and fraternal than either avuncular or paternal; although their feelings for each other remain ambivalent, the possibility of a romantic or erotic connection between Nikita and Michael can safely be alluded to by other characters and by suggestive camera shots. Indeed, such an ambiguous relationship is perfectly consistent with that of the heroes of La *Femme Nikita*'s Sunday-night companion on the USA Network, *Silk Stalkings*, a show whose dubbed version on French television rivals in popularity such longtime French favorites as *Dynasty*, *Dallas*, and *Santa Barbara*.

Still, what originality there is in *La Femme Nikita*, the television series, appears to stem at least as much from cultural dislocation as from the change in the size of the screen. This American Nikita has a moral conscience that predates her government makeover and dominates her characterization. As she reminds us at the beginning of each episode, she is the innocent victim of government error and oppression: "I was falsely accused of a hideous crime and sentenced to life imprisonment. One night I was taken from my cell to a place called Section One, the most covert anti-terrorist group on the planet. Their ends are just, but their means are ruthless. If I don't play by their rules, I die." Thus Nikita is no longer a convicted murderer who must learn to redirect her violent instincts toward more worthwhile targets, but a woman whose inability to kill puts her job and therefore her life in danger in every episode. Moreover, not only is the heroine herself constantly on the verge of a nervous breakdown, but the moral dilemma is often reflected in the situation of the supporting characters as well. This shift in ethical attitudes, which recalls our earlier discussion of the relationship between Tacchella's *Cousin, Cousine* and Schumacher's *Cousins*, once again focuses less on the question of right and wrong than on the issue of freedom. Madeline (Alberta Watson), for example, the expert psychologist of Section One, attributes Nikita's persistent psychological problems to her inability to abandon her belief in individual freedom: "There's no free will in here." In another episode, Michael tells an abused wife, whose unsuspecting betrayal of her husband has led to his assassination by Section One, that his death has released her from "prison": "You're free. I'm not free. Nikita's not free." The fact that Nikita no longer appears to have a life, let alone a lover, outside the confines, physical as well as metaphoric, of Section One, reinforces this important subtext of the television series: Nikita's metaphysical battle to regain the freedom to make her own choices and to act for herself. The show's strong emphasis on teamwork, on the latest technological developments in information gathering and communication, on elaborate disguise and deception, and on plots dependent on seemingly impossible entrances and exits, together will immediately remind viewers old enough to remember of the original *Mission Impossible* television series. This reference may serve indirectly and by contrast to characterize the potentially more ambiguous moral climate of *La Femme Nikita*. In a postmodernist and post–Cold War world, the actions of government agents bear a disturbing resemblance to those of the international terrorists they oppose, and the primacy of a collective good and of solidarity in the face of a common enemy seems less evident and absolute.

Yet, to return to Besson's film and its American remake, even in circumstances that would seem to make explicit comparison of the two films as irrelevant as the existence of two versions, critics apparently cannot resist the desire to establish a context that subsequently allows them to assess the relative quality of the two films and to announce a preference for the original or (less likely) the copy. What interests me is not the fact of the judgment itself, which I understand to be part of the reviewer's responsibilities, or even the characteristic subjectivity and superficiality of the evidence on which it tends to be based. (In the case of *La Femme Nikita* and *Point of No Return*, the critic's preference for, or, more typically, dislike of a particular actor in a given role seems to constitute the only grounds available on which to form an opinion.) Rather, what interests me is the sense that comparison itself matters, that, in fact, it matters so much that it continues to take place even in circumstances where its practice has become theoretically impossible.

Stanley Kauffmann provides a fascinating example of this urge to compare in his review of *Point of No Return*, which he ironically presents as a slightly "adjusted" version of his own earlier analysis of *La Femme Nikita*: "If Hollywood can remake films, why can't critics remake reviews" ("Making Over")? In a general introduction Kauffmann recalls that American popular theater "fed on remakes" of French and German plays throughout the nineteenth century: "Some diligent scholar, I'm sure, has done a comparative study to see whether the originals gained or suffered in translation." Because what follows comes unnervingly close to an explicit commentary on the project that informs this book and yet differs radically in what it assumes to be the appropriate focus and purpose of such a study, I quote much of Kauffmann's next two paragraphs in their entirety:

> And some diligent film scholar, I'm sure, is investigating the modern equivalent, comparing American remakes of foreign films with their originals. The results may be grim. Offhand I can think of only one truly memorable remake, *Some Like It Hot* by Billy Wilder and I. A. I. Diamond (1959). It's a great film, but I don't know its French and German forebears and can't do any comparing.
>
> Remake River flows on. The latest wavelet is *Point of No Return* . . . this remake seems stale and, I think, will seem so even to those who didn't see the French original.

What an astonishing series of methodological contradictions these few brief sentences contain. Initially, Kauffmann assumes that the cross-national comparison of film, a context he explicitly establishes, serves not to identify areas of cultural difference or similarity but only to determine the relative aesthetic merit of two related works. Although he clearly accepts the superiority of the original as the general norm, Kauffmann does not articulate the criteria according to which such a conclusion might be reached nor can one assume that it somehow automatically emerges from the comparative context itself. When Kauffmann does qualify a remake as "great," he simultaneously affirms his total ignorance of the original film(s) that would presumably allow him to arrive at this judgment in the first place. Subsequently, moreover, Kauffmann appears to consider such knowledge unnecessary, or rather, much more curiously, to presume that it is somehow either intuitively present in the film viewer, or immediately inducible from the remake itself, or both. The affirmative response to the rhetorical question with which Kauffmann closes his review of Badham's *Point of No Return*, itself intentionally conceived more to repeat than to compare, confirms this surprising conclusion: "Does comparative criticism matter if most of the audience never saw the original? Only if, as may well be the case here, the audience finds something lacking in the remake and wonders why the original deserved another version."

Does a tree falling in a forest make any noise if there is no one there to hear it? Is a remake a remake if the public never saw the original? This new cinematic version of a classic conundrum apparently found a ready response on the set of the American remake of Clouzot's *Les Diaboliques*. In the context of a special issue devoted to the waning international influence of French culture ("Que reste-t-il de notre rayonnement à l'étranger?" [What remains of our influence abroad?]), *Le Nouvel Observateur* reports that one of the producers actually used this argument to justify the Hollywood version of the French original: "Americans have never seen the film with Signoret in it; therefore we're not making a remake" (Forestier, "La France" 27). According to this reasoning, which obviously confuses the production of a film with its eventual reception, the existence of a remake depends not on its textual relationship to an earlier work but on the actual viewing experience of any given moviegoer. In that case, however, the quotation above requires a remake of its own: some Americans—I for one—*have* seen the film with Signoret in it; therefore the producers of *Diabolique are* making a remake. Of late Hollywood has discovered a less convoluted and more convincing way to discourage comparative criticism. American studios have begun to block the U.S. distribution of French films that are destined to be remade. Touchstone, for example, purchased distribution as well as remake rights to Francis Veber's *Les Fugitifs* but has neither released the original film, which played only at the Sarasota film festival, nor allowed anyone else to do so.[1] Critics commonly assume, with Molly Haskell, that "studios don't want the original competing with the remake, which is invariably inferior" (qtd. in Young), an assumption—that comparison serves only to confirm the inescapable superiority of the original—which we have already encountered on a number of previous occasions and which now merits a closer look.

Is the original French film presumed to be superior because it is *original* (that is, novel, unusual, as well as first in time) or because it is *French*? Further discussion of Francis Veber's work, imperative in any case, may help resolve this question. Veber virtually incarnates the remake phenomenon entirely on his own. He represents as an individual what Touchstone Pictures does as a studio, except that Veber's influence extends cross-culturally on a far broader scale. In France he has been equally successful as a screenwriter (*Le Jouet, La Cage aux folles, Le Grand Blond avec une chaussure noire*) and as a director (*La Chèvre, Les Compères, Les Fugitifs*); and in both cases his films have consistently inspired Hollywood remakes. Moreover, Veber is the first French filmmaker hired to remake his own original film; indeed, he reportedly agreed to direct *Three Fugitives* (1988) before he had even begun to shoot *Les Fugitifs* (1986) (Canby, "Movies Lost"). Thus Hollywood's two favorite strategies—the purchasing of remake rights to foreign films and the importing of foreign directors to make movies in English—converge in Veber's case.[2] This would seem to be another instance in which we can expect a remake and its original to be so fundamentally similar that comparative textual analysis is unlikely to reveal much of interest or significance about cross-cultural difference or specificity.[3] In this case, after all, unlike that of *La Femme Nikita* and *Point of No Return*, the French and the American films were both written and directed by the same man. This also means, however, that for the first time the *American* version was directed by a *French* man. What difference, if any, does this make?

Obviously, Veber makes superficial changes in adapting *Les Fugitifs* to the American screen. For example, Seattle and the Canadian border replace Bordeaux and the Italian border; the three heroes—Lucas (Gérard Depardieu), Pignon (Pierre Richard), and Jeanne (Anaïs Bret)—become Lucas (Nick Nolte), Perry (Martin Short), and Meg (Sarah Rowland Doroff); the characters speak English rather than French. Upon reflection, almost all of the alterations made by Veber, and not just the last, might in some sense be considered essentially linguistic. (I don't mean to suggest that Seattle is indistinguishable from Bordeaux—nor, for that matter, that Pierre Richard looks like Martin Short, only that the visual differences are of no importance; indeed, spectators who can't read or who leave before the final credits may never know where either film takes place.) In general, *Three Fugitives* and a dubbed version of *Les Fugitifs* would be hard to tell apart, as the following generic description makes clear. Lucas, just released from prison after serving a sentence for armed robbery, has a very bad first day of freedom. When he tries to open a bank account, he is taken hostage by a thoroughly incompetent bank robber (Pignon/Perry), and the police naturally assume that Lucas is the one responsible for the holdup. In their subsequent attempt to escape, Pignon/Perry accidentally shoots Lucas in the leg and leaves him with a veterinarian who "treats" him, both literally and metaphorically, like a dog. Meanwhile Pignon/Perry collects his young daughter (Jeanne/Meg) who has refused to speak since her mother's death three years earlier and whose expensive private school explains her father's desperate need for money. Jeanne/Meg turns out to be so fond of Lucas that she speaks to him almost immediately, but the further misadventures of the two heroes result in her being placed in a children's home under police guard. Lucas and Pignon/Perry eventually join forces to rescue her and then escape to a foreign country disguised as a nuclear family with Lucas as "father," Pignon/Perry in drag as "mother," and Jeanne/Meg with cropped hair as "son."

Given this basic resemblance between *Les Fugitifs* and *Three Fugitives*, there would seem to be nothing to invite comparative analysis, even if the French version were readily available in the United States. Yet the critical desire to proclaim the superiority of the original is evidently irresistible. Indeed, as in the case of Kauffmann above (and below), reviewers do not need to have seen *Les Fugitifs* in order not only to prefer it to the remake but even to explain *why* they find the latter inferior. In the absence of knowledge, they are quite willing to proceed by pure conjecture, as in the case of Pauline Kael: "My guess is that Veber desperately threw in his repertory of tricks and that, working in this country, he didn't have the instinctive understanding to blend the different elements." Alternatively, according to Josh Young, the second-rate quality of the remake stems less from Veber's insufficient Americanness than from his excessive Frenchness: "Mr. Veber tried to stick closely to his original film, causing the remake to stumble over cultural differences." Nolte's "flawed" performance, which figures most prominently among what Young qualifies as "cultural differences," serves to justify the judgment of most other reviewers as well. Kauffmann confidently asserts that "one way of describing *Three Fugitives* is to say that the role originally played by the vital Gérard Depardieu is done here by the null Nick Nolte" ("Late Winter"), only to reveal later that he "didn't see the French original." Young, who apparently did, nonetheless settles for citing an earlier review by his colleague Vincent Canby in order to support the same opinion: "Mr. Nolte more or less suggests Mr. Depardieu in physique but without any of the self-aware, comic reckless-ness that distinguishes Mr. Depardieu's not easily imitated, quintessentially French performance" ("Movies Lost"). Even Canby, however, appears to find actual knowledge of the Veber original, including his own, somehow irrelevant, and proceeds to illustrate the "quintessential Frenchness" of Depardieu's performance in *Les Fugitifs* by inviting his readers to conjure up a nonexistent remake of a very different film by another director: "To get the picture, try to imagine Mr. Nolte carrying off Mr. Depardieu's role as the love-smitten drag queen in 'Ménage.'"[4]

The insistence on Depardieu's mere presence or absence as incontrovertible evidence of a film's superiority or inferiority no doubt follows directly from the fact that in the United States the actor has come to represent cinematic Frenchness itself, an association on which Resnais's *I Want to Go Home* depends. In fact, all three Veber films in which Depardieu appears (*La Chèvre*, *Les Compères*, *Les Fugitifs*) also star Pierre Richard, who always gets top billing. Praising Depardieu is therefore simply another way of saying that French films are inherently better, an opinion shared by French and American critics, though perhaps for somewhat different reasons.[5] Although I have resisted the widespread temptation to use comparative analysis to reach relative value judgments of "better" or "worse," it has never been my intention to suggest that films such as Veber's merit study because they are cinematic masterpieces. I simply don't think that the question of quality can or should be posed in comparative terms; in the case of *Les Fugitifs* and *Three Fugitives*, the French original and the American remake are equally mediocre and formulaic. Nor are they alone among the films included in this study; Caryn James appropriately cites *Trois Hommes et un couffin* as proof that "not all French films exist in intellectual and artistic utopia; the French mega-hit was as silly as its American remake."

Although the refusal of American studios to release the original version of the French films to which they have purchased remake rights understandably angers the French film industry, the practice may well have the unintentional consequence of protecting the prestige of French cinema in the United States. When Richard Roud talks about "a feeling" among Americans that "we all know what a French film is like" (15), he is clearly not referring to the popular comedies of a Veber or a Serreau but to a long tradition of thematically sophisticated, stylistically innovative, and intellectually challenging works associated with such auteurs as Renoir, Carné, Godard, Truffaut, Resnais, and Rohmer, to cite only a few. In France, too, French cinema is classified as art rather than entertainment, but in this case the category also includes comedy, which the French take very seriously. What matters, in other words, is not the genre of the film but its national identity, so that any French film (such as *Trois Hommes et un couffin*) belongs, by definition, to "high" culture; since this domain is further constituted in direct and permanent opposition to Hollywood, commercial American cinema (such as *Three Men and a Baby*) is simultaneously relegated to the sphere of "low" or mass culture.

This is what the conflict over GATT was all about; and it no doubt reinforced France's reputation for producing films that appeal only to a cultured elite. As Jeffrey Goodell put it in a report on the GATT negotiations, "the French are great at making movies that satisfy directors, but lousy at making movies that satisfy mass audiences" (135). In reality, popular comedy has become the mainstay of French cinema, every bit as responsible for the survival of the French film industry, according to Ginette Vincendeau, as the state

Double Takes

subsidies and quota systems that Hollywood finds so irritating ("Gérard Depardieu" 345). Jean-Marie Poiré's *Les Visiteurs* (1992), "comédie lourdingue"
(predictable, clumsy) even according to *Le Monde*, was the biggest French hit
in twenty years, and in general only comedies can compete with American
imports at the box office. In May 1996, Etienne Chatiliez's *Le Bonheur est
dans le près* and Didier Bourdon's *Les Trois Frères*, both decidedly lightweight
comedies, were the only French films to have attracted over a million spectators in the previous year. At that time the audience for each of those films not
only exceeded that of Disney's *Pocohontas* but, perhaps more important, more
than doubled that of three far more interesting and demanding French films,
all top award-winners that year: Claude Sautet's *Nelly et M. Arnaud* (César
1996, the French equivalent of the Oscar, for best director and best actor);
Mathieu Kassovitz's *La Haine* (César 1996 for best film); and Jean-Paul
Rappeneau's *Le Hussard sur le toit* (César 1996 for best cinematography).

The commercial success of French comedies is obviously not a secret in
Hollywood either, especially to Touchstone Pictures and Universal Studios.
But the French want credit for their own original creations in a way that they
believe the current remake practice denies them; and they may soon get it.
David Seale, the president of American Multi-Cinema, reportedly plans to
show at least ten dubbed French films a year at AMC theaters in California
and Florida, beginning with *Les Visiteurs* (Cohen, "Aux Armes"). Frédéric Gol-
chan, a French producer based in Hollywood, is attempting to form a video
company for the purpose of distributing French comedies; if he succeeds, this
will mean, as Josh Young points out, that "some parents and children will be
able to compare the American remakes with their foreign forbears." Most reviewers will be able to do so as well, however, a situation that may ultimately
please the French less than they expect. In the long run, most mainstream
French comedies are unlikely to garner any higher critical praise in the United
States than their American remakes do now. Even the most resolute of Fran-
cophile critics, who now insistently attribute all perceived flaws to the fact
that the film has been remade in Hollywood, will be forced to acknowledge
that a great many of the same defects are present in the French original.[6]

At the same time, wider availability of the French comedies that inspired
American remakes is essential to cross-cultural comparison and therefore
understanding, regardless of the aesthetic quality or the cinematic importance of either version. As I noted earlier, Jim Collins suggests in the introduction to *Film Theory Goes to the Movies* that the inclination of film scholars
to abandon the analysis of contemporary movies to the world of popular reviewing has tended to "preclud[e] consideration of the cultural significance
of those texts." If we have encountered repeated examples of this phenomenon in circumstances that clearly encourage even popular reviewers to try to
consider questions of "cultural significance," their inability to compare across

cultures provides at least part of the explanation. Pauline Kael's review of *Three Fugitives* offers a case in point. Although she too proclaims her dislike for the American version of Veber's film, Kael differs from most other reviewers in that she actually cites textual evidence from the remake to justify her opinion. Meg's preference for Lucas over her own father particularly troubles Kael, who concludes: "Everything in [*The Three Fugitives*] seems designed to humiliate the father, and you can't tell what's going on when Short—ostensibly for the purpose of disguise—is dressed as a woman and the three form a nuclear family." Even without having seen the French original, you really can "tell what's going on" in the final sequence of the film, but certainly this is also the point at which cross-cultural analysis proves particularly revelatory. Curiously, Kael almost seems to feel the lack of such comparison, since her discontent focuses on the single episode in which Veber made significant changes in adapting *Les Fugitifs* for an American public. Although the situation itself remains the same, the two films end quite differently.

Kilday displays similar perspicacity in labeling *Three Fugitives* "the two-men-and-a-baby comedy." In 1988 Touchstone Pictures released the remakes of both Veber's *Les Fugitifs* (1986) and Serreau's *Trois Hommes et un couffin* (1985), which also date from essentially the same time period; and the four films show exceptional patterns of similarity, both in terms of intracultural resemblance and of cross-cultural differences. This broader comparative context validates a number of the conclusions about divergent Franco-American discourses of gender that I first proposed on the basis of a single set of films. Veber's two films, like Serreau's *Trois Hommes*, portray the reconstruction of the nuclear family by an all-male parental couple, which nonetheless continues to respect the traditional gender roles and the conventional notions of masculinity and femininity that characterize the heterosexual norm. The process occurs even more explicitly in Veber's case than in Serreau's, where Michel figures as the "female" half of the couple he forms with Pierre primarily because he works at home and is good at domestic tasks. In both *Les Fugitifs* and *Three Fugitives*, however, the oppositional (if complementary) nature of the character and behavior of the two male leads, consistent with traditional gender stereotypes, structures the entire film. Lucas represents masculinity at its most elementary: he is big, strong, tough, often violent, and independent. Despite the unfeeling and self-sufficient façade he maintains, however, he is also competent, dependable, and protective of women and children. Pignon/Perry (P/P), in contrast, is physically fragile, frequently helpless, and somewhat vain—he cries when he's happy and then worries about how he looks. His life revolves entirely around his young daughter, whom he is nonetheless unable to support financially. Thus Lucas and P/P's literal impersonation of husband and wife in the final sequence of the film(s) simply makes visual reality conform with a relationship whose nature has been evident virtually from the beginning. In a much more daringly meta-phoric scene than that of the comic cross-dressing, for example, Lucas carries both P/P and his daughter, equally sick and weak, up a staircase.

Veber's stereotypical portrayal of femininity includes its traditional deval-orization in the face of masculinity. The clearest example is provided by the little girl, who turns out to be suffering not from the loss of a mother—a role adequately filled by P/P—but from the lack of a father; the child recovers the ability to speak in order to keep Lucas from leaving. Pauline Kael's confusing statement that "everything in [*Three Fugitives*] seems designed to humiliate the father" thus reflects a basic misunderstanding of the role reversals that structure the film. In fact, everything in the film is designed to *glorify* the "father," represented by Lucas. Despite his biological paternity, P/P actually functions as "mother" so that the humiliation to which Kael refers metaphori-cally targets traditional womanhood.[7] Not only is femininity devalued when portrayed by a man, but in Veber's films, as in Serreau's, real women are also either eliminated or marginalized and always portrayed negatively. P/P's wife proves herself to be a bad mother and an irresponsible spouse by virtue of the disastrous consequences that her inconsiderate death has for her husband and child. The policewoman assigned to guard Jeanne/Meg in the children's home treats her with insensitivity, even cruelty. As in *Trois Hommes et un couffin*, this link between bad parenting and conventional law enforcement officers clears the way for the formation of the "unlawful" or "fugitive" couple formed by Lucas and P/P.

The homoerotic subtext, which necessarily accompanies a relationship between two men that is explicitly modeled on the heterosexual couple, comes to full realization in the films' final masquerade in which Lucas and P/P, dressed as a woman, definitively escape beyond legal boundaries. This is also the point at which Veber's two films take different paths. In the closing sequence of the French original, Lucas catches up with Pignon and Jeanne as they head toward the Italian border. Although he announces his decision to accompany them as temporary—"I can't spend my whole life with you, you know? I have a hell of a lot of other things to do"—the sly smile exchanged by "mother" and daughter, even as they pretend to concur with Lucas, marks the triumph of two wily female allies who have successfully trapped their man. More important, since Pignon is still dressed as a woman, he and Lucas form a travesty of the most conventional of heterosexual couples, who, in the most conventional of Hollywood endings, head off arm in arm to the accompani-ment of decidedly romantic music. *Les Fugitifs* reaches closure in a way that makes it a much more coherent film than its American remake, which may explain why Kael senses something amiss in the latter. The series of ironic re-versals, confusions, or what might best be qualified as cases of "mistaken identity" that recur throughout the French original—the confusion, for example, between man and dog, veterinarian and doctor, or kidnapper and hostage—carefully prepare and support the ultimate reversal, the one that really matters: the "inversion" of man and woman, father and mother, masculine and feminine.

But the explicit homoeroticism of the ending of the French film must have appeared to Veber far too disturbing to be acceptable to an American audience.[8] In the passage from *Trois Hommes et un couffin* to *Three Men and a Baby*, Serreau's story of "male mothering" becomes so threatening to traditional American masculinity that the three heroes of Nimoy's remake must constantly find ways to prove their virility. Something similar occurs in *Three Fugitives*. In contrast to the original film, Veber's remake ends not with the maintenance—indeed, the consecration—of the traditional nuclear family but with its breakup. In the final sequence of the American film, Perry has reinvested his male identity; he is dressed as a man and he informs Meg that she "can call [him] Daddy again." Lucas's decision to stay, which originally had no situational motive, now occurs only because Perry has been taken hostage in his turn in another bank holdup. Thus Veber reminds us that the relationship between two men with which the film began is entirely innocent of either sexual or effeminate overtones, and in any case (should any such suspicions remain), criminal and illicit. In addition, Lucas remains alone with Meg so that the final shot of the film unambiguously portrays a father holding his daughter. Perry and Lucas may have changed places, but they have not joined forces; both, therefore, can remain men. This final reversal reinforces the greater emphasis that the structure of the American film devotes to establishing direct parallels between the two heroes rather than surrounding them with analogous cases of mistaken identity.[9]

Somewhat surprisingly, language more explicitly furthers the affirmation of the heroes' heterosexuality in the English version of the film than in the French original. Lucas's insistence in the opening scene of the film that he is "going straight" (that is, becoming *law-abiding* but also *heterosexual*) takes on new resonance as the film subsequently flirts with homoeroticism, especially since the person whose mocking doubts he is trying to overcome ("Yeah, Lucas, you'll be the straightest man in the world") is his former arresting officer, the representative of traditional law and order.[10] Similarly, at the very end of the film, Lucas justifies his separation from Perry by his refusal to go on living beyond conventional boundaries, both legal and geographical: "I can no longer live as a fugitive" (that is, a refugee from the law). Veber also ever so slightly recontextualizes the scene in which Perry cross-dresses as a woman to suggest that his sex change is also "fugitive" (that is, fleeting, ephemeral). Although the false passports in both films require the transformation of the little girl into a boy, the American remake adds a brief scene in which we actually see Lucas cutting Meg's hair, as he promises her that "it will grow back." Meg's subsequent repetition of the same line to reassure her father, now in drag, similarly suggests that his "femininity" is also nothing more than a temporary disguise. More generally, the parallel sex changes of daughter and father help to neutralize, to render harmless, the one change that is truly threatening, that of man into woman. At the same time, both serve to validate Lucas's paternity; if a man (especially *this* man ["Even at the convention of transvestites, I'd be arrested"]) and a girl can pass for a woman and a boy—a success evidenced, significantly, by their ability to fool two police officers—then Lucas's credibility as a father goes without saying.

Throughout the final credit sequence of *Les Fugitifs*, Veber's camera holds on a shot, taken from the mountain perspective of the film's three heroes, of the valley that lies below and represents their freedom. Although the border in question is that of Italy rather than Switzerland, the remarkable resemblance of narrative situation and visual image inevitably recalls, as it is surely intended to, the ending of Jean Renoir's *La Grande Illusion* (1937). Whether or not one agrees with Robin Buss that Maréchal and Rosenthal "reconstitute their own version of the ideal family," let alone one that includes "an element of sublimated homosexuality" (83–84), Veber's allusion to Renoir encapsulates a national film history in which male couples more often function as a pseudo-family than as the "buddies" characteristic of a similar tradition in Hollywood (See Jeffords, *Hard Bodies*; and Fuchs). Moreover, *Les Fugitifs* helps to create a microcosmic version of such a tradition that is specific to a single director's career. As the most recent of three films that Veber wrote and directed starring Richard and Depardieu, in some sense *Les Fugitifs* represents both a remake and a sequel in relationship to *La Chèvre* (1981) and *Les Compères* (1983). The many similarities of both characterization and plot that link the three films confirm in yet another context that Veber is writing a discourse of gender whose consistency and popularity suggest that it is rooted in the values of the national culture.

Although fourteen years separate *Les Compères* from *Father's Day* (1997), Ivan Reitman's recent remake retains the central plot device of the original French film. Colette Andrews (Nastassja Kinski), the former lover of both Jack Lawrence (Billy Crystal) and Dale Putley (Robin Williams), separately contacts both men years later to tell each of them that he is the father of her runaway teenage son and to ask each of them to track down the missing boy. Reitman also borrows Veber's oppositional construction of the characters of the two heroes of this plot, whose differences serve as the principal focus of audience laughter. As Jack's and Dale's paths quickly converge in the search for Scott (Charlie Hofheimer), they join forces to separate him from the unworthy girl he is pursuing and to protect him from the drug dealers who are pursuing him in turn. This schematic story line, however, primarily provides a context into which a series of set comedic pieces can be inserted.

For once it would seem that the director of an American remake actually hired a comic team that can hold its own in the inevitable comparison with Depardieu and Richard. Janet Maslin implicitly attributes the long delay in remaking Veber's film to the search for the right comic talent: "Enter Billy Crystal and Robin Williams: for American audiences, the casting couldn't be any more right than that." Indeed, for Maslin, the cultural specificity of the Hollywood remake lies in the nationality of the stars or, perhaps more precisely, in their style of acting. In Crystal's case, for example, she is particularly insistent, noting that as a result of successfully hosting the Academy Awards ceremony, he is "rapidly approaching national treasure status." This stature is further confirmed by Crystal's own revelation that he studied the work of such classic American comedians as Jack Benny and George Burns in order to prepare for his role in *Father's Day* ("Fathers"). No doubt Robin Williams's position as the current leading man of American comedy and the successor of Burns and Benny can be safely assumed from his past work without further evidence. Although Maslin's focus on the casting and the comic performances of Crystal and Williams is perfectly consistent with the general approach of American reviewers to the discussion of remakes, differences of theme and character, here as elsewhere, better identify the locus of cross-cultural interest.

In *Les Compères* Richard and Depardieu once again play François Pignon and Jean Lucas, even though the characters of the earlier film are unrelated to their namesakes in *Les Fugitifs*. The use of the same names identifies not specific individuals but rather a particular construction of masculinity. Lucas and Pignon again form two halves of a contrasting couple respectively coded as "masculine" and "feminine" in ways fully comparable to those previously discussed in relation to *Les Fugitifs*. Despite the title of the film, the putative story of two "fathers" in search of a runaway child whom each believes to be his biological son actually turns out, once again, to be the story of a "father" and a "mother." Pignon is scrawny, weak, divorced, unemployed, incompetent, and prone to suicidal depression that frequently causes him to dissolve into tears for no apparent reason. He is also kind, sentimental, and sensitive. Lucas is big, strong, physically aggressive, attractive to women, and a successful journalist. As in *Les Fugitifs* he must constantly rescue Pignon from aggressors and compensate for the mistakes he makes. Lucas denounces what he considers his co-father's overly protective attitude toward their "son" as inappropriately maternal: "It's possible you're his father, not his mother." Pignon does not actually masquerade as a woman here, but when his own clothes are ruined, he is forced to wear one of Lucas's suits, which is far too large to fit him properly.

The contrast between the weak but sensitive Pignon and the strong but violent Lucas is directly linked in Veber's film to masculinity, both as gender construction and as paternal heritage. Lucas and Pignon simultaneously seek reflections of their own selves in the behavior of their "son" Tristan (Stéphane Bierry) and attempt to enact two opposing theories of *éducation*. Lucas's, for example, would reproduce traditional masculine strength and emotional control—"don't cry, my son, men don't cry"; Pignon's, in contrast, would create a sensitive "new man" in touch with his feelings—"cry, my son, you'll feel better." Pignon denounces his rival's strategies as "macho bullshit" while Lucas fears Tristan's imminent emasculation: "You're going to turn him into a faggot." The simultaneous devalorization and usurpation of traditional feminine values are here as in other films we have explored accompanied by an explicitly antifemale subtext. Tristan's mother is essentially irrelevant from the beginning—her son runs away to find a father—and she soon conveniently disappears. Even the one right that is presumably uniquely hers—to identify the biological father of her child—is taken away by her son. In the course of the film, Tristan also recovers from his early infatuation with an obviously worthless girl in order to reintegrate the all-male world of his "fathers."

In the American remake of *Les Compères*, Jack and Dale function far less like a cross-gendered couple. Although Dale initially tends, like his French counterpart, to be both ineffectual and excessively emotional, the American version of this character is portrayed as essentially neurotic, at once a hopeless romantic and an uninhibited free spirit who is still living the bohemian lifestyle of 1960s youth. Dale, that is, may well be an unstable *man*, but he is not specifically feminized as a result. Indeed, the different personas that Robin Williams successively embodies in front of his mirror, in a series of imaginary first meetings with his newly discovered "son," are all comic variations on stereotypical masculinity whose range from the rap singer to the working-class buddy to the European aristocrat cuts across boundaries of class and race. In keeping with an American discourse of masculinity whose consistency clearly transcends the work of any single director, the focus of Reitman's *Father's Day* on certain aspects of what I have called the feminist "New Man" recalls in many ways Ardolino's *Three Men and a Little Lady* and Schumacher's *Cousins* far more than it does Veber's *Les Compères*.

The opening and closing sequences of *Father's Day* both establish the importance of family and make it clear that the Andrews family will ultimately be more a model to be imitated than a problem to be solved. After a shot of Scott's birth certificate, which immediately confirms the paternity of Colette's husband Bob (Bruce Greenwood), we see a series of photos that take Scott from babyhood to adolescence. This opening montage illustrates a doctrine of childhood that depends upon the raising of the child within the context of a supportive family. Scott is frequently pictured with his parents in close-ups and tightly framed photos that emphasize emotional closeness and tenderness. This message is reiterated toward the end of the film after Jack and Dale bring Scott home to his parents. As Jack and Dale look through the same photo album and admire what both now describe as "[a] nice family," the family itself reaffirms its privileged bonds in another part of the house.

Still, if Jack and Dale remain isolated from this particular family reunion, it is largely because they are now prepared to raise children of their own in new family structures of their own making. Unlike Veber's French film, which focuses on biological fatherhood (albeit in the virtual absence of Tristan's natural father) and on exclusive father-son relationships, Reitman's American version reveals paternity to be less a natural right than a matter of merit and of learned behavior. Jack, the successful lawyer, must give up his obsession with order and control in order to prove that he is finally ready to have children with his third wife. When he threatens to abandon the search for Scott, Carrie (Julia Louis-Dreyfus), whose active presence throughout *Father's Day* emphasizes the importance of traditional parenting, turns her husband's frustration into a symptom of personal and (possible) paternal failure: "You don't like anything that's annoying. Would you give up on our own kid if he was this annoying?" In this context, Jack's partnership and, ultimately, friendship with Dale serves as a metaphoric initiation into the messy and emotional world of modern fatherhood.

That Dale's open expressions of love and need constitute not only a model for successful parenting but the core of male bonding as well is confirmed by the adventures of Bob. Scott's biological father logically plays a much more active role in the American remake than in the French original, since he too must prove by his actions that he deserves to raise a son. Although Bob also sets out to bring his son home in *Father's Day*, the excessive severity with which he has treated Scott in the past requires punishment, which takes the form both of failure and of his extensive involvement, always as victim, in a comic subplot characterized by farce and scatological humor. After a series of misadventures, which include being pushed over a cliff in a port-a-potty, Bob is finally redeemed by the burly truck driver who rescues him and drives him home. Both the parting hug and the advice with which Calvin leaves Bob confirm a change in masculinity that cuts across differences in class and temperament: "Stop being so stiff. Lighten up. Take the pickle out of your butt. It's not enough to love them; you have to show them." If Dale, who best illustrates this new sensitivity, is ironically still without a family of his own at the end of Reitman's film, the final sequence of *Father's Day* reaffirms the mediating role he has played throughout. Unlike Jack, who instantly interprets Scott's identification of him as his real father as a lie designed to make him "feel good," Dale is quite willing to be deceived and to project a future of substitute fatherhood. At the same time, however, his final encounter with an available woman, who seems to share his romanticism and spontaneity, suggests that Dale, like Jack, may be able to establish the committed relationship in which he too can become a father who will "be there from the beginning." Thus, unlike Veber's *Les Compères* or Serreau's *Trois Hommes*, Reitman's "three men" do not need to discredit or usurp traditional femininity or motherhood in order to become responsible fathers. Indeed, when men can be fathers, not "mothers," mothers can be valorized as good parents in general.

Even *La Chèvre*, the earliest of the three films that Veber constructed around the same two actors, indirectly introduces the parental motif that will be of primary importance in *Les Compères* and *Les Fugitifs*. Perrin (Richard) and Compagnard (Depardieu) are hired by a father to find his accident-prone daughter, whose disappearance while on vacation in Mexico is perfectly consistent with her extraordinary propensity for bad luck. A psychological consultant convinces the father that only someone like Perrin, an inept company accountant as unlucky as the missing daughter, will be able to find her by virtue of his inadvertent re-creation of whatever incidents have befallen her. Perrin, who believes himself to be in charge of the investigation, is sent off to Mexico in the reluctant care of Compagnard, a private detective. The ensuing comic adventures consist of a series of pratfalls and mishaps that focus our attention on the relationship between the two men, whose contrasting characters and appearance and difficult interaction prefigure the polarized couples of the later films. Perrin, for example, essentially functions as an equally unlucky substitute for the young woman who has disappeared; and Compagnard must constantly rescue him from misfortune. Still, the fundamental opposition that structures *La Chèvre*, in contrast to the two later films, is explicitly philosophical in nature. Compagnard's commitment to logic, reason, and science confronts Perrin's incarnation of a theory of luck and coincidence. As Compagnard explains it in one of his many experiences with either frustration or bewilderment or both: "I don't believe in magic. I believe in logic. I'm a rational, Cartesian man. I don't depend on woolly-headed coincidences." Although this contrast between the rational and the capricious no doubt has gendered connotations, its most important context is specific to national culture. At least since the seventeenth century, France has defined itself as the privileged realm of Reason; and Frenchness continues to be strongly associated with scientific methodology and Cartesian logic.

Despite the cultural specificity of *La Chèvre*, which was never released in the United States, Universal Pictures chose to produce not only an American version but one that is virtually indistinguishable from the original. Perhaps this was inevitable, given that absolute repetition is already the structural foundation of Veber's film; Perrin and Compagnard succeed in their mission only because, metaphorically speaking, lightening does strike twice. Nadia Tass's *Pure Luck* (1991) no doubt also resulted, at least in part, from the commercial success of *Three Fugitives*. Indeed, in partial imitation of Veber's original casting, Martin Short reappears as the unlucky Proctor, a

role parallel to the one he played in the earlier remake. Danny Glover, however, takes over the Depardieu/Nolte role of Campanella, a choice that immediately identifies the one important way in which Tass's remake differs from
Veber's original: in *La Chèvre*, as opposed to *Les Compères* and *Les Fugitifs*,
the male couple is only indirectly constructed on a familial model, which
leaves room for Hollywood to substitute a racially mixed team.[11] The introduction of interracial buddies, however, arguably codes *Pure Luck* as an
American film in much the same way that the philosophical subtext points to
La Chèvre's Frenchness. Not only are such pseudo-friendships particularly
prevalent in recent American films and especially those that feature teams of
police officers or detectives (Veber recasts a black actor, James Earl Jones, as
Lucas's arresting officer in *Three Fugitives*), but race relations constitute the
key opposition that has historically divided—and continues to divide—American society.

Indeed, Susan Jeffords argues that the white hero is invariably constructed
as superior to his black partner in Hollywood's interracial buddy films, including very recent ones (*Hard Bodies*). Although this is certainly not true in *Pure
Luck*, the film nonetheless manages to respect this pattern on the surface,
since Proctor is led to believe that he is in charge of the investigation and repeatedly objects whenever his black "assistant" seems to overstep his authority. In addition, the interracial pairing also introduces potentially racist overtones into the American version of the film. In one key scene, for example,
Proctor returns to the airport restaurant from a visit to the men's room and
proceeds to sit down across from *another* black man whose vague similarity to
Campanella in physical size and color of clothing appears designed to convey
the implicit message that "all blacks look alike." Moreover, the shot is framed
in such a way—the camera shows us Campanella from the back and then reverses angle to reveal Proctor sitting down across from a man whose arm and
partial profile alone are visible—that Tass seems to be encouraging the audience to make the same error. As Proctor says, as he rejoins the real Campanella, "That was a little awkward, wasn't it?"

Even *Cahiers du cinéma*, whose interests still lie far more with auteur cinema
than mainstream comedy and which has recently dared to suggest that "Veber
is overrated," nonetheless continues to praise him as a gifted writer (H.I.R.).
His influence in this domain is such that American reviewers in particular
tend to attribute the authorship of Edouard Molinaro's *La Cage aux folles*
(1978) to Veber, even though the latter only collaborated on the adaptation of
Jean Poiret's play with three other writers, including Molinaro and Poiret
themselves.[12] Indeed, the success enjoyed in the United States by the original
French version of *La Cage aux folles* helped establish Veber's own reputation
as a source for Hollywood remakes long before it led to an American remake,

Double Takes

Mike Nichols' recently released *The Birdcage* (1996), adapted by Elaine May. This may help to explain why the American version of *La Cage aux folles* illustrates Veber's general understanding of the process of the remake at least as well, if not better, than do some of his own films: "Doing a remake can be compared to cooking. It's like adding crème fraîche to foie gras" (qtd. in Bishop 22). Other than its excessive richness, however, Nichols's remake, like those of Veber's films, so closely resembles the original French film, to which I devoted an essay some years ago, that I am tempted to claim the same right to repetition that Stanley Kauffmann has: "If Hollywood can remake films, why can't critics remake reviews?" (see Durham, "Inversion").[13]

Although Nichols moves the action from St. Tropez to South Beach, Florida, and changes the names of his characters, the structure and plot of the American film rigorously respect those of the French original. Armand (Robin Williams) and Albert (Nathan Lane) own the club of the film title in which Albert is featured as Starina in the nightly transvestite reviews. As they are about to celebrate their twentieth year as lovers and companions, Armand's son Val (Dan Futterman) arrives to announce his intention to marry the daughter of Senator Keeley (Gene Hackman), co-founder and vice-president of the ultraconservative Coalition for Moral Order. Val insists that during an impending get-acquainted visit with his future in-laws, Armand must send Albert away, get their maid Agador out of drag, and transform himself into a straight diplomat. This proposal provokes hurt and indignation in Albert, whose jealousy is further aroused by Armand's decision to invite Val's mother Katie (Christine Baranski) in an effort to create the illusion of an apparently traditional family. When Katie is delayed, however, Albert takes her place at dinner, and the ensuing complications eventually lead to the exposure of Armand's and Albert's real identity and lifestyle. Fortunately for the young lovers, Keeley is involved in a political scandal and must dress in drag to escape from the nightclub without being spotted by reporters. Thus the film can end happily with the marriage of Val and Barbara (Calista Flockhart).

With *The Birdcage*, there is for once no need to speculate on the reasons for the remake. The film's multiple references to the contemporary political issues in the United States, ranging from abortion to school prayer to gays in the military, make it clear that Nichols considers *La Cage aux folles*, a fifteen-year-old French comedy, ideally suited to explore America's current obsession with "family values."[14] But it is precisely the possibility that stereotypes and attitudes, whose exaggeration and ambivalence already seemed anachronistic in 1979, either can—or should—be identically reproduced in 1996 that makes the existence of this remake particularly astonishing. Although Nichols, like Molinaro before him, no doubt believes that *Cage* delivers a progressive message—one that Richard Corliss, for example, characterizes as a "sweet parable of family values" that is "gently supportive" of gays ("The Final Frontier"

46)—both versions of the film are characterized by an underlying ideological discourse, both homophobic and misogynistic, that invites us at the very least to examine what lies behind our (continued—and cross-cultural) willingness to laugh.

The original *La Cage aux folles* begins with a metaphor: a shot of the stage, where the nightly transvestite show is underway, seen from the perspective of the nightclub audience—middle-class, liberal, and above all, heterosexual. In 1979 the audience on screen seemed to represent the general public for sophisticated French comedies about homosexuality, and also, if less deliberately, the usual American public for subtitled foreign films. In both cases, however, there was a clear discrepancy of ideals and values between the performer and the spectator, between the homosexual transvestite and the heterosexual couple, between the film *La Cage aux folles* and the public at which it was aimed. In 1996 Nichols reinforces, if anything, this complicity between the straight audience on camera and that in movie theaters nationwide by singling out two tables of guests to serve as our official representatives: a couple celebrating its fiftieth wedding anniversary and members of one of America's most infamously heterosexual families, the Kennedys ("the young ones"), who are regular clients of the Birdcage ("I wish we could get Ted," Armand laments). The distance established between audience and actors makes it clear that we are still invited to laugh *at* gays rather than *with* them. "In short," as Corliss concludes, "this new version [of *La Cage aux folles*] is no more threatening to mainstream sentiments than the pro-Indian *Pocohontas*" (46).

Perhaps the most serious symptom of both Molinaro's and Nichols's ambivalence about homosexuality is the making—and remaking—of a film that implicitly advocates heterosexuality. Armand offers only the briefest defense of the lifestyle he has chosen, a single sentence asserting his own identity ("Yes, I'm a middle-aged fag, but I know who I am; it took me twenty years to get here"), before totally acquiescing to Val's plan of disguise, denial, and deception. If Armand's—and eventually Albert's—deliberate denial of their own reality is no doubt intended to prove their commitment to such "family values" as self-sacrificing devotion to one's children, it also reinforces a message we encountered, for example, in *Trois Hommes et un couffin* and *Les Fugitifs*: the traditional, that is, heterosexual, nuclear family is the only acceptable societal model. Albert's jealousy of Val's mother proves, moreover, extremely well justified. On the first afternoon they spent together, Armand and Katie conceived Val; at their second meeting twenty years later, they are well on their way to a repeat performance when Albert's sudden entrance into Katie's office interrupts them. *Cage* thus delivers the clear message that Armand's instincts are heterosexual. Given the ease with which Katie seduces him at their every encounter, we might well conclude that he lives with Albert as a homosexual only because he has not had ready access to the "right" woman. In the American remake Nichols adds to Albert's humiliation by repeatedly crosscutting between the seduction itself and Albert in the waiting room; the lengthy sequence of shots that contrast the perfectly toned bodies of Katie, who heads "Archer Bodyworks," and of her sexy young secretary to Albert's puffy plumpness makes Armand's preference for a "real" woman painfully understandable. Armand's son, representative of the next generation, chooses heterosexuality openly. Armand and Albert specifically sacrifice their gay lifestyle to Val's happiness so that the film can end with a wedding, the celebration *par excellence* of the institution of heterosexuality.

Although the American gay community certainly voiced greater opposition to the Hollywood remake than it did to the French original, which was generally well received by homosexual audiences in the United States (see Durham, "Inversion"), such condemnation has been far from universal. Some critics thought gays themselves responsible for the success of *La Cage aux folles*, and it seems reasonable to assume that at least some percentage of the thousands of spectators who have already made *Birdcage* a runaway hit are homosexual. If gays themselves can laugh at what Bruce Bawer describes as the reduction of gay characters to "cartoons" (qtd. in Forestier, "Le Phénomène"), it is no doubt in large part because neither *La Cage aux folles* nor *The Birdcage*, unlike the Jean Poiret play that the American remake also claims as its principal source, is really about homosexuality at all. The standard gender roles played by the "husband" Armand and the "wife" Albert not only permit this apparently nonconformist couple to be subsumed in the heterosexual norm that the film generally advocates, but also make women the authentic, if covert, subject of attack. Indeed, identities that in Molinaro's film are primarily articulated through the occasional use of gendered pronouns are immediately and explicitly announced in Nichols's remake; the first time they appear on screen together, Albert complains to Armand: "I know what you're thinking. You know everything because you're a man and I know nothing because I'm a woman." Just as the laughter of straight spectators at the conservative Keeley family produces a self-chastisement that frees them to retain their prejudices against gays, so the underlying mockery of women achieves an even more important catharsis that in a still male-oriented culture ultimately permits all laughter at males, homosexual or heterosexual, to pass as harmless. In this context, the literal realization of the homosexual couple may actually serve to defuse the homoerotic anxiety that underlies the representation of all-male couples in such films as *Three Fugitives* or *Three Men and a Baby*.

The primary focus of laughter in Nichols's film, as in Molinaro's, is the "female" homosexual whose identification as woman is evident in the description of straight reviewers who find Albert "flamboyantly effeminate" (Zoglin), and "a tempestuous wife, a doting mother and every inch the great lady" (Corliss, "The Final Frontier" 48). If these characterizations appear to be far more favorable than the adjectives that fifteen years ago cast his original French model as "outrageously bitchy" (*Newsweek*) and "a menopausal hysteric" (*Time*), Albert nonetheless continues to offer a virtual paradigm of stereotypical female behavior, a complete catalogue of conventional feminine flaws. Nichols does not simply portray Albert as the tyrannical and spoiled *prima donna*, a type as often male as female, that he originally represented in Poiret's play and that somewhat influenced Molinaro's interpretation of the character. Rather, from the first, Albert incarnates the typical shrewish wife, vain and unreasonable. On the basis of Armand's failure to appreciate his efforts to lose weight, for example, Albert proceeds to launch a traditionally female series of accusations: you're neglecting me, you're taking me for granted, you don't love me anymore, you're cheating on me. At the end of this tirade, Albert encourages Armand to strike him ("Go ahead, hit me; that's what you want to do"), a wish that is satisfied as the cut to the next scene reveals Albert, transformed into Starina, happily making her grand entrance on stage. *The Birdcage* is certainly not the first film to deliver a doctrine as clear as it is dangerous: not only does violence against women keep them in their place, they like it; in fact, they ask for it. The message proves no less threatening for being concealed in a light-hearted comedy (apparently) about gay men.[15]

The second most important comic character in *The Birdcage*, the Guatemalan maid Agador, cross-dresses as a woman and displays exaggerated and stereotypically feminine mannerisms. If it is already sufficiently astonishing that Nichols retains the black servant he inherits from Poiret and Molinaro as non-white, the American director actually manages to reinforce the implicit racism of his predecessors. Poiret's play at least allows Jacob a number of lines in which he openly mocks his "masters" for their racism. In the original transposition to the screen, Molinaro abandons the exorcism effected by these explicit accusations, so that the filmed stereotype silently reinforces conventional attitudes. Nichols, in contrast, adds new references that openly associate Agador's race with nothing less than savagery. If Agador, now the son of a tribal chief and a high priestess, can't walk properly in shoes, no doubt it is for the same reason that Armand refuses to let him perform in his nightclub, despite a singing voice far superior to Albert's: he is "too primitive." The fact that Agador, like Jacob, dresses "like a whore" is also significant, since the threat to Senator Keeley's career takes the form of Agador's female counterpart; Keeley's colleague, the co-founder and president of the Coalition for Moral Order, has been found dead in the arms of an underage black prostitute. Even if in 1996 the prospective bride is no longer a virgin (indeed, she admits to having had "the test"), Mrs. Keeley (Dianne Wiest) quickly realizes that "a big *white* wedding" can still erase the (*black*) stain left on her husband's reputation by the prostitute. In general, although Albert and Agador are the primary focus of the laughter directed against women, Nichols also uses female characters to further his critique. Notably, as in *Trois Hommes et un couffin*, Val's biological mother is denounced, in her own words, as "not exactly maternal." (Albert, in contrast, is described as "practically a breast.") Not only has she not made any effort to see her son in twenty years, but in the American remake we learn that she originally "traded" him to his father in exchange for the capital she used to found "Archer's Bodyworks."

The use that Nichols makes of Keeley himself, who within his own milieu plays a fool's role comparable to that of Albert, is also revealing. With their initial appearances on camera and long before they actually meet, Nichols begins to establish a parallel between the two men and between both to stereotypical femininity. Throughout the film we see Keeley stuffing himself with the chocolates he is not supposed to eat, in imitation of the similarly self-indulgent, weak-willed, and hysterically nervous Albert; and in the film's finale, Keeley is forced to dress in drag to escape the photographers and reporters who lie in wait outside the club. In Poiret's play, everyone, including the Armand and Val characters, puts on female clothes, but Molinaro and Nichols keep their ideological message pure: only those who are ridiculed and ridiculous are women or, one is tempted to deduce, only women are ridiculous. Moreover, in the American remake, in which Keeley is clearly attracted to Albert in drag—to the point, in fact, of arousing his own wife's jealousy—what might have led to a potentially promising reversal of conventional assumptions is undermined by Nichols's absolute insistence on the heterosexual model of the couple. In order, no doubt, to defuse any suggestion that Keeley's transformation might point to his own latent homosexuality, once Keeley dresses as a woman, Albert appears in public for the only time in the film in traditional male attire. Thus, if the American version of *La Cage aux folles* manages to be every bit as misogynistic as the French original, it manages to be even more openly homophobic.[16] In which case, one can only hope that the French are wrong to predict that the extraordinary success of *The Birdcage* will inevitably lead to the same series of sequels that followed the triumph of Molinaro's film in France.

Still, in anticipation of further repetition, I want to close by citing the final paragraph that originally concluded my discussion of *La Cage aux folles* and its first sequel. ("If Hollywood can remake films, why can't critics remake reviews?") I would not say it the same way today—feminist criticism has matured in the meantime and softened a certain tone that now sounds needlessly militant to me; unfortunately, however, the content of my remarks still applies, which suggests that filmmakers may have changed somewhat less. In 1982 I wrote the following:

Such remarks as I make here normally call forth the protestation that the critic is "missing the point," focusing on clearly secondary aspects of the film or not dealing with the film as a whole on the terms that it sets out for itself as an artistic work. Moreover, some readers will surely suspect that I lack a sense of humor. But, of course, it is precisely those elements of *La Cage aux folles* [and *The Birdcage*] that are "beside the point," "secondary"—and therefore never confronted openly—that constitute its ideology and so permit the constant reinforcement of attitudes unacceptable if voiced aloud. We can laugh at *La Cage aux folles*, [at its remake,] and even at its sequel; indeed, it is hard not to. But laughter need never blind us to the discreet social and political messages contained in the most entertaining of films, for these messages function best when we show our willingness to ignore them. (Durham, "Inversion" 6)[17]

Given the importance of Hollywood's recent practice of remaking French films, deciding which texts to consider in a comparative study potentially becomes as arbitrary as deciding how many to include. That these questions refer me back to my methodological origins is no doubt appropriate at this point in my discussion. In *The Great Cat Massacre*, Robert Darnton also worries that there is "something arbitrary" in his selection of material and therefore "something abusive in drawing general conclusions from it" (262). In contrast to Darnton, however, I am either less troubled by what he calls "the problem of representativeness" (261) or, rather, more fully convinced that I never intended this study to be any more representative than exhaustive. This does not mean, however, that the conclusions I have reached are without meaning or, even, significance. To paraphrase Jean-Philippe Mathy's position in the introduction to *Extrême-Occident*, one need not examine all of the texts produced within a given universe of discourse in order adequately to account for it (11).

Initially, I sought a selection of directors and of films that would represent the variety and the diversity of the remake phenomenon. In this context, for example, I wanted to achieve some balance between the works of critically acclaimed cineastes with international reputations (such as Resnais, Godard, and Truffaut) and those of mainstream filmmakers virtually unknown outside of France (such as Veber, Serreau, and Tacchella). To the extent possible, I took similar concerns into consideration in relation to the directors of remakes, although here my choices were clearly far more limited. Still, I preferred Truffaut's *L'Homme qui aimait les femmes*, for example, to other possibilities (such as *Jules et Jim*) because of the relative prominence of Blake Edwards among American filmmakers. Similarly, I was interested in comparisons in which the virtual contemporaneity of the original and the remake promised to highlight cross-cultural differences (as in *Trois Hommes et un couffin* and

Double Takes

Three Men and a Baby) as well as those in which the passage of time could be expected to interact significantly with cultural constants (as in *A Bout de souffle* and *Breathless*). In other cases, the variables in question were far more specific. *A Bout de souffle*, for example, refers back to the New Wave, whose stylistic innovations still dominate the content of many French film courses taught on the campuses of American colleges and universities. In contrast, the Oscar awarded to *Cousin, Cousine* led, at least potentially, to the nationwide distribution of French comedies within the United States. In the case of Nimoy and Serreau, the director changed sex as well as nationality; in that of Veber, the director of the French original remade his own film in Hollywood; and so on.

Gradually, however, a focus on gender and, more specifically, on the cultural construction of masculinity began to emerge from my study. The fact, for which the reader will to some extent obviously have to take my word, that the revelation of this thematics resulted not from a prior selection process, but rather from the practice of comparative analysis itself, has interesting implications. Neither of the two most common theories about Hollywood's current passion for the remake has ever struck me as fully convincing, in part, no doubt, because they are mutually contradictory. Rather than reproducing French films in order to "cash in on guaranteed hits" (Pall)—a foreign "guarantee," of course, that U.S. audiences may or may not honor—or, alternatively, to exploit a source of "new, offbeat material" (Young), the American film industry, my experience suggests, is attracted to foreign films precisely to the extent that they resist foreignness and represent concerns and interests fully consistent with the cultural climate of the United States. From this perspective, the otherwise astonishing decision to remake *La Cage aux folles*—years after the French original was either successful or innovative—actually makes perfect sense. *The Birdcage* is in many ways the logical continuation of Hollywood's ongoing exploration of the homoerotic subtext that both consistently underlies the development of male friendships on screen and accompanies changes in traditional masculine roles within the family.

In addition to the further comparative study of the many American remakes of French films that I have omitted from these pages, whose consideration may well produce a different dynamics of cross-cultural differences and similarities, a number of other methodological approaches should be explored.[18] Although my specific interest in textual analysis and cross-cultural comparison led me to focus on contexts more revelatory of differences than of similarities, virtually identical films also raise a number of potentially intriguing questions. Notably, the fact that two texts are similar does not necessarily mean that their reception will be too; French and American audiences, for example, may well laugh at different times or for different reasons. To assume otherwise leads to what Philip Schlesinger has identified as "the *fallacy of distribution*, according to which it is supposed that distributing the same cultural product leads to an identity of interpretation on the part of those who consume it" (qtd. in Elteren 62; see also Tomlinson). The frequency with which my own research has led me to the work of certain particularly prominent film critics (such as Canby, Ansen, and Kauffmann) suggests that the remake phenomenon might also be intriguingly explored through systematic analysis of the responses of one or more popular media reviewers to both French films and their Hollywood remakes.

Ultimately, I think that the notion of the "remake" could be usefully extended to include other films that lend themselves, if less obviously, to cross-cultural comparison. One might, for example, compare Claire Denis's *Chocolat* (1988) to Harry Hook's *Kitchen Toto* (1988), both of which are first feature films coded as autobiographical accounts of growing up in colonialist Africa; or Euzhan Palcy's *A Dry White Season* (1989) and Chris Menges's *A World Apart* (1988), which offer parallel accounts of South Africa. A Franco-American comparison of recent jazz films—Bertrand Tavernier's *Round Midnight* (1986), Clint Eastwood's *Bird* (1989), and Spike Lee's *Mo' Better Blues* (1990)—similarly promises to illuminate both the intricate ways in which race, culture, class, and gender are interconnected and the alternative ways in which this relationship is structured depending on the racial and national identity of the culture on which a particular film focuses. In the context of an even broader cultural base of comparison, I am also intrigued by the curious phenomenon by which two directors—one British, Stephen Frears, and one Polish-American, Milos Forman—simultaneously elected to film in 1988 and 1989 new English-language versions of *Les Liaisons dangereuses*, Choderlos de Laclos's eighteenth-century novel about class conflict and sexual politics on the eve of the French Revolution, originally translated into (French) film by Roger Vadim in 1959. I suspect that these three very different cinematic interpretations of what is nonetheless the same story might reveal with particular clarity the ways in which culture and ideology come to be inscribed in visual technique.

In conclusion, we are also left with the question of varying, indeed, distinctively different, national responses to the remake phenomenon as a whole. As the American film industry acquires remake rights with increasing voracity, the French cultural establishment continues to fluctuate between resignation, despair, and outright anger. Ultimately, the attitudes of both partners in the process, as well as the process itself, may reflect deeply embedded cultural characteristics. In a discussion of attitudes toward immigration, Ted Morgan, whose personal metamorphosis from his original identity as Sanche de Gramont curiously reproduces the cultural remake on the level of the individual, sets in opposition an America that absorbs new arrivals to a France that defends against impurities (216). To some extent, the very fact that a

Double Takes

French film *can* be remade, regardless of how well or how successfully, must irritate and puzzle a nation whose identity is and always has been grounded in an absolute belief in French cultural distinctiveness (see, for example, Bernstein). Of late, the notion of *appellation contrôlée*, which once served primarily to distinguish the champagne and the cognac of France from supposedly similar products produced elsewhere, has been vastly extended in an apparent attempt to establish the inimitable Frenchness of everything from cassoulet to Camembert. Indeed, the recent practice of producing big-budget, state-supported, historical films could be interpreted as the application of this politics of *appellation contrôlée* to the domain of French cinema. Films such as Rappeneau's *Cyrano* (1990) and *Le Hussard sur le toit* (1995) or Molinaro's *Beaumarchais l'Insolent* (1995) resemble officially patented products of France that are surely unlikely to be reproduced, if not impossible to reproduce, in a different national culture.

In recalling the role played by Touchstone and Universal Studios in the production of Hollywood remakes, Marc Mancini comments that "Disney, in fact, seems to have concocted a particularly arcane cultural equation; bring Paris cinema here, build Disney-World there" (37). Since I first drafted the introduction to this book, I have had occasion to visit Euro Disney at Marne-la-Vallée. It is, I am assured, virtually identical in size, layout, and choice of attractions to the original park in California, and French visitors of all ages appeared to be appropriately enchanted on the day I was there. Since I have never seen an American Disneyland, I am painfully aware that I am about to put myself in the position of the many reviewers I have chided for bemoaning the inferiority of a remake without any direct knowledge of the original and, moreover, to illustrate my own "compulsion to compare." Still, perhaps it was my imagination, but, in my view, the Disney characters moved about with an identifiably more sedate Gallic gait and their gestures and speech, even in disguise, somehow managed to convey something closer to the mildly sardonic and somewhat disabused tones of Paris than to the childlike wonder and wide-eyed optimism that I had always associated with the original American dream. I mean this not as a criticism, of course, but as yet another example of the limits of either the transplantation or the translation of one national culture into another.

There are, of course, less subjective differences. Notably, Tomorrowland of the American amusement park has been replaced outside Paris by "Discoveryland," which features Leonardo da Vinci, H. G. Wells, and Jules Verne, in what Miles Orvell suggests, consistent with a distinction we have often encountered, may be "the result of seeing Europe as a more traditional, a more literary culture, one more interested in the history of discovery than its future" (250). Similarly, Orvell is surely right to point out that the very experience of Disneyland varies with its geographical context. If, for example, a

Fantasyland situated in California or Florida invites its visitors to escape into "a realm of imagined European culture," characterized by castles, fairy tales, and figures of royalty, then the very proximity of the *châteaux* of the Loire valley makes any directly parallel evasion in France highly unlikely (252). From this perspective, the similar positioning of the Loire *châteaux* and of Euro Disney within their respective Michelin guides may be the only common ground on which the two can meet.

Richard Pells singles out Euro Disney as an exemplary illustration of how the success of American products in France depends upon their ability to adapt to French culture. Moreover, Pells and others point out that not only does France participate in the "Europeanizing" of American exports in ways that enable it to preserve its cultural distinctiveness both in relation to the United States and within Europe, but that the cultural exchange is not nearly as one-sided as France's political and intellectual establishment would have the world believe. "In the modern world," notes Elteren, "a 'national culture' is never purely locally produced, it always contains the traces of previous cultural borrowings or influences which have been part of a thorough assimilation process and have become 'naturalized'" (68). In this cultural context, which could well serve as a metaphor for the kind of complex, dynamic, and palimpsestic interactions that, as we have seen, characterize an "original" film and its "remake," French journalists need not worry that the "Americanization" of their cinema marks the waning influence of their own culture in the United States, nor should American reviewers lament that soon all films will end up looking alike. On the contrary, the contemporary practice of remaking French comedies in Hollywood offers a unique opportunity for cross-cultural comparisons that (to date at least) foreground the endurance, even in an increasingly international world, of Franco-American differences, and thus the resilient distinctiveness of both nations' particular identities. In this context, Disney's cultural equation becomes eminently explicable, fully understandable, indeed, anything but "arcane."

Notes

Introduction: Disneyland Comes Home to Paris

1. All translations from the French are my own, unless otherwise indicated.
2. The word *entertainment* appears in English in the original.
3. The original French reads: "Celui-ci [le modèle américain] ne conçoit la différence qu'à travers l'intégration, l'enrôlement culturel, l'absorption d'un langage dans un autre, prétendu universel, où tout repose sur le spectacle. Ce langage culturel— qui conçoit le melting-pot—n'a pour autant nulle peur de s'affronter à ce qui relève encore de quelques traces de civilisation, en offrant le seul salut possible: la vulgar- isation." In a recent essay on the effects of American popular culture in Western Europe, Mel van Elteren concurs that "American culture is characterized by an aesthetics of performance" (66) whose further dissemination in Europe could in- deed lead to "a deeper transformation of everyday culture." At the same time, how- ever, Elteren views this "culture of performance and expressive individualism" as inherent to Western modernity in general and therefore unrelated to any threat of the "colonization" of "European" cultural identity by the influx of U.S. popular cul- ture in Europe (71).
4. See, for example, the special issue that *SubStance* devoted in 1995 to "France's Identity Crisis." *Time* has published two special issues on France in recent years: "The New France" (15 July 1991) and "La France Peut-elle s'en sortir?" (4 Decem- ber 1995). See also Bernstein, Kuisel, and Mathy.
5. *Assimilation*, from the Latin *assimilare*: to make *similar* to by absorbing into the prevailing culture; *integration*, from the Latin *integrare*: to make *whole* by bringing all parts together into equal association. Unless otherwise specified, all future defi- nitions and etymologies are also cited from *The American Heritage Dictionary of the English Language*. For French words, similar references are to *Le Nouveau Petit Robert*.
6. See Tomlinson for a particularly insightful discussion of the complex and proble- matic concept of "cultural imperialism."
7. *Trois Hommes et un couffin* earned $3.5 million in the United States in its subtitled French version; *Three Men and a Baby* earned $170 million (Cohen, "Aux Armes").
8. I am speaking primarily of mainstream cinema and of reviews; in the domain of art or auteur cinema, as we will see, there exist a great many detailed scholarly studies of what makes French film(s) specifically French. What may be relevant here, however, is the general tendency of the French to equate "cinema" with "art." The high critical praise with which some American reviewers have welcomed such re- cent French exports as Coline Serreau's *Romuald et Juliette* might suggest that this equation also plays some role in shaping American expectations of French

205

films. The origin of this very project lies in my initial reaction of anger after viewing an earlier Serreau film, *Trois Hommes et un couffin*. (As Ellis says, "Dislike of a film is usually a very aggressive feeling" [86].) Unlike the French press and my own Parisian friends, not only did I fail to perceive the highly praised "originality" of Serreau's comedy but I eventually realized that it deeply offended my own sense of French cinema as "art film."

9. Capretz and Lydgate suggest that "American cultural imperialism" is directly related to American sexism: "Because of historical and economic reasons that are now some two centuries old, the ways in which Americans view other cultures are analogous to the ways in which men have traditionally viewed women . . . [as] something subjectless, something with demands that need not be attended to, something to be sampled for delight or anathematized in disgust, but something whose integrity need not be taken into consideration" (10). In France, the nation is symbolized by the image of Marianne, whose particular features change over time to conform to those of living models of ideal French womanhood. That these women have often been actresses, as in the case of Brigitte Bardot and Catherine Deneuve, emphasizes once again the connection between the French nation, its culture, and its cinema.

10. In 1996, even as France regained its status as the most popular tourist destination in the world, only Mont St. Michel topped Disneyland Paris as the most frequently visited site in France. With 11,800,000 foreign visitors, Disneyland Paris came out ahead of both Beaubourg and the Louvre—in keeping, ironically, with the relative importance advocated in the Michelin guidebooks for *Euro Disney Resort*.

Comic Strips and Cultural Stereotypes: Alain Resnais's *I Want to Go Home*

1. According to Thomas, Resnais modeled the character of Gauthier on what the director described as the "demented brain of Umberto Eco" (314).

2. I assume that Vincendeau's omission of *I Want to Go Home* from her recent article on Depardieu simply means that she (too) never had an opportunity to see it. Not only does Resnais's film explicitly illustrate her thesis that the actor "to some extent defines contemporary French cinema" but *Home* also combines the work in comedy and in auteur films that Vincendeau sees as the key to Depardieu's exceptional status. One could argue, in fact, that in some sense the role of Christian Gauthier—at once a populist, a comic, and an intellectual hero—embraces multiple aspects of Depardieu's own film career. I will return to the question of the actor's representative Frenchness in a subsequent essay.

3. As we have already seen, Elsie's list of great French writers also includes Sartre and Beauvoir but only on a first-name basis, which suggests a familiarity and an accessibility foreign to canonization. Seventeenth-century France, in contrast, was the production site of what must surely be the most ambitious "remake" project ever undertaken: the transformation of the Greco-Roman culture at the origin of Western civilization into a new and specifically French classicism. Moreover, the contemporaneous creation of the French Academy institutionalized the protection of

this modern version of *civilisation*, lest it become in turn the target of the very tactics that had brought it into being.

4. According to Thomas, it was important to Resnais that Hepp Catt and Sally Catt "specifically call to mind at all times the comic strip and not the animated cartoon" (295).

5. Herman Lebovics borrows the concept of "wrapping" from Frederic Jameson to describe how France incorporated the native cultures of its colonies into European high culture in the 1930s (57, n. 14). More recently, in an article on the French-led opposition to the GATT, Mel van Elteren depicts the reception of American culture in Europe in terms of what he calls "processes of creolization" (67). Joelle Attinger points out contemporary France's continued ability to absorb and transform foreign influences, although her examples tend to be frivolous: "Even as French politicians rail against the cultural imperialism of others—particularly the American variety—foreign strains are continually passed through an invisible sieve, gaining veneers of sophistication even their creators never dreamed of. Where else would one find lowly catsup elevated to a rarefied condiment . . . ?" (42; see also Kuisel 232–33; and Tomlinson 90ff). I will return to this question in my conclusion.

6. Through "Bambi," one of the primary examples Terry cites of Disney's "tragic vision," *I Want to Go Home* finds a curious resonance in Spielberg's explanation of why he decided to do a remake of an earlier American film (*A Guy Named Joe*): "It was the second movie that ever made me cry that didn't have a deer in it" (Pall). Elteren confirms Gauthier's assessment of American popular culture as more widely representative: "Protagonists of European 'high' culture have sometimes valued American popular culture differently than the guardians of high culture in America—think of Picasso's affection for the Katzenjammer Kids cartoon strip . . . or the impact of Hollywood *film noir* on the French "new novel" (69).

7. The fact that Joey presents such potential American virtues as sincerity, friendliness, easy intimacy, and so on, only in their exaggerated and therefore flawed forms may be culturally significant in itself. In Terry's words: "You Americans are fond of your own shortcomings—and the French, of course, are fond of those of others."

8. In English in the French-language version of the film.

9. Nostrand argues that Anglo-Saxon culture as a whole is characterized by a habit of thought he calls "particularism," that is, the "emphasis on the concrete case as a primary independent reality" (469).

10. See David Finkle's column for an amusing take on the frustration of not being allowed to speak French in France. Finkle explicitly raises the question of whether the persistence of this practice is somehow reflective of "a need to hang on to national identity." See also Mathy 274.

11. "*Botte* de foin, Miss," insists the secretary, when Elsie uses the otherwise perfectly acceptable (and, certainly, perfectly understandable, even here) word "*meule* de foin" in the idiomatic expression "chercher une aiguille dans une botte de foin" (to look for a needle in a haystack).

12. In France, moreover, names are not simply a matter of personal—or parental—

choice. The Napoleonic Code officially made first names "immutable" from birth. In recent years, as Bernstein notes, foreigners who acquire French citizenship have been allowed to *"franciser"* their names so that "presumably, [a] hypothetical Mohammed could decide to call himself Maurice or Michel but not Mahsoud or Muammar, which are Arabic names" (101).

13. I do not mean to belabor my own disorientation, but to be honest this description does not entirely make sense to me. If, as Mazabrard says, "the entire film is in English," then "the American" is not "lost in a foreign language," at least not in this version of the film. I would think that a more accurate analogy might center around Elsie, whose experience, as we have already seen, makes the film's audience an integral part of its own diegesis. The only difference in the original version of *I Want to Go Home* (for which Laura Benson, unlike Green and Lavin, dubbed her own role) is that there are now a whole series of "Elsies" speaking a language that is not their own.

14. Given the prominence of *La Règle du jeu*, I have relegated this brief summary to the notes. Renoir's film focuses on the lives of a group of aristocrats and their servants who spend a weekend at the country home of Robert de la Chesnaye and his wife Christine. Among the guests are André Jurieu, an aviator in love with Christine, and Octave, an old friend of hers. In the servants' quarters, Robert's gamekeeper tries to keep Marceau, the poacher-turned-valet away from his own wife, who is Christine's maid. In the final scene, the gamekeeper shoots Jurieu in error, mistaking him for Octave, whom he wrongly confuses with Marceau as the seducer of his wife.

Jim McBride's "Breathless In L.A.": Remaking Jean-Luc Godard's Narrative of Gender

1. I have verified my citation of the last two lines of the film with the published script. Some reviewers hear Michel's line as "T'es vraiment déguelasse," which is certainly consistent with the meaning of the scene and with my interpretation; and I initially understood the detective's line as "Il a dit: vous êtes vraiment déguelasse(s)." My argument remains essentially the same; in the latter case, the police officer repeats a "singular" insult, which Michel addresses directly to Patricia, as a general comment that indirectly targets all women. Although a reasonable translation of the first and last lines of the film might produce something like "I'm a bloody fool" and "You're rotten to the core," both of these expressions also invite a more gender-specific interpretation that simultaneously (re)inscribes the two poles of Godard's emplotment of gender: the man's self-aware victimization—"What a cunt I am"—and the woman's readiness to betray—"You're a real bitch."

2. To be exact, we also glimpse a Clark Gable poster in passing, a reference fully consistent with that to Flynn—and to the Silver Surfer.

3. In her memoir about her love affair with France and its language, Alice Kaplan describes "existentialism," at once as signifier, signified, and referent, as constitutive of Frenchness itself: "A different kind of landmark: in 1966 I first heard the word

'existentialism' . . . It was the longest word I had ever heard. French was this, too, always—even in beginning French classes you knew there was a France beyond the everyday, a France of hard talk and intellect, where God was dead and you were on your own, totally responsible" (138).

4. Thomas Schatz argues that such a "radical amalgamation of genre conventions" (23) is generally characteristic of American cinematic narrative in the 1970s, a period when films also exhibit a "strong nostalgic quality" (16). Hollywood's growing fascination with the remake, beginning in the 1980s, may then be the logical sequel to this earlier trend.

5. "Tout à l'heure, dans *France-Soir*, j'ai lu un truc pas mal. Un receveur d'autobus qui avait volé 5 millions pour séduire une fille. Il se faisait passer pour un riche imprésario. Ils sont descendus ensemble sur la Côte. En trois jours, ils ont grillé les 5 millions et là, le type, il s'est pas dégonflé. Il a dit à la fille: 'C'est de l'argent volé. Je suis un voyou, mais je t'aime.' Et ce que je trouve de formidable, c'est que la fille l'a pas laissé tomber. Elle lui a dit: 'Moi aussi je t'aime bien.' Ils sont remontés ensemble à Paris et on les a pincés alors qu'ils cambriolaient les villas à Passy. C'est gentil de sa part."

Three Takes on Motherhood, Masculinity, and Marriage: Serreau's Original, Nimoy's Remake, and Ardolino's Sequel

1. Since 1988, the situation has twice recurred, albeit in reverse. Mary Agnes Donoghue directed *Paradise* (1991), the remake of Jean-Loup Hubert's *Le Grand Chemin* (1987); and Nadia Tass directed *Pure Luck* (1991), the remake of Francis Veber's *La Chèvre* (1982).

2. Of the many reviewers or critics who note the change in directors, Mancini is, to my knowledge, the only one to hazard any explanation. Raymonde Carroll maintains that Serreau continued to act as "production consultant" throughout the filming of the Hollywood remake ("Film et Analyse" 346).

3. I mean this only metaphorically; the fundamental problem is that of the indifference to culture that appears to accompany most feminist film criticism that is psychoanalytically informed. Lucy Fischer's recent analysis of *Trois Hommes* in her *Cinematernity* (118–28) has the same problems as Modleski's reading of *Three Men*, although in reverse. Fischer now focuses exclusively on the French film but without ever wondering what might be specifically French about this particular version of what she sees as a virtual "subgenre" of comedy in general: "those comic films that sustain female absence, while positioning maternity at center stage" (118). Moreover, by virtue of focusing on one version to the exclusion of the other, Fischer exaggerates the significance of certain elements that, if present in *Trois Hommes*, are nonetheless much more typical of the American remake.

4. That the French should sometimes disagree about the significance of Serreau's sex is not necessarily inconsistent with some of the cultural beliefs we will see reflected in the film. In the opinion of André Dussollier, who plays the role of Jacques, "only a woman can have written this film" (qtd. in Serreau 101), although

the only explanation he offers in support of this conviction—the fact that Serreau had recently given birth to a baby girl and therefore had to take care of her (104)—seems, if anything, directly contradicted as a specifically female issue by the very subject matter of *Trois hommes et un couffin*. More generally, Serreau's reputation as a "feminist filmmaker," mostly as a result of her 1975 documentary, *Mais qu'est-ce qu'elles veulent*, tends to cause French reviewers to confuse her ideological positions with her sex. In relation to *Trois hommes* specifically, Serreau has said "I'm not a professional feminist. I'm a filmmaker; I'm not out to indoctrinate spectators" (105).

5. Richard Corliss begins a review of John Sayles's *Passion Fish* with what he (no doubt appropriately) characterizes: "Humongous generalization of the week: Hollywood movies are masculine; foreign and independent films are feminine" ("What Dreams Come To").

6. Irma Garcia offers a particularly comprehensive overview of French feminist theory; see also the essays anthologized in *New French Feminisms* (Marks & Courtivron), *The Future of Difference* (Eisenstein & Jardine), and *French Connections* (Duchen). On the pro-natalist campaign waged by the French government in the summer of 1985, see, for example, Zeldin (94); and Dudovitz (161). Although pro-natalist propaganda resurfaces periodically throughout modern French history, the billboard campaign of 1985 nonetheless stands out, not only for its intensity and visual appeal but as the first example of such a politics since the election of a Socialist president in 1981.

7. In January 1987, at a time when Serreau was still working for Walt Disney Studios, *Avant-Scène* published an excerpt from her projected screenplay for the American remake. Despite the editors' assertion that Serreau has entirely rewritten and re-conceived her original film to adapt it to an American public and that the pharmacy sequence, in particular, is "totally different," the changes seem relatively superficial. The pharmacy is replaced by a Safeway, but Peter is questioned and advised not only by a female employee, as in Nimoy's version, but by two female customers as well. Thus, women as a group retain their authority as "natural" experts on motherhood; indeed, the scene ends with their sudden realization of the only plausible explanation for Peter's "fatherhood": "You know what? It's a kidnaping" (Serreau 87–88).

8. As with French feminism, the sources are many and diverse. See, for example, Carolyn Durham (*The Contexture of Feminism*), Toril Moi, and Elaine Showalter ("Feminist Criticism"), all of whom explicitly contrast French and American feminist theory; and Nancy Chodorow, who reworks traditional Freudian psychoanalysis into a "sociology of gender." Note that all three American films—Belslawski's and Ford's *Three Godfathers* and Nimoy's *Three Men and a Baby*—resemble each other and differ from Serreau's in one particularly significant way: fatherhood is not limited to the biological and both the right and the ability of men to "mother" is unproblematically assumed.

9. Lucy Fischer draws on Northrop Frye's argument that comedies often duplicate the structure of legal confrontations to suggest that "the male maternal comedy enacts a symbolic court case—a custody battle" (*Cinematernity* 123). In fact, this

characterization applies much more clearly to John Ford's version of *Three God-fathers* than to either *Trois Hommes* or *Three Men*.

10. To the extent that Serreau reconstructs the couple on an explicitly *heterosexual* model, it also serves one of the same functions as Nimoy's narrative of virility. Both directors appear equally homophobic in their desire to diffuse any suggestion of homosexuality, although once again they adopt revealingly different strategies to achieve a common end.

11. I am reminded of Vincent Canby's witty column satirizing French assertions that the poor reception reserved for *Trois Hommes et un couffin* by New York film critics was politically motivated in protest of France's refusal to allow U.S. planes to fly over French territory during the 1986 raid on Libya ("How France's 'Cradle'").

12. Only in the American films does the mother's nationality differ from that of the three fathers. The choice of a British identity for Sylvia represents both the initial "foreignness" of the mother and of maternity and the possibility of their cultural recuperation, precisely through a return to our origins, at once gendered, cultural, and cinematic.

At the Franco-American Crossroads of Gender and Culture: Where Feminism and Sexism Intersect

1. All references are to this official version of the report, which is available, upon request, from the chair of the Yale French department. Although the Yale students subsequently sent copies of their letters of complaint (originally submitted to the Women's Studies department and the Sexual Harassment Grievance Board as well as to the French department) to other institutions who had adopted *French in Action*, I have chosen not to identify the students by name in citing representative examples of their complaints.

2. Because the purpose of *French in Action* is to teach the French language, I have included the original French version of all quotations followed by their English translation.

3. Unfortunately, this particular version of the doctrine of "separate spheres" continues to replicate itself within the structure of the Modern Language Association. Although one can fairly assume that the annual convention is designed to represent the diverse interests of the membership as a whole, the many papers presented on explicitly pedagogical issues never find their equivalent reproduced in essay form in the pages of *PMLA*, the same organization's official professional journal. Moreover, this omission recurs at a time when the traditional subjects of *PMLA* essays have themselves turned to the writing of textbooks, literally so in the case of Alain Robbe-Grillet's *Djinn*, reprinted with Yvonne Lenard in textbook format as *Le Rendez-vous*. This is a particularly fascinating text for any exploration of the relationship between culture and gender, since the particular set of formal "generative constraints" that Robbe-Grillet imposes on himself—that is the respect of the grammatical and lexical limitations of a beginning to intermediate foreign-language student (9)—not only produces a content grounded in Franco-American

differences but, more specifically, engenders a cross-cultural "battle of the sexes" (19).

4. See, for example, Elaine Marks & Isabelle de Courtivron. For more recent discussions and bibliographies, see Toril Moi; Carolyn A. Durham, *The Contexture of Feminism*; and Nancy Fraser & Sandra Lee Bartky.

5. The commitment to social change, an element common to different feminisms, constitutes a particularly serious obstacle to the study of a foreign language and culture, whose goal, as George Santoni points out, is directly antithetical: "Our primary concerns are not to motivate social changes but discussions, acceptance of other ways, awareness of the concepts of otherness" ("Visual Images" 72). Thus Alice Kaplan, although she appears to agree with the charges of sexism directed against *French in Action*, cannot finally support them, precisely because of the cultural authenticity of the Capretz method: "I've been willing to overlook in French culture what I couldn't accept in my own, for the privilege of living in translation" (140; see 125–41).

6. Silence is precisely the approach recommended to American women in *Let's Go France: 1989*, the popular student travel guide published by Harvard University: "Your best answer to verbal harassment is no answer at all" (qtd. in Capretz & Lydgate, "A Statement" 6).

7. As Claire J. Kramsch's work has revealed, most existing foreign language textbooks employ "culture-learning strategies" that derive from the assumption that "the foreign culture is basically the same as the native culture" ("Cultural Discourse" 82). With this in mind, initial student blindness, resistance to any view of a foreign culture that challenges American ethnocentrism, or both, are not surprising. See also Santoni, "Visual Images."

8. Jean-Pierre's dismissal of Mireille a few moments later—"ah non, pas la blonde dans cette horrible jupe rouge de Prisunic" (oh no, not the blond in that horrible red skirt from Prisunic [a French K-Mart])—confirms that he has correctly interpreted her earlier remark as a rejection.

9. The identical outcome of Mireille's successive encounters with Jean-Pierre and Robert—in the latter case she abruptly flees from the Jardin du Luxembourg as well—underlines not only their parallelism as such, but also the apparently omnipresent male fantasy that makes it possible. Left to his own devices, Robert quickly proceeds to (super)impose verbal uniform-ity on the visual diversity of all immediately available women: "Les Parisiennes portent des pulls blancs et des jupes rouges" (Parisian women wear white sweaters and red skirts) (Lesson 14).

10. Although beginning language students would not use the terminology and might well not understand the particular theoretical frameworks that inform this analysis, they do, in my experience, arrive at the same conclusions. They might not know, for example, what is meant by "the deconstruction of the discourse of masculinity" or "the subversion of the heterosexual romance narrative," but they clearly understand that Mireille is "moqueuse" and that her gentle mockery of Jean-Pierre and Robert undermines both them and their romantic pretensions. To put it more simply, *French in Action* is funny; the video makes students laugh and they understand, without ever having read Robert Darnton, that laughter is subversive. In this

context, Jean-Pierre emerges as the classic comic figure whose endless repetition of the same act to the same predictable end marks his behavior as every bit as mechanical, automatic, and conventionally formalistic as that of the "guignol" or the mime who reappear in every lesson to define on a broader scale the comic function and functioning of male figures within *French in Action*. Student familiarity with MTV also translates into a ready ability to read postmodernist parodic strategies accurately. Finally, the dependence of *French in Action* on repetition, the reinforcement of narrative content by associated lexical and grammatical exercises, further assures student complicity with the active and critical stance required of them.

11. Mireille's actual meeting with Robert is similarly coded as conventionally literary, literary convention, or both by the use of experimental film techniques (such as, the slow-motion insistence on the traditional shot/countershot sequence; the musical parody of the romantic score; and the visual irony of the mime's ceremonious salute).

12. An embedded bilingual allusion relevant to gender and culture may be in play here. The term *chauvinism* originates in excessive devotion to Napoleon, and the French word no doubt continues to evoke extreme patriotism. Feminist influence, however, has altered its usage in English, where *chauvinism* is more likely to identify a commitment to the superiority of men than to that of the United States. Robert, of course, is of bicultural heritage.

13. Although intriguing intertexual parallels between the narrative of *French in Action* and that of Godard's *A Bout de souffle* have, I assume, been clear at several earlier points in this discussion, the following one is sufficiently curious to merit specific mention: Michel, also arguably a professional *dragueur*, refuses Patricia's request that he buy her a dress "chez Dior" with the assertion that "what you find at Prisunic is a lot better."

14. The interference of American cultural values not only leads students to reinterpret class issues as a fact of gender but also affects their understanding of gender itself, when it is at issue, by leading them to misread the textual reversal of stereotypical gender roles as their reinscription. Thus, objections to Georgette's portrayal as a "stereotypical spinster" typically cite as evidence her dislike of children; in fact, her open assumption that she has every right to dislike children seems anything but stereotypically "feminine." Similarly, Guillaume's fondness for children not only challenges stereotypically masculine values but makes him, if anyone, the unfulfilled object of pity unmarried women have so often been.

15. Although a full consideration of the intricate textual and contextual functioning of "Pierre Capretz" would require a detailed study of its own, we can begin to see how the complex attributes and multiple roles of the intradiegetic professor of *French in Action* work to undermine any automatic assumptions about male pedagogical authority in the extradiegetic classroom as well. The ongoing critique of masculinity, which necessarily includes "Pierre" in his own incarnations of both actor and director, inevitably extends to embrace the clearly analogous role of teacher, especially since this particular "performance" has a certain French charm not unrelated to the flirtatiousness associated with Jean-Pierre and Robert. At the same time, how-

ever, as we have seen on a number of occasions, the professor consistently draws on the pedagogical and linguistic authority he retains to point out to us, to reinforce, and to participate in that very critique.

16. The prominent role played by the visual objectification of the female body in images of popular culture suggests that it is extremely difficult to avoid entirely, and certainly students have a valid objection to *French in Action*'s perpetuation of a conventionally dichotomous portrayal and evaluation of women, alternatively idealized as beautiful and ridiculed as ugly. Although the men are figured similarly, perhaps because the French have unusually strong respect for a particularly narrow range of cultural "norms" that define appropriate appearance and behavior, such a depiction is unquestionably more detrimental for women, given its broad and constant cultural reinforcement. I will point out, however, that the only remotely erotic shot in Lesson 11 is the repeated view of a nearly-nude Robert getting out of bed. On the other hand, I am also aware of a unique pedagogical problem that results almost inevitably from the use of *French in Action*. Because the completion of a coherent sequence rather than the specific on-screen visual content most often determines when the instructor puts the video on "pause," this act can produce fragmented images of the female body that refocus visual attention in potentially voyeuristic ways. It is often possible, however, to avoid this effect and always easy to rectify it quickly. In any event, the problem arises only from a particular classroom use to which the text is put and not from the text itself.

Jean-Charles Tacchella's and Joel Schumacher's Kissing Cousins: In/Fidelity in Family and Film

1. These scenes have a famous literary ancestor in the *fête mystérieuse* of *Le Grand Meaulnes* (1913) at which authority is also delegated to children and which culminates in a masquerade ball. Alain-Fournier's celebrated novel, whose narrative structure depends on the dynamics of fantasy and reality, focuses, of course, on adolescence; indeed, many historians of French literature argue that we owe the interwar phenomenon of the *roman d'adolescence* to its example and its influence.

2. The emphasis that Tacchella places on pleasure and play in *Cousin, Cousine* does suggest another possible explanation for Jacques's heart attack. Prior to the slide show, he has spent his limited "leisure" time ("I work all week long in a travel agency, so on weekends I want to enjoy nature") jogging and digging huge rocks out of a pit to make a swimming pool. It may be this atypical commitment to work, a trait more American than French, that his sudden death punishes.

3. The historical origins of French film lie precisely at the juncture of reality and fantasy, with the contemporaneous appearance of the realistic documentaries of the Lumière Brothers and the supernatural fictions of Georges Méliès. French comedy, in particular, may continue to reflect the paradoxes of this double tradition. Thus *Cousin, Cousine* is at once a social satire and a romantic comedy.

4. In a further example of irony, however, Clinton's unusual ability to survive the allegations of sexual misconduct, which have ended the careers of other American

politicians, may also have to do with culturally specific notions of seduction. Unlike France, where intelligence and a prestigious education are highly prized qualifications for positions of leadership, Clinton's Rhodes scholarship and Yale law degree arguably did him little good in the United States. American culture most consistently associates "manhood" with economic power; with physical prowess and courage, whose heroic manifestations often include violence; and with sexual seductiveness. Unlike most other male candidates for national office, Clinton didn't meet the first two criteria. He wasn't rich—in fact, he was financially dependent on his wife—and he was neither a war hero nor an athlete. But he was reputed to be a womanizer; and I would suggest that what in any other circumstances would have been a tremendous, and probably insurmountable, liability has become in Clinton's case a kind of asset: the "proof," however unspoken and unspeakable, that he really is a "man" after all.

5. Although some reviewers tend to attribute the changes in attitudes toward adultery in the two films more to historical context than to cultural difference, I think Schumacher is right to insist on the latter. (For example, Manohla Dargis of *The Village Voice* asserts that "any difference between *Cousins* '75 and '89 is due less to the transatlantic shift than to the social and psychic distance between the mid-'70s and late '80s"; see also Ansen, "Love.") Certainly fourteen years separate the 1970s, a decade characterized by exceptional tolerance for sexual freedom, from a period now deeply concerned about sexually transmitted diseases. Still, I would cite an even more recent American film, Clint Eastwood's *The Bridges of Madison County* (1995), as evidence of Hollywood's apparent need to find adultery *per se* unthinkable at any or, rather, at every point in time. That sexual infidelity in Iowa in the 1950s should be a source of scandal is hardly surprising, but the contemporary reactions of disbelief, shock, and outrage, which Eastwood attributes to the young adults who learn about their mother's affair years later, are, frankly, unbelievable, indeed, so unrealistic as to border on the ridiculous. Since most Americans do now at least know that such things happen, even sometimes in their own families, one must assume that Eastwood's only interest lies in the expression of moral disapproval at any cost, including that of implausibility. Similarly, one might note the cultural consistency between *Cousin, Cousine* and a film made ten years earlier, Claude Lelouche's *Un Homme et une femme* (1966).

6. This message also finds expression in Maria's now frequent tears. Her counterpart in *Cousin, Cousine* also complains early in that film that she has never been able to cry—Marthe even explicitly hopes that Ludovic will someday make her cry—but the heroine's desire becomes reality only in the American remake.

7. The influence of French feminism seems far less direct in the case of *Cousin, Cousine*, but the compatibility is the same. In France, the early seventies marked the most militant moment of recent feminist history. In keeping with the still powerful influence of Simone de Beauvoir, feminist groups encouraged women to develop their identity as individuals; the family was analyzed as the cause of women's specific oppression; and, according to Claire Duchen, "feminists almost universally agreed that motherhood, defining and limiting women, had to be rejected" (*Feminism* 49). In 1971, a number of prominent women, including Beauvoir, published a

manifesto indicating that they had had illegal abortions; and a large demonstration against Mother's Day was held in 1972.

8. Bill Clinton, to return one final time to the American president, has fared less well in similar circumstances. Clinton, too, might be seen as a representative "New Man," given such factors as his financial dependence on his wife and his opposition to the war in Vietnam. His leadership style—the bus and train tours that bring him into contact with "real" people; the national conferences and town meetings that encourage a kind of participatory politics and highlight the President's apparent willingness to listen to average citizens; the focus of Clinton's first national campaign and, to some extent, his first term in office on domestic issues rather than foreign policy; even his need to be liked, his desire to please, and his preoccupation with his public image—has also been more characteristic of, or, at least, more acceptable for women. In Clinton's case, however, such feminized qualities in a man have been more often perceived as signs of vulnerability and weakness than of modernity. Moreover, in keeping with cultural habits of gender dichotomization, Hillary Rodham Clinton has been simultaneously attacked for her unseemly "masculine" character and behavior.

Other Ways of Looking: Re-Visions of Feminism and Film Theory in François Truffaut's and Blake Edwards's *The Man Who Loved Women*

1. As Jean Collet points out, Truffaut's hero's very name (*Morane*) identifies him with death (*la mort*) (136).
2. Truffaut, as I have noted, originally relates the story of such a death in *Tirez sur le pianiste*. Bob Fosse reproduces the visual version at the end of *All That Jazz* (1979) to kill off his own hero, another "man who loved women." I rather suspect this is a frequently reproduced deathbed story of the same order as that other apocryphal tale of masculinity that literally equates orgasm with death and which I have heard told about men ranging from Philippe d'Orléans to the former president of a university where I used to teach.
3. In *Le Cinéma selon François Truffaut* the director addresses this issue: "One has the same relationships with women that one had with one's mother. I wanted to go beyond the fact that Bertrand had simply suffered from a detestable mother. He was also strongly attracted to her, and that's what he seeks to recreate with the women he meets" (356).
4. See, for example, Sherry Turkle's *Psychoanalytical Politics: Freud's French Revolution* in which she develops her interpretation of a specifically "French Freud" within the comparative context of American ego psychology.
5. Curiously, in an inversion similar to one already seen in the comparison of *Cousin, Cousine* and *Cousins*, in at least one sense Edwards' film literally begins where Truffaut's ends. The central idea of Geneviève's final speech in *L'Homme qui aimait les femmes* ("Bertrand loved all these women for what they were") reappears in Marianna's opening one in *The Man Who Loved Women* ("He really and truly loved all these women"). Perhaps such a conception of the relationship between the two

films would also help justify Edwards's failure to cite Truffaut's film anywhere in the credit sequences of the remake, an omission presumably in keeping with the French director's own wishes (Canby, "Tidying Up").

6. Given the extensive cinematic intertexuality that informs Rainer's film, it does not seem too farfetched to suggest that the name *Deller* also intentionally recalls that of Charles *Denner*, the actor who plays the lead role in Truffaut's *L'Homme qui aimait les femmes*. This probability is increased by the fact that Trisha explains her hero's name during a conversation that focuses on Jean-Pierre Leaud, an actor whose repeated portrayals of Antoine Doinel came to identify him as Truffaut's alter ego, and on Jean Eustache's *La Maman et la putain* (1933), a film whose title appears to foreshadow the portrayal of the hero's mother in *L'Homme qui aimait les femmes*. Jill Forbes cites Eustache as one of several filmmakers who "might almost be said to have been 'invented' by Truffaut" but interprets *La Maman et la putain* as "clearly an attempt to come to terms with this paternal heritage by rejecting it" (109), that is, as something more like Rainer's own *The Man Who Envied Women*.

7. The new importance of feminist studies of masculinity (see also Jeffords, *Hard Bodies*; Showalter, *Speaking of Gender*; Vincendeau; and Cook & Dodd) complements the appearance of late of a number of works on national identity (see Anderson and Greenfeld, among many others). Just as the latter, however, have tended to ignore gender by the implicit and nonproblematic equation of "man" and "citizen," so too have the former, until recently, ignored cultural differences and continued to treat masculinity as monolithic.

8. Raymonde Carroll argues in *Cultural Misunderstandings* that the art of seduction serves the same powerful function within French culture that money does within American culture. Notably, financial success and amorous seduction are both charged with multiple meanings and defined as activities accessible to everyone within their respective cultures; each also leads to reciprocal reactions of shock and accusations of bad taste in the other culture (128–33).

9. In an intriguing coincidence of visual image, ideological significance, and etymology, *mannequin* derives from a Middle Dutch term meaning "little man," even though, as the *American Heritage Dictionary* points out, "a department store mannequin is often not a man and often not little." In this context, the implications of the synonym *dummy* seem relevant as well.

10. It was important to Truffaut that his hero be a writer and that the visual and the verbal texts eventually merge. According to Truffaut, he had long wanted "to show in a film how a book gets written" (*Le Cinéma* 360).

11. In the clearest example of this process, when Bertrand asks the copy editor to change the color of a young girl's dress in the text of his book, we see the transformation occur simultaneously on screen.

12. This is the full text of Geneviève's response to her colleagues: "C'est simplement *un homme*. Effectivement ce livre est plein de détails qui se contredisent mais, comme il est évident que rien n'est inventé, il faut bien admettre que ce sont les contradictions de la vie. Vous dites: 'On ne voit pas ce qu'il veut prouver.' Mais il ne veut rien prouver. Il raconte, sans faire de discrimination entre les détails qui signifient quelque chose et d'autres qui illustrent seulement le saugrenu de la vie. Mon-

sieur Bétany, c'est un manuscrit instinctif et sincère, l'auteur ne se met jamais en valeur . . ." On characteristically "feminine" writing, see, for example, Aptheker; Juhasz; and Durham, *The Contexture of Feminism*.

13. Elsewhere, Truffaut has said, "Besides, I hope it will be contradictory, that some people will say the film is phallocratic. Then I will be amused if others say exactly the opposite. It's a feminist film in its own way" (*Le Cinéma* 360). He has also said, however, that in his own mind the film was "classified in the category of films about criminals, about men who kill women" (*Le Cinéma* 367).

14. Truffaut responded to a suggestion that *L'Homme qui aimait les femmes* eluded conventional generic categories by insisting that "*Pariscope* will certainly classify it as a '*comédie dramatique*'" (*Le Cinéma* 360).

15. For Lawrence O'Toole, for example, *The Man Who Loved Women* includes "the funniest sequence of the year"; David Ansen refers to the same scene as "one of [Edwards's] classic slapstick routines" ("Don Juan") and Vincent Canby describes it as "one hilarious slapstick sequence" ("Rev. of *The Man Who*"). To be exact, Canby also finds Truffaut's *L'Homme qui aimait les femmes* "boisterously funny" ("'Accessible' Films") and Charles Denner "very, very funny" in the title role ("Rev. of *L'Homme*")—again, however, without explanation.

Conclusion: Contemporary French-to-American Comedy or the Compulsion to Compare

1. October Films reports that it tried unsuccessfully to acquire the distribution rights from Touchstone (Young).

2. Coline Serreau was originally hired by Touchstone Pictures to direct *Three Men and a Baby*. Marc Mancini asserts, though without providing any evidence, that her subsequent withdrawal shortly before shooting was scheduled to begin "set rumors swirling, since it is well known that Hollywood feels that a French adaptor is less likely than an American to write fluent dialogue, conjure well-situated characters or capture the American cultural idiom" (33). French directors who have recently been recruited by Hollywood include Jean-Jacques Annaud and Luc Besson.

3. In the case of two essentially identical texts, extradiegetic concerns—casting, audience reception—may, of course, be of considerable interest; but that is not the focus of this study.

4. The reference is to Bertrand Blier's *Tenue de Soirée* (1986), which was retitled *Ménage à trois* for its U.S. distribution.

5. The American remake of Gérard Langier's *Mon Père ce héros* (1991) must therefore create a real dilemma for critics given to comparative evaluation, since Gérard Depardieu reprises the role he played in the original. In fact, one conclusion would seem to be that not even Depardieu can play Depardieu in an American remake. Although Janet Maslin acknowledges that the actor "acquits himself with remarkably good cheer," she also describes the sight of "France's greatest living film actor mak[ing] a fool of himself on waterskis" as "providing a graphic illustration of what troubled the French during the GATT talks" ("A Bahamian Vacation"). Veber's

cross-cultural career takes yet another turn here since he wrote only the English-language version of Steve Miner's *My Father the Hero* (1994).

6. In addition, if Hollywood studios have bought up remake rights relatively indiscriminately, they appear to have shown somewhat greater discretion in the actual exercise of those rights. Notably, the decision to abandon projected American versions of Serreau's *Romuauld et Juliette* (1989) and Chatiliez's *La Vie est un long fleuve tranquille* (1987) suggests some sensitivity to comic portrayals of race and class so foreign to mainstream American values as to prove inevitably offensive to the vast majority of moviegoers. Despite the extraordinary success of *Les Visiteurs* in France, an American remake strikes me as unthinkable; and I would predict that the U.S. distribution of a dubbed or subtitled version of a film whose essential purpose is to vaunt the superiority and justify the privileges of the (supposedly *ancienne*) *noblesse*, and whose primary comic effects depend upon the ability to distinguish speech patterns by social class, will prove to be a resounding critical and commercial failure.

7. The failure to understand Lucas's paternal role no doubt also explains why Kael qualifies the scene in which the little girl sleeps in his arms as "near-obscene" and complains about the film's "queasy pedophiliac overtones." Although such connotations would not necessarily be unexpected in this context—certainly they are present in *Three Men and a Baby*—here, I think, they are unjustified.

8. The following comment by Veber suggests that he indeed had cultural differences in the portrayal of masculinity in mind: "It's a sin in this country for a man to be a wimp. In France it's delightful. I had to remake the characters a lot in *Three Fugitives*" (Bishop). The only example he cites, however, is a scene in a police station that ends with a display of physical force by Pignon/Perry as well as Lucas; moreover, the direct comparison of two essentially identical scenes does not support Veber's claim that the American version differs significantly from the French.

9. For example, the only extended scene that Veber adds to the American version of the film introduces an inebriated doctor whose connection to Lucas corresponds to that of Perry's with the deluded veterinarian.

10. In the French film, in contrast, the police officer implicitly condones the homoerotic couple. During the period when Jeanne is in the children's home and Lucas and Pignon separated, the detective shows up one day at Lucas's apartment to ask "When are you going to get married and have kids?" "Je vais me ranger," the French equivalent of "I'm going straight," has similar connotations of conventional domesticity. At the comparable moment in the American remake, Veber settles for intercutting between shots of Lucas and Perry to imply that the evident unhappiness of each man alone has something to do with the absence of the other. Lucas, of course, also plays "straight man" to Perry in this comic team.

11. As it is, the substitution forces a change in one of the last lines of the film, which serves to confirm the affection that has developed between the mismatched heroes. When Compagnard leaves the unconscious Perrin at the hospital, he identifies himself as "one of the family." Campanella must settle for being "a close friend."

12. Marcello Donan also worked on the screen adaptation of Poiret's play. Veber wrote

the dialogue and again collaborated on the screenplay with Poiret and Danon for Molinaro's sequel, *La Cage aux folles II* (1980). Neither Molinaro nor Veber contributed to *La Cage aux folles III* (1985), directed by Georges Lautner and written by Michel Audiard.

13. In the clearest example of "crème fraîche," Nichols's gay heroes are now Jewish as well so that religion becomes a further source of potential discrimination.

14. In an interview on French television just before the remake was released in France, Robin Williams noted that *The Birdcage* fits the current climate in America "like a condom." Ironically, the character of Armand urgently needs to see the very film in which he stars: Nichols asks us to believe that a gay man in 1996 has never heard of Keeley, his coalition, nor, presumably, the growing conservatism of America.

15. If Nichols omits the visible evidence of the black eye that Albin (Albert) displays in *La Cage aux folles*, he compensates by adding an earlier scene in which Armand breaks down the door of the bedroom when Albert is late for his nightclub number.

16. In contrast, the contemporary French counterpart to the original *La Cage aux folles* is represented by such films as Gabriel Aghion's *Pédale douce* (1995). Although it won the audience prize at the Chamrousse Humor Festival in 1996, *Pédale douce* is a much more serious and realistic film about homosexuality than its famous predecessor. Aghion deals openly with the question of homophobia, in particular by showing how plausibly any one of us might be "mistaken" for gay in certain circumstances. Although scenes featuring characters in drag figure significantly in *Pédale douce*, the important roles assigned independently to women (indeed, Fanny Ardant won the César for Best Actress in a comic performance) prevent any substitution of misogyny for homosexuality as the source of the film's humor. Moreover, the concern that aging brings loss of beauty and desirability is treated sensitively and specifically in relation to gay men.

17. In her recent discussion of *Three Men and a Baby*, Lucy Fischer notes that feminist film theory has rarely been used to study comedy, "as though the topic of misogyny were too grave to consider within a jocular light" (*Cinematernity* 112).

18. See *CinémAction* and Mancini for listings, comprehensive at the time of their publication, of recent American remakes of French films.

Works Cited

Alain-Fournier. *Le Grand Meaulnes*. Paris: Livre de poche, 1913.

Altman, Rick. *The Video Connection: Integrating Video into Language Teaching.* Boston: Houghton Mifflin, 1989.

The American Heritage Dictionary of the English Language. 3d ed. Boston: Houghton Mifflin, 1992.

Anderson, Benedict. *Imagined Communities: Reflections on the Origin and Spread of Nationalism.* Rev. ed. London: Verso, 1991.

Andrew, Dudley. "Au Début du souffle: le culte et la culture d'*A bout de souffle.*" *Revue belge du cinéma* 16 (1986): 11–21.

Ansen, David. "Don Juan in Limbo." *Newsweek* 2 Jan. 1984: 58.

———. "Lovers on the Lam." *Newsweek* 23 May 1983: 54.

———. "Love with the Proper Relative." *Newsweek* 20 Feb. 1989: 65.

———. "Oscar Looks Abroad." *Newsweek* 12 March 1990: 86–87.

Aptheker, Bettina. *Tapestries of Life: Women's Work, Women's Consciousness, and the Meaning of Daily Experience.* Amherst: University of Massachusetts Press, 1989.

Arthur, Paul. "Don't Play it Again, Sam!" *USA Today* (Sept. 1988): 93.

Ashour, Linda. *Speaking in Tongues.* New York: Simon and Schuster, 1988.

Attinger, Joelle. "Savoir-Vivre." *Time* 15 July 1991: 42–43.

Aumont, Jacques. "The Fall of the Gods: Jean-Luc Godard's *Le Mépris* (1963)." In *French Films: Texts and Contexts*, edited by Susan Hayward and Ginette Vincendeau, 217–29. New York: Routledge, 1990.

Baby, Yvonne. "Propos recueillis." *Le Monde* 18 Jan. 1960. *Avant-Scène* 356 (January 1987): 197–98.

Baron, Dennis. *Grammar and Gender.* New Haven: Yale University Press, 1986.

Barzini, Luigi. *The Europeans.* London: Penguin Books, 1983.

Bergstrom, Janet. "Rereading the Work of Claire Johnston." In *Feminism and Film Theory*, edited by Constance Penley, 80–88. New York: Routledge, 1988.

———, and Mary Ann Doane, eds. "The Spectatrix." Special issue. *Camera Obscura* 20–21 (May–September 1989).

Bernstein, Richard. *Fragile Glory: A Portrait of France and the French.* New York: Alfred A. Knopf, 1990.

Betton, Gérard. *Esthétique du cinéma.* Paris: Presses universitaires de France, 1983.

Bishop, Tom. "I Love You, Moi Non Plus." Special issue: France's Identity Crises. *SubStance* 76/77 (1985): 21–29.

Boujet, Michel. "Le Cinéma cocooning." *Evénement du Jeudi* 23–28 Nov. 1989: 110.

Bowles, Gloria, and Renata D. Klein, eds. *Theories of Women's Studies.* London: Routledge & Kegan Paul, 1983.

Works Cited

Boxer, Marilyn. "For and About Women: The Theory and Practice of Women's Studies in the United States." *Signs* 7 (1982): 661–95.

Brooks, Peter. *Reading for the Plot: Design and Intention in Narrative.* New York: Alfred A. Knopf, 1984.

Buss, Robin. *The French Through Their Films.* London: Batsford, 1988.

Canby, Vincent. "'Accessible' Films." *New York Times* 9 Oct. 1977.

———. "Bachelor Fathers." *New York Times* 25 April 1986.

———. "How France's 'Cradle' Was Rocked." *New York Times* 11 May 1986.

———. "Ici Se Habla Euro-English." *New York Times* 4 June 1989.

———. "It Takes More Than Gimmicks." *New York Times* 26 July 1983.

———. "Movies Lost in Translation." *New York Times* 12 Feb. 1989.

———. Rev. of *The Man Who Loved Women. New York Times* 6 Dec. 1983.

———. Rev. of *L'Homme qui aimait les femmes. New York Times* 1 Oct. 1977.

———. "Stomach in the Air." *New York Times* 13 May 1983.

———. "Tidying Up a Few Matters as '83 Fades from the Screen," *New York Times* 1 Jan. 1984.

Capretz, Pierre J. (with Béatrice Abetti, Marie Odile Germain, and Lawrence Wylie). *French in Action: A Beginning Course in Language and Culture.* New Haven: Yale University Press, 1987, 1992.

———, and Barry Lydgate. "A Statement from M. Pierre J. Capretz of Yale University and Prof. Barry Lydgate of Wellesley College, co-authors of *French in Action.*" 16 April 1990.

Caraway, Nancy. *Segregated Sisterhood: Racism and the Politics of America.* Knoxville: University of Tennessee Press, 1991.

Carroll, Raymonde. *Cultural Misunderstandings: The Franco-American Experience.* Translated by Carol Volk. Chicago: University of Chicago Press, 1988.

———. "Film et analyse culturelle: Le Remake." *Contemporary French Civilization* 13 (Summer/Fall 1989): 346–59.

Chidley, Joe. "Killer in a Miniskirt." *Maclean's* 29 March 1996: 46.

Chodorow, Nancy. *The Reproduction of Mothering: Psychoanalysis and the Sociology of Gender.* Berkeley: University of California Press, 1978.

Clifford, James. *The Predicament of Culture: Twentieth-Century Ethnography, Literature, and Art.* Cambridge: Harvard University Press, 1988.

Cohan, Steven, and Ina Rae Hark, eds. *Screening the Male: Exploring Masculinities in Hollywood Cinema.* New York: Routledge, 1993.

Cohen, Roger. "Aux Armes! France Rallies to Battle Sly and T. Rex." *New York Times* 2 Jan. 1994.

———. "When You Wish Upon a Deficit." *New York Times* 18 July 1993.

Collet, Jean. *François Truffaut.* Paris: L'Herminier, 1988.

Collins, Jim. "Introduction." In *Film Theory Goes to the Movies*, edited by Jim Collins, Hilary Radner, and Ava Preacher Collins. New York: Routledge, 1993.

———. *Uncommon Cultures: Popular Culture and Post-Modernism.* New York: Routledge, 1984.

Cook, Pam. "Border Crossings: Women and Film in Context." In *Women and Film: A Sight and Sound Reader*, edited by Pam Cook & Philip Dodd, ix–xiii. Philadelphia: Temple University Press, 1993.

————. "Approaching the Work of Dorothy Arzner." In *Feminism and Film Theory*, edited by Constance Penley, 46–56. New York; Routledge, 1988.

Corbett, James. *Through French Windows: An Introduction to France in the Nineties*. Ann Arbor: University of Michigan Press, 1994.

Corliss, Richard. "Fellini go home!" *Time* 13 Jan. 1997: 69–70.

————. "The Final Frontier." *Time* 18 March 1996: 46–48.

————. "Voilà! Disney Invades Europe. Will the French Resist?" *Time* 20 April 1992: 82–83.

————. "What Dreams Come To." *Time* 25 Jan. 1993: 69.

Crapanzano, Victor. "Hermes' Dilemma: The Masking of Subversion in Ethnographic, Description." In *Writing Culture: The Poetics and Politics of Ethnography*, edited by James Clifford and George E. Marcus, 51–76. Berkeley: University of California Press, 1986.

Daly, Robert. *Portraits of France*. New York: Little, Brown and Co., 1991.

Daninos, Pierre. *Les Carnets du Major W. Marmaduke Thompson: Découverte de la France et des Français*. Paris: Hachette, 1959.

Dargis, Manohla. "Spawned." *The Village Voice* 21 Feb. 1989: 77.

Darnton, Robert. *The Great Cat Massacre and Other Episodes in French Cultural History*. New York: Vintage, 1985.

Dejean, Jean, and Nancy K. Miller, eds. "The Politics of Tradition: Placing Women in French Literature." Special issue. *Yale French Studies* 75 (1988).

Delbanco, Nicholas. *Running in Place: Scenes from the South of France*. New York: Atlantic Monthly Press, 1989.

Denby, David. "Bang Bang, Ho Hum." *New York* 30 May 1983: 78–80.

Doane, Mary Ann, Patricia Mellencamp, and Linda Williams, eds. *Re-vision: Essays in Feminist Film Criticism*. New York: Oxford University Press, 1984.

Dondelinger, Jean. *Les Rencontres cinématographiques de Beaune*. 17–21 October 1991. Unpublished proceedings.

Douglas, Susan J. *Where the Boys Are*. New York: Random House, 1995.

Duchen, Claire. *Feminism in France: From May '68 to Mitterrand*. London: Routledge and Kegan Paul, 1986.

————, ed. and trans. *French Connections: Voices from the Women's Movement in France*. Amherst: University of Massachusetts Press, 1987.

Dudovitz, Resa L. *The Myth of Superwoman*. London: Routledge, 1990.

Durham, Carolyn. *The Contexture of Feminism: Marie Cardinal and Multicultural Literacy*. Urbana: University of Illinois Press, 1992.

————. "The Inversion of Laughter." *Jump Cut* 27 (1982): 4–6.

————. "Taking the Baby Out of the Basket and/or Robbing the Cradle: 'Re-making' Gender and Culture in Franco-American Film." *French Review* 65 (April 1992): 774–84.

"Editors' Choice: Silver Surfer," *TV Guide* 15 March 1997: 54.

"Editors' Choice: La Femme Nikita," *TV Guide* 27 Sept. 1997: 37.

Ehrenreich, Barbara. *The Hearts of Men: American Dreams and the Flight from Commitment*. New York: Anchor Press, 1983.

Eisenstein, Hester, and Alice Jardine, eds. *The Future of Difference*. Boston: Hall, 1980.

Works Cited

Ellis, John. *Visible Fictions*. New York: Routledge, 1982.

Ellwood, David W., and Rob Kroes, eds. *Hollywood in Europe: Experiences of a Cultural Hegemony*. Amsterdam: Vrij Universiteit P., 1994.

Elteren, Mel van. "GATT and Beyond: World Trade, the Arts and American Popular Culture in Western Europe." *Journal of American Culture* 19 (Fall 1996): 59–73.

Euro Disney Resort. Paris: Guide Vert Michelin, 1992.

"L'Europe à la question." *Cahiers du cinéma* 455/456 (May 1992): 103–109.

Ewell, Barbara C. "Empowering Otherness: Feminist Criticism and the Academy." In *Reorientations: Critical Theories and Pedagogies*, edited by Bruce Henricksen and Thaïs Morgan, 43–62. Champaign: University of Illinois Press.

Faludi, Susan. *Backlash: The Undeclared War against Women*. New York: Crown Publishers, 1991.

Finkle, David. "Plus Ça Change, More She Is the Same." *New York Times* 31 March 1991.

Fischer, Lucy. *Cinematernity: Film, Motherhood, Genre*. Princeton: Princeton University Press, 1997.

———. *Shot/Countershot: Film Tradition and Women's Cinema*. Princeton: Princeton University Press, 1989.

Fischer, Michael M. J. "Ethnicity and the Post-Modern Arts of Memory." In *Writing Culture: The Poetics and Politics of Ethnography*, edited by James Clifford and George E. Marcus, 194–203. Berkeley: University of California Press, 1986.

Flitterman-Lewis, Sandy. *To Desire Differently: Feminism and the French Cinema*. Urbana: University of Illinois Press, 1990.

Forbes, Jill. *The Cinema in France: After the New Wave*. Bloomington: Indiana University Press, 1992.

Forestier, François. "La France fait de la Résistance." *Le Nouvel Observateur* 21–27 March 1996: 27.

———. "Le Phénomène 'Birdcage.'" *Le Nouvel Observateur* 2–8 May 1996: 54.

"La France peut-elle s'en sortir?" Special issue. *Time* 4 Dec. 1995.

Frank, Barbara, and Bill Krohn. "Sortie des Marges: Entretien avec Jim McBride." *Cahiers du cinéma* 350 (Aug. 1983): 30–34, 64–66.

Fraser, Nancy, and Sandra Lee Bartky. *Revaluing French Feminism: Critical Essays on Difference, Agency, and Culture*. Bloomington: Indiana University Press, 1992.

"French Course Termed Sexist, Will Be Revised." *New York Times* 15 April 1990.

Friedan, Betty. *The Feminine Mystique*. New York: Dell, 1963.

———. *The Second Stage*. New York: Summit Books, 1981.

Fuchs, Cynthia. "The Buddy Politic." In *Screening the Male: Exploring Masculinities in Hollywood Cinema*, edited by Steven Cohen and Ina Rae Hark, 194–207. New York: Routledge, 1993.

Fussell, Paul. *Class*. New York: Ballantine, 1983.

Garcia, Irma. *Promenade femmelière: Recherches sur l'écriture féminine*. 2 vols. Paris: des femmes, 1981.

Gaudin, Colette, Mary Jean Green, Lynne Anthony Higgins, Marianne Hirsch, Vivian Kogan, Claudia Reeder, Nancy Vickers, eds. "Feminist Readings: French Texts/American Contexts." Special issue. *Yale French Studies* 62 (1981).

Gibaldi, Joseph, ed. *Introduction to Scholarship in Modern Languages and Literatures.* New York: Modern Language Association, 1992.

Gillain, Anne. "The Script of Delinquency: François Truffaut's *Les 400 Coups* (1959)." In *French Film: Texts and Contexts*, edited by Susan Hayward and Ginette Vincendeau, 187–99. New York: Routledge, 1990.

———. *François Truffaut: Le Secret perdu.* Paris: Hatier, 1991.

Godard, Jean-Luc. "À Bout de souffle." *L'Avant-Scène du cinéma* 79 (1968).

Goodell, Jeffrey. "Salut Suckers." *Première* (April 1994): 13, 132–38.

Gramont, Sanche de. *France in the 1980's.* London: Secker and Warburg, 1982.

Grazia, Victoria de. "Mass Culture and Sovereignty." *Journal of Modern History* 61 (March 1989): 53–87.

Greenfeld, Liah. *Nationalism: Five Roads to Modernity.* Cambridge: Harvard University Press, 1992.

Hall, Catherine. "Gender, Nationalisms and National Identities: Bellagio Symposium, July 1992." *Feminist Review* 44 (Summer 1993): 97–103.

Hartman, Elwood. "A Profile of French National Character." *Contemporary French Civilization* 4 (Fall 1979): 45–65.

Hayward, Susan. *French National Cinema.* New York: Routledge, 1993.

Hayward, Susan, and Ginette Vincendeau. "Introduction." In *French Film: Texts and Contexts*, edited by Susan Hayward and Ginette Vincendeau, 1–5. New York: Routledge, 1990.

Henricksen, Bruce, and Thaïs Morgan, eds. *Reorientations: Critical Theories and Pedagogies.* Champaign: University of Illinois Press, 1990.

H.I.R. Rev. of *Les Fugitifs. Cahiers du cinéma* 391 (Jan. 1987): 55–56.

Hornblower, Margot. "Foreign Overdose." *Time* 15 July 1991: 26–27.

Hutcheon, Linda. *The Poetics of Postmodernism: History, Theory, Fiction.* New York: Routledge, 1988.

James, Caryn. "When Film Becomes a Feast of Words." *New York Times* 30 July 1989.

Jardine, Alice, and A. M. Menke. "Exploding the Issue: 'French' 'Women' 'Writers' and 'the Canon'? Fourteen Interviews." *Yale French Studies* 75 (1988): 229–58.

Jeffords, Susan. *Hard Bodies: Hollywood Masculinity in the Reagan Era.* New Brunswick: Rutgers University Press, 1994.

Johnson, Barbara, ed. "The Pedagogical Imperative: Teaching as a Literary Genre." Special issue. *Yale French Studies* 63 (1982).

Johnson, Diane. *Le Divorce.* New York: Dutton, 1997.

Johnston, Claire, "Dorothy Arzrier; Critical Strategies." In *Feminism and Film Theory*, edited by Constance Penley, 36–45. New York: Routledge, 1988.

———. "Women's Cinema as Counter-Cinema." In *Notes on Women's Cinema*, edited by Claire Johnston, 24–31. London: Society for Education in Film and Television, 1973.

Jousse, Thierry, and Nicolas Saada. "Entretien avec Adolph Green." *Cahiers du cinéma* 422 (Sept. 1989): 59–64.

Juhasz, Suzanne. "Toward a Theory of Form in Feminist Autobiography: Kate Millet's *Flying* and *Sita*; Maxine Hong Kingston's *The Woman Warrior*." In *Women's Autobiography*, edited by Estelle C. Jelinek, 221–37. Bloomington: Indiana University Press, 1980.

Works Cited

Kael, Pauline. Rev. of *Cousins*. *The New Yorker* 6 March 1989: 97–98.

————. Rev. of *Three Fugitives*. *The New Yorker* 20 Feb. 1989: 98.

Kaplan, Alice. *French Lessons: A Memoir*. Chicago: University of Chicago Press, 1993.

Kaplan, E. Ann. *Women & Film: Both Sides of the Camera*. New York: Methuen, 1983.

Kauffmann, Stanley. "Late Winter Roundup." *The New Republic* 6 March 1989: 25.

————. "Making Over, Making New." *The New Republic* 19 April 1993: 28.

Kilday, Gregg. Rev. of *The Three Fugitives*. *American Film* May 1989: 14.

Kramsch, Claire J. "The Cultural Discourse of Foreign Language Textbooks." In *Northeast Conference on the Teaching of Foreign Language: Toward a New Integration of Language and Culture*, edited by Alan J. Singerman, 63–88. Middlebury: Northeast Conference, 1988.

————. "Language Acquisition and Language Learning." In *Introduction to Scholarship in Modern Languages and Literatures*, edited by Joseph Gibaldi, 53–76. New York: Modern Language Association, 1992.

Kritzman, Lawrence D., ed. Special issue: France's Identity Crises. *SubStance* 76/77 (1995).

————. "Identity Crises: France, Culture, and the Idea of the Nation." *SubStance* 76/77 (1995): 5–20.

Kuisel, Richard F. *Seducing the French: The Dilemma of Americanization*. Berkeley: University of California Press, 1993.

Labro, Philippe. *Un Eté dans l'ouest*. Paris: Gallimard, 1988.

————. *L'Etudiant étranger*. Paris: Gallimard, 1986.

Laclos, Choderlos de. *Les Liaisons dangereuses*. Paris: Garnier Flammarion, 1960.

Lebovics, Herman. *True France: The Wars Over Cultural Identity, 1900–1945*. Ithaca: Cornell University Press, 1992.

Len. "I Want To Go Home." *Variety* 13–19 Sept. 1989: 32+.

Levy, Shawn. "The Nutty Professor, Emeritus, Returns." *New York Times* 6 March 1994.

Mancini, Marc. "French Film Remakes." *Contemporary French Civilization* 13 (Winter/Spring 1989): 32–46.

Marie, Michel. "'It really makes you sick!': Jean-Luc Godard's *A bout de souffle* (1959)." In *French Film: Texts and Contexts*, edited by Susan Hayward and Ginette Vincendeau, 201–15. New York: Routledge, 1990.

Marks, Elaine, and Isabelle de Courtivron, eds. *New French Feminisms*. New York: Schocken Books, 1981.

Martin, Marcel. Rev. of *A bout de souffle*. *Cinéma* May 1960. "Dossier de presse." *L'Avant-scène du cinéma* 79 (1968): 195–213.

Maslin, Janet. "A Bahamian Vacation for Gérard Depardieu." *New York Times* 2 Sept. 1994.

————. "Fathers Going Farther (Or Is It Further?)" *New York Times* 9 May 1997.

Mathy, Jean-Philippe. *Extrême-Occident: French Intellectuals and America*. Chicago: University of Chicago Press, 1993.

Mayle, Peter. *Choosing Cézanne*. New York: Knopf, 1997.

————. *Toujours Provence*. New York: Knopf, 1991.

————. *A Year in Provence*. New York: Knopf, 1990.

Mayne, Judith. "Review Essay: Feminist Film Theory and Criticism." *Signs* 11 (Autumn 1985): 81–100.

Mazabrard, Colette. "La Modernité d'être vieillot." *Cahiers du cinéma* 422 (Sept. 1989): 54–56.

McCarthy, Todd. "Point of No Return." *Variety* 22 March 1993: 50.

Miller, Nancy K. "The French Mistake." In *Getting Personal*, edited by Nancy K. Miller. New York: Routledge, 1991. 48–55.

Mills, Sara, Lynne Pearce, Sue Spaull, and Elaine Millard. *Feminist Readings/Feminists Reading*. Charlottesville: University Press of Virginia, 1989.

Modleski, Tania. "Three Men and Baby M." *Camera Obscura* 17 (May 1988): 69–81. Reprinted in *Feminism Without Women: Culture and Criticism in a "Postfeminist" Age*, edited by Tania Modleski, 76–89. New York: Routledge, 1991.

Moi, Toril. *Sexual/Textual Politics: Feminist Literary Theory*. London: Methuen, 1985.

Mordore, Michel. "Portrait de star en bébé." *Le Nouvel Observateur* 22–28 Nov. 1985: 106.

Morgan, Ted. *On Becoming American*. New York: Paragon House, 1988.

Mulvey, Laura. "Afterthoughts on 'Visual Pleasure and Narrative Cinema.'" In *Feminism and Film Theory*, edited by Constance Penley, 69–79. New York: Routledge, 1988.

———. "Visual Pleasure and Narrative Cinema." In *Feminism and Film Theory*, edited by Constance Penley, 57–68. New York: Routledge, 1988.

"The New France." Special issue. *Time* 15 July 1991.

Newmark, Kevin, Denis Hollier, Lynne Huffer, and Eliza Nichols. *Report of the Ad Hoc Committee on French 115*. New Haven: Yale University, French Department, 26 March 1990.

Nostrand, Howard L. "French Culture's Concern for Relationships: Relationism." *Foreign Language Annals* (May 1973): 469–80.

Le Nouveau petit Robert. Paris: Dictionnaires Le Robert, 1993.

O'Brien, Tom. "Bland Isn't Beautiful." *Commonweal* 24 March 1989: 177–78.

Oms, Marcel. "Le Remake à l'épreuve de l'histoire." *CinémAction* 53 (October 1989): 63–67.

Orvell, Miles. "Understanding Disneyland: American Mass Culture and the European Gaze." In *Cultural Transmissions and Receptions: American Mass Culture in Europe*, edited by R. Kroes, R. W. Rydell, and D. F. J. Bosscher. Amsterdam: Vrij Universiteit P., 1993.

O'Toole, Lawrence. "The Painful Curse of Perfection." *Maclean's* 26 Dec. 1983: 44.

Pall, Ellen. "Are Some Remakes Much, Much More Than Meets the Eye?" *New York Times* 11 March 1990.

Parker, Andrew, Mary Russo, Doris Sommer, and Patricia Yaeger, eds. *Nationalisms & Sexualities*. New York: Routledge, 1992.

Pascal, Francine. *If Wishes Were Horses*. New York: Bantam Books, 1994.

Pells, Richard H. *Not Like Us: How Europeans Have Loved, Hated, and Transformed America Since World War II*. New York: Basic Books, 1997.

Penley, Constance, ed. *Feminism and Film Theory*. New York: Routledge, 1988.

Penley, Constance, and Sharon Willis, eds. *Male Trouble*. Minneapolis: University of Minnesota Press, 1993.

Works Cited

Pertié, Olivier. "Un Couffin pour cent millions de dollars." *Le Nouvel Observateur* 29 Jan.–4 Feb. 1988: 80–81.

Philippon, Alain. "A Bout de Souffle Made in U.S.A." *Cahiers du cinéma* 350 (Aug. 1983): 43–44.

Poiret, Jean. *La Cage aux folles*. Paris: Presses Pocket, 1979.

Protopopoff, Daniel. "'A bout de souffle' en version américaine." Special issue: "Le Remake et l'Adaptation." *CinémAction* 53 (Oct. 1989): 122–23.

———. "Sur Quelques Films récents." *CinémAction* 53 (Oct. 1989): 110–11.

———, and Michel Serceau. "Les Remakes américains de films européens: une greffe stérile." *CinémAction* (Oct. 1989): 98–107.

"Que Reste-t-il de notre rayonnement à l'étranger? Culture: Ces Français Que le Monde Nous Envie." Special issue. *Le Nouvel Observateur* 21–27 March 1996.

Raby, Michael J. "'I Lost it at the Movies': Teaching Culture Through Cinematic Doublets." *French Review* 68 (April 1995): 837–45.

Rafferty, Terrence. "A Critic At Large: The Essence of the Landscape." *New Yorker* 25 June 1990: 80–92.

Rainer, Yvonne. *The Films of Yvonne Rainer*. Bloomington: Indiana University Press, 1989.

"Le Remake et l'Adaptation." Special issue. *CinémAction* 53 (Oct. 1989).

Rich, Ruby B. "Feminism and Sexuality in the 1980's." *Feminist Studies* 12 (Fall 1986): 525–61.

Robbe-Grillet, Alain. *Djinn: Un Trou rouge entre les pavés disjoints*. Paris: Minuit, 1981. Reprinted, with Yvone Lenard, as *Le Rendez-vous*. New York: CBS, 1988.

Rosenbaum, Mitchell. "Interview with Yvonne Rainer." In *The Films of Yvonne Rainer*. Bloomington: Indiana University Press, 1989.

Roud, Richard. *Rediscovering French Film*. New York: Museum of Modern Art, 1983.

Sadoul, Georges. Rev. of *A bout de souffle*. *Lettres françaises* 31 March 1960. "Dossier de presse." *L'Avant-Scène du cinéma* 79 (1968): 195–213.

Santoni, Georges. "Stéréotypes, contextes visuels et dimensions sociales." *Le Français dans le monde* 181 (Nov.-Dec. 1983): 84–94.

———. "Visual Images and Imagination in Pursuit of Mimesis and French Society." *Studies in French Culture* 14 (Winter/Spring 1990): 63–79.

Schafer, Roy. *A New Language for Psychoanalysis*. New Haven: Yale University Press, 1976.

Schatz, Thomas. "The New Hollywood." In *Film Theory Goes to the Movies*, edited by Jim Collins, Hilary Radner, and Ava Preacher Collins. New York: Routledge, 1993.

Schuster, Marilyn R., and Susan R. Van Dyne, eds. *Women's Place in the Academy: Transforming the Liberal Arts Curriculum*. New York: Rowman and Allanheld, 1985.

Serceau, Daniel. "Hollywood à l'heure de Paris." *CinémAction* 53 (Oct. 1989): 113–23.

Serceau, Michel. "Un Phénomène spécifiquement cinématographique." *CinémAction* 53 (Oct. 1989): 6–11.

Serreau, Coline. "Trois Homme et un couffin." *Avant-Scéne* 356 (January 1987).

Sherman, Jeffrey. "Kissing Cousins." *Vogue* March 1989: 268.

Showalter, Elaine. "Feminist Criticism in the Wilderness." *Critical Inquiry* 8 (1981): 179–205.

————. "Introduction: The Rise of Gender." In *Speaking of Gender*, edited by Elaine Showalter, 1–13. New York: Routledge, 1989.

The Silver Surfer 3. New York: Official Magazine Corp., 1968.

Skorecki, Louis. "Nos Couffins d'Amérique." *Libération* 22 Feb. 1988: 44.

Stanley, Alessandra. "Can 50 Million Frenchmen Be Wrong?" *New York Times Magazine* 21 Oct. 1990: 41+.

Stanton, Domna C. "Language and Revolution: The Franco-American DisConnection." In *The Future of Difference*, edited by Hester Eisenstein and Alice Jardine, 73–87. New Brunswick: Rutgers University Press, 1980.

Steinem, Gloria. *Revolution From Within: A Book of Self-Esteem*. Boston: Little, Brown, and Co., 1992.

Thomas, François. *L'Atelier d'Alain Resnais*. Paris: Flammarion, 1989.

Tocqueville, Alexis de. *Democracy in America*. New York: Doubleday, 1969.

Tomlinson, John. *Cultural Imperialism: A Critical Introduction*. Baltimore: Johns Hopkins University Press, 1991.

Toubiana, Serge. "L'Europe! l'Europe! l'Europe." *Cahiers du cinéma* 455/456 (May 1992): 38–41.

Truffaut, François. "Une Certaine Tendance du cinéma français." *Cahiers du cinéma* 31 (Jan. 1954): 15–28.

————. *Le Cinéma selon François Truffaut*. Textes réunis par Anne Gillain. Paris: Flammarion, 1988.

————. *L'Homme qui aimait les femmes*. Paris: Flammarion, 1977.

————. *Truffaut par Truffaut*, edited by Dominique Rabourdin. Paris: Editions du Chêne, 1985.

Turkle, Sherry. *Psychoanalytic Politics: Freud's French Revolution*. New York: Basic Books, 1978.

Valenti, Jack. "Statement of Jack Valenti, President and CEO, Motion Picture Association of America." News release, 14 Dec. 1993.

Varenne, Hervé. *Americans Together: Structured Diversity in a Midwestern Town*. New York: Teachers College Press, 1977.

Vinay, J. P., and J. Darbelnet. *Stylistique comparée du français et de l'anglais*. Paris: Didier, 1973.

Vincendeau, Ginette. "Gérard Depardieu: The Axiom of Contemporary French Cinema." *Screen* 33 (Autumn 1992): 343–61.

————. *Jean Gabin, Anatomie d'un mythe*. Paris: Editions Nathan, 1993.

Vogue, "Jean Seberg" (March 1990): 362–75.

Watson, Richard. *The Philosopher's Demise: Learning French*. Columbia: University of Missouri Press, 1995.

Wolf, Naomi. *The Beauty Myth: How Images of Beauty Are Used against Women*. New York: William Morrow, 1991.

Young, Josh. "The Best French Films You'll Never See." *New York Times* 30 Oct. 1994.

Zeldin, Theodore. *The French*. New York: Vintage Books, 1984.

Zoglin, Richard. "Nathan Lane—Uncaged." *Time* 25 March 1996: 70.

Films Cited

3 *Godfathers*. Screenplay by Frank S. Nugent, Laurence Stallings (adapted from the novel by Peter B. Kyne). Dir. John Ford. Argosy Pictures/MGM, 1948.

10. Screenplay by Blake Edwards. Dir. Blake Edwards. Warner Bros./Orion Pictures Corporation, 1979.

A Bout de souffle. Screenplay by Jean-Luc Godard, François Truffaut. Dir. Jean-Luc-Godard. Perf. Jean-Paul Belmondo, Jean Seberg. Imperia/Les Films Georges de Beauregard/SNC/Société Nouvelle de Cinéma, 1959.

All That Jazz. Screenplay by Robert Alan Aurthur, Bob Fosse. Dir. Bob Fosse. 20th Century Fox/Columbia Pictures Corporation, 1979.

An American In Paris. Screenplay by Alan Jay Lerner. Dir. Vincente Minnelli. Perf. Gene Kelly, Leslie Caron. MGM, 1951.

L'Année dernière à Marienbad. Screenplay by Alain Robbe-Grillet, Alain Resnais. Dir. Alain Resnais. Terra Film/Société Nationale des Films Comoran/Précitel/Como-Films/Argos Films/Les Films Tamara/Cinétel/Silver Films/Cineriz, 1961.

Beaumarchais, l'insolent. Screenplay by Jean-Claude Brisville, Sacha Guitry, Edouard Molinaro. Dir. Edouard Molinaro. France 2 Cinéma/France 3 Cinéma/Le Studio Canal+, 1996.

Bird. Screenplay by Joel Oliansky. Dir. Clint Eastwood. Warner Bros./The Malpaso Company, 1988.

The Birdcage. Screenplay by Elaine May. Dir. Mike Nichols. Perf. Robin Williams, Gene Hackman, Nathan Lane. United Artists/MGM, 1996.

Le Bonheur est dans le pré. Screenplay by Florence Quentin. Dir. Étienne Chatiliez. Le Studio Canal+/Téléma, 1995.

Breathless. Screenplay by L. M. Kit Carson, Jim McBride. Dir. Jim McBride. Perf. Richard Gere, Valérie Kaprisky. Orion Pictures Corporation, 1983.

The Bridges of Madison County. Screenplay by Robert James Waller, Richard LaGravenese, Barbara Benedek. Dir. Clint Eastwood. Warner Bros./Amblin Entertainment/Malpaso Productions, 1995.

La Cage aux folles. Screenplay by Marcello Danon, Edouard Molinaro, Jean Poiret, Francis Veber. Dir. Edouard Molinaro. Perf. Michel Galabru, Rémi Laurent, Benny Luke. Da Ma Produzione/Les Productions Artistes Associés, 1978.

La Cage aux folles II. Screenplay by Jean Poiret. Dir. Edouard Molinaro. Columbia Pictures Corporation/Da Ma Produzione/Les Productions Artistes Associés, 1980.

La Cage aux Folles 3: The Wedding. Screenplay by Jacques Audiard, Michel Audiard, Christine Carère, Marcello Danon. Dir. Georges Lautner. Ingram International Films, 1985.

La Chèvre. Screenplay by Francis Veber. Dir. Francis Veber. Perf. Pierre Richard, Gérard Depardieu. Conacine, S.A. DE C.V./Fideline Films/Gaumont International, 1981.

Films Cited

Un Chien andalou. Screenplay by Luis Buñuel, Salvador Dalí. Dir. Luis Buñuel. Hollywood Home Theater, 1929.

Chocolat. Screenplay by Claire Denis, Jean-Pol Fargeau. Dir. Claire Denis. Wim Wenders Productions/Le F.O.D.I.C. Cameroun/Caroline Productions/Cerito Films/Cinémanuel/La Sept Cinéma/MK2 Productions/TF1 Films Productions, 1988.

Les Compères. Screenplay by Francis Veber. Dir. Francis Veber. Perf. Pierre Richard, Gérard Depardieu. D.D. Productions/E.F.V.E. Films/Fideline Films, 1983.

Cousin, Cousine. Screenplay by Jean-Charles Tacchella, Danièle Thompson. Dir. Jean-Charles Tacchella. Perf. Marie-Christine Barrault, Victor Lanoux, Marie-France Pisier. Gaumont, 1975.

Cousins. Screenplay by Stephen Metcalfe. Dir. Joel Schumacher. Perf. Ted Danson, Isabella Rossellini, Sean Young. Paramount Pictures, 1989.

Cyrano de Bergerac. Screenplay by Jean-Claude Carrière, Jean-Paul Rappeneau (adapted from the play by Edmond Rostand). Dir. Jean-Paul Rappeneau. Union Générale/Caméra One/D.D. Productions/Hachette Première, 1990.

Dangerous Liaisons. Screenplay by Christopher Hampton (adapted from the novel by Choderlos de Laclos). Dir. Stephen Frears. Warner Bros./Lorimar Film Entertainment/NFH Productions, 1988.

Dead Poets Society. Screenplay by Tom Schulman. Dir. Peter Weir. Silver Screen Partners IV/Touchstone Pictures, 1989.

Diabolique. Screenplay by Don Roos. Dir. Jeremiah Checknik. Warner Bros./Marvin Worth Productions/Morgan Creek Productions/ABC Productions, 1996.

Les Diaboliques. Screenplay by Pierre Boileau, Henri-Georges Clouzot, Frédéric Grendel, Jerome Géronimi, René Masson, Thomas Narcejac. Dir. Henri-Georges Clouzot. Vera Films/Filmsonor, 1954.

Diva. Screenplay by Jean-Jacques Beineix, Delacorta, Jean Van Hamme. Dir. Jean-Jacques Beineix. Films A2/Greenwich Film Production/Les Films Galaxie, 1981.

A Dry White Season. Screenplay by Euzhan Palcy, Colin Welland (adapted from the novel by André Brink). Dir. Euzhan Palcy. MGM, 1989.

Father's Day. Screenplay by Francis Veber, Lowell Ganz, Babaloo Mandel. Dir. Ivan Reitman. Perf. Robin Williams, Billy Crystal, Julia-Louis Dreyfus. Warner Bros./Northern Lights Entertainment/Silver Pictures, 1997.

La Femme Nikita. Screenplay by Luc Besson. Dir. Luc Besson. Perf. Anne Parillaud, Tchéky Karyo, Jeanne Moreau. Cecchi Gori Group/Gaumont/Tiger Cinematografica, 1990.

Four Weddings and a Funeral. Screenplay by Richard Curtis. Dir. Mike Newell. Working Title Films/Polygram Filmed Entertainment, 1994.

Les Fugitives. Screenplay by Francis Veber. Dir. Francis Veber. Perf. Pierre Richard, Gérard Depardieu. D.D. Productions/E.F.V.E. Films/Fideline Films/Orly Films, 1986.

Le Grand Blond avec une chaussure noire. Screenplay by Yves Robert, Francis Veber. Dir. Francis Veber. Gaumont, 1972.

Le Grand Chemin. Screenplay by Jean-Loup Hubert. Dir. Jean-Loup Hubert. Flach Films/Séléna Audiovisuel/TF1 Films Productions, 1987.

La Grande Illusion. Screenplay by Jean Renoir, Charles Spaak. Dir. Jean Renoir. R.A.C., 1937.

La Haine. Screenplay by Mathieu Kassovitz. Dir. Mathieu Kassovitz. Gramercy Pictures/Les Productions Lazennec/Le Studio Canal+/La Sept Cinéma/Kasso Inc. Productions, 1995.

Un Homme et une femme. Screenplay by Claude Lelouch, Pierre Uytterhoeven. Dir. Claude Lelouch. Les Films 13, 1966.

L'Homme qui aimait les femmes. Screenplay by Michel Fermaud, Suzanne Schiffman, François Truffaut. Dir. François Truffaut. Perf. Charles Denner, Brigitte Fossey, Nelly Borgeaud. Les Films du Carrosse, 1977.

Le Hussard sur le toit. Screenplay by Jean-Claude Carrière, Nina Companéez, Jean Giono, Jean-Paul Rappeneau. Dir. Jean-Paul Rappeneau. Perf. Juliette Binoche, Isabelle Carré. Centre Européen Cinématographique Rhone-Alpes/France 2 Cinéma/Hachette Première, 1995.

I Want to Go Home. Screenplay by Jules Feiffer. Dir. Alain Resnais. Perf. John Ashton, Laura Benson, Gérard Depardieu. Films A2/La Sept Cinéma/MK2 Productions, 1989.

La Jetée. Screenplay by Chris Marker. Dir. Chris Marker. Argos Films, 1962.

Le Jouet. Screenplay by Francis Veber. Dir. Francis Veber. E.F.V.E. Films/Andrea Films/Renn Productions, 1976.

Jules et Jim. Screenplay by Jean Gruault, Henri Pierre Roché, François Truffaut. Dir. François Truffaut. Les Films du Carrosse/SEDIF, 1961.

The Kitchen Toto. Screenplay by Harry Hook. Dir. Harry Hook. Cannon/British Screen/Film Four International, 1988.

Les Liaisons dangereuses. Screenplay by Claude Brulé, Roger Vadim, Roger Vailland (adapted from the novel by Choderlos de Laclos). Dir. Roger Vadim. Ariane Distribution, 1959.

Mais qu'est ce qu'elles veulent? Screenplay by Coline Serreau. Dir. Coline Serreau. Copro Film/INA, 1977.

The Man Who Envied Women. Screenplay by Yvonne Rainer. Dir. Yvonne Rainer. Perf. Bill Raymond, Larry Loonin, Trisha Brown. Zeitgeist Films, 1985.

The Man Who Loved Women. Screenplay by Blake Edwards, Geoffrey Edwards, Milton Wexler. Dir. Blake Edwards. Perf. Burt Reynolds, Julie Andrews, Kim Basinger. Columbia Pictures, 1983.

The Man with One Red Shoe. Screenplay by Robert Klane, Yves Robert, Francis Veber. Dir. Stan Dragoti. 20th Century Fox, 1985.

La Mariée était en noir. Screenplay by Jean-Louis Richard, François Truffaut, Cornell Woolrich. Dir. François Truffaut. Dino de Laurentis Cinematografica/Les Films du Carrosse/Les Productions Artistes Associés, 1967.

Mo' Better Blues. Screenplay by Spike Lee. Dir. Spike Lee. Universal Pictures/40 Acres & a Mule Filmworks, 1990.

Mon Père ce héros. Screenplay by Gérard Lauzier. Dir. Gérard Lauzier. Paravision International, S.A./D.D. Productions/Film Par Film/Orly Films/TF1 Films Productions, 1991.

My Father the Hero. Screenplay by Gérard Lauzier, Charlie Peters, Francis Veber. Dir. Steve Miner. Touchstone Pictures, 1994.

The Naked Gun: From the Files of Police Squad. Screenplay by Jim Abrahams, Pat Proft, David Zucker, Jerry Zucker. Dir. David Zucker. Paramount Pictures, 1988.

Films Cited

Nelly et Monsieur Arnaud. Screenplay by Jacques Fieschi, Claude Sautet, Yves Ulmann. Dir. Claude Sautet. Cecchi Gori Group/Les Films Alain Sarde/Prokino Filmproduktion/TF1 Films Productions/Tiger Cinematografica, 1995.

Paradise. Screenplay by Mary Agnes Donoghue, Jean-Loup Hubert, Scott Kroopf, Patrick J. Palmer. Dir. Mary Agnes Donoghue. Buena Vista Pictures, 1991.

Point of No Return. Screenplay by Robert Getchell, Alexandra Seros. Dir. John Badham. Perf. Bridget Fonda, Gabriel Byrne, Olivia d'Abo. Warner Bros./Art Linson Productions, 1993.

Pure Luck. Screenplay by Herschel Weingrod, Timothy Harris. Dir. Nadia Tass. Perf. Martin Short, Danny Glover, Harry Shearer. Universal Pictures/Sean Daniel Company, 1991.

Les Quatre Cent Coups. Screenplay by François Truffaut, Marcel Moussy. Dir. François Truffaut. Les Films du Carrosse/SEDIF, 1959.

La Règle du jeu. Screenplay by Henry Cartier, Camille François, Carl Koch, Jean Renoir, André Zwoboda. Dir. Jean Renoir. Perf. Nora Gregor, Mila Parély, Roland Toutain, Jean Renoir. Nouvelle édition française, 1939.

Romuald et Juliette. Screenplay by Coline Serreau. Dir. Coline Serreau. Cinéa/Eniloc Films/FR 3, 1989.

'Round Midnight. Screenplay by David Rayfiel, Bertrand Tavernier. Dir. Bertrand Tavernier. Little Bear/Odessa Films/Films A2, 1984.

Three Fugitives. Screenplay by Francis Veber. Dir. Francis Veber. Perf. Nick Nolte, Martin Short, Sarah Rowland Doroff. Touchstone Pictures, 1989.

Three Godfathers. Screenplay by Edward E. Paramore Jr., Manuel Seff (adapted from the novel by Peter B. Kyne). Dir. Richard Boleslawski. MGM, 1936.

Three Men and a Baby. Screenplay by Jim Cruickshank, James Orr. Dir. Leonard Nimoy. Perf. Tom Selleck, Steve Guttenberg, Ted Danson. Interscope Communications/Silver Screen Partners III/Touchstone Pictures, 1987.

Three Men and a Little Lady. Screenplay by Charlie Peters. Dir. Emile Ardolino. Perf. Tom Selleck, Steve Guttenberg, Ted Danson, Nancy Travis. Interscope Communications/Touchstone Communications, 1990.

Tirez sur le pianiste. Screenplay by David Goodis, Marcel Moussy, François Truffaut. Dir. François Truffaut. Les Films de la Pléïade, 1960.

Trois Hommes et un couffin. Screenplay by Coline Serreau. Dir. Coline Serreau. Perf. Michel Boujenah, André Dussollier, Roland Giraud. Flach Films/Soprofilms/TF1 Films Productions, 1985.

Les Trois Frères. Screenplay by Didier Bourdon, Bernard Campan, Michel Lengliney. Dir. Didier Bourdon, Bernard Campan. Canal+ Productions/Renn Productions/TF1 Films Productions, 1996.

Twelve Monkeys. Screenplay by David Webb Peoples, Janet Peoples. Dir. Terry Gilliam. Universal Pictures/Atlas Entertainment, 1995.

Valmont. Screenplay by Jean-Claude Carrière, Jan Novàk (adapted from the novel by Choderlos de Laclos). Dir. Milos Forman. Burrill Productions/Renn Productions, 1989.

La Vie est un roman. Screenplay by Jean Gruault. Dir. Alain Resnais. Fideline Films/Filmédis/Films A2/Les Films Ariane/Soprofilms, 1983.

Les Visiteurs. Screenplay by Christian Clavier, Jean-Marie Poiré. Dir. Jean-Marie Poiré. Alpilles Productions/France 3 Cinéma/Gaumont International/Amigo Productions, 1993.

A Wedding. Screenplay by Robert Altman, John Considine, Allan F. Nicholls, Patricia Resnick. Dir. Robert Altman. 20th Century Fox/Lion's Gate Films, 1978.

A World Apart. Screenplay by Shawn Slovo. Dir. Chris Menges. Working Title Films/ British Screen Productions/Hippo Films/Zimbabwe/Channel Four Films/Atlantic Entertainment Group, 1988.

Index

Index

Nichols, Mike, 194. See also *The Birdcage* (1996)

Nimoy, Leonard, 71. See also *Three Men and a Baby* (1988)

Nostrand, Howard L., 36, 67

Objectification of men, 152, 162–63. *See also* Femininity

Objectification of women, 79, 144–47, 154–55, 157, 176, 214n16. *See also* Male gaze

Oedipus complex, 150–51, 155

Optimism, American, 66

Orvell, Miles, 202

Parallel patterning, 145

Parent/child relationship: *Les Compères/ Father's Day*, 190–92; *Cousins*, 118–19, 122, 132–33; *La Femme Nikita/Point of No Return*, 176; *Les Fugitifs/Three Fugitives*, 186–88. *See also* Childhood; Fatherhood; Mother; Motherhood

Parisian culture, stereotype of, 29

Particularism, American, 36–37, 56, 67, 68, 207n9

Patriarchy, and American feminism, 103, 159

Pedagogical issues, 93–113, 212nn5 & 7

Pells, Richard, 6, 203

Personalization, as emblematic of American culture, 36–37. *See also* Interpersonal relationship

Philippon, Alain, 51

Philosopher's Demise: Learning French, The (Watson), 91

Philosophical themes, in French films, 60, 66, 192, 193, 208–9n3

Point of No Return (1993), 175–80

Poiret, Jean, 193

Popular culture: American exportation of, 3; vs. art, 81, 183; comic strip as thematic of, 33–34, 58; as language of culture, 20–21; vs. literary, 32–33, 42, 68, 183–84

Postmodernism, 16–17, 26, 95–96, 105–6, 111

Pragmatism, American, 36, 42, 72

Prostitution, 146, 147, 152

Protopoff, Daniel, 51

Psychoanalytic approach: in feminist film criticism, 19, 150; *The Man Who Envied Women*, 155–57; *The Man Who Loved Women*, 151–55; and neglect of cultural analysis, 71, 209n3

Pure Luck (1991), 192–93

Puritanism, American, 112, 128, 131, 132. *See also* Moral issues

Raby, Michael J., 114

Racial issues: in *La Cage aux folles*, 197–98; in France, 3, 4, 37, 38–39, 39, 201; in *French in Action*, 103; importance in American film, 193, 219n6; as neglected by American feminism, 102–3

Rainer, Yvonne, 142, 147, 155. See also *The Man Who Envied Women* (1985)

Realism: American preference for, 81, 99–101, 104; feminist debate over, 20; French filmmakers' challenge to, 61–62; French vs. American attitudes, 125

Reality vs. fantasy in *Cousin, Cousine*, 125, 214n3

Reciprocity of perspective, 51

Rediscovering French Film (Roud), 61

Referential imagery, 99–100, 104, 105–6

Règle du jeu, La (1939), 43–46, 208n14

Reitman, Ivan, 188. See also *Father's Day* (1997)

Relationships, interpersonal. *See* Interpersonal relationship

Remake, film: and complications of sequels, 81–82; constructing theory of, 21, 140; as cross-cultural analysis tool, 16–17, 21–24, 70, 114, 199–203; cultural issues as significant to, 12, 71; determining origin of, 26; and French fears of cultural imperialism, 5, 7, 10–11; and repetition/revision movement, 142; repetition with a difference as result of, 50, 58, 63–64; as self-reflexive, 51; textual vs. viewer relationship to, 180

Renoir, Jean, 43–44

Reorientations: Critical Theories and Pedagogies (Henricksen & Morgan), 94

Repetition, internal, 64, 121, 124, 130, 146. See also *Mise en abyme*

Index

Touchstone Pictures, 5, 70, 82, 180, 184, 185, 202

Trois Hommes et un couffin (1985): aesthetic quality of, 183; directorial assignment for, 70–71; narrative structure of, 73–77, 78, 79–80, 81; *Three Men and a Little Lady* as remake of, 82, 84, 89

Truffaut, François, 66, 141–42, 159, 174. See also *L'Homme qui aimait les femmes* (1977)

Universal Studios, 184, 202

Vadim, Roger, 174

Van Dyne, Susan R., 94, 102

Varenne, Hervé, 13, 134–35

Veber, Francis, 10, 180, 181–83. See also *La Chèvre* (1981); *Les Compères* (1988)

Vie est un roman, La (1982), 43

Vigo, Jean, 93

Vinay, J. P., 72

Vincendeau, Ginette, 15, 30, 61, 162, 174, 183

Visual imagery: American preference for, 42, 68; and American's passive viewing habits, 99–100; international appeal of, 42; interpretive force of, 105; vs. written language, 33

"Visual Pleasure and Narrative Cinema" (Mulvey), 19, 109, 147

Voice-over narration, 157–58

Voyeurism, 149–50, 155. *See also* Male gaze

Watson, Richard, 91–92, 95

Weir, Peter, 93

Williams, Robin, 189

Woman, ideal, 144–45, 147, 149–50

Women: devaluation of, 146–47, 150–51; objectification of, 144–47, 154–55, 157, 176, 214n16; reproductive creativity of, 164; stereotypical portrayals of, 157. *See also* Femininity; Misogyny; Mother; Motherhood

"Women's Cinema as Counter-Cinema" (Johnston), 106

Women's Place in the Academy (Schuster & Van Dyne), 94, 102

Women's Studies, 96, 98–99, 102–3

Yale French Department, 93–94, 98, 109

Yale French Studies, 95

Young, Josh, 11, 182, 184

Zéro de conduite (1933), 93

University Press of New England publishes books under its own imprint and is the publisher for Brandeis University Press, Dartmouth College, Middlebury College Press, University of New Hampshire, Tufts University, and Wesleyan University Press.

Library of Congress Cataloging-in-Publication Data
Durham, Carolyn A.
  Double takes : culture and gender in French films and their
American remakes / Carolyn A. Durham.
      p.   cm. — (Contemporary French culture and society)
    Filmography: p.
    Includes bibliographical references and index.
    ISBN 0–87451–873–3 (cl : alk. paper). -- ISBN 0–87451–874–1 (pbk.
  : alk. paper)
    1. Motion picture remakes.   2. Motion pictures—France.   3. Motion
  pictures—United States.   4. Sex role in motion pictures.
  I. Title.   II. Series.
  PN1995.9.R45D87   1998
  791.43'75'0944—dc21   98-3920